CONNECTING HISTORIES

CARIBBEAN
STUDIES
SERIES

Anton L. Allahar and Natasha Barnes
SERIES EDITORS

CONNECTING HISTORIES

*Francophone Caribbean Writers
Interrogating Their Past*

Bonnie Thomas

University Press of Mississippi / Jackson

www.upress.state.ms.us

The University Press of Mississippi is a member
of the Association of American University Presses.

Copyright © 2017 by University Press of Mississippi
All rights reserved

First printing 2017

∞

Library of Congress Cataloging-in-Publication Data

Names: Thomas, Bonnie, 1975– author.
Title: Connecting histories : Francophone Caribbean writers interrogating their past / Bonnie Thomas.
Other titles: Francophone Caribbean writers interrogating their past
Description: Jackson : University Press of Mississippi, 2017. | Series: Caribbean studies series | Includes bibliographical references and index.
Identifiers: LCCN 2016035689 (print) | LCCN 2016058052 (ebook) | ISBN 9781496810557 (hardback) | ISBN 9781496810564 (epub single) | ISBN 9781496810571 (epub institutional) | ISBN 9781496810588 (pdf single) | ISBN 9781496810595 (pdf institutional)
Subjects: LCSH: Caribbean literature (French)—20th century—History and criticism. | Caribbean literature (French)—21st century—History and criticism. | Caribbean literature (English)—20th century—History and criticism. | Caribbean literature (English)—21st century—History and criticism. | Authors, Caribbean—20th century—Biography. | Authors, Caribbean—21st century—Biography. | Identity (Psychology) in literature. | Psychic trauma in literature. | Memory in literature. | History in literature. | BISAC: LITERARY CRITICISM / Caribbean & Latin American. | BIOGRAPHY & AUTOBIOGRAPHY / Literary. | HISTORY / Caribbean & West Indies / General.
Classification: LCC PQ3940 .T56 2017 (print) | LCC PQ3940 (ebook) | DDC 840.9/9729 [B] —dc23
LC record available at https://lccn.loc.gov/2016035689

British Library Cataloging-in-Publication Data available

CONTENTS

ACKNOWLEDGMENTS IX

INTRODUCTION
HISTORY, MEMORY, AND TRAUMA IN THE FRANCOPHONE CARIBBEAN 3

CHAPTER 1
MARYSE CONDÉ: Filling in the Gaps of "Herstory".. 24

CHAPTER 2
GISÈLE PINEAU: Writing as Therapy 50

CHAPTER 3
PATRICK CHAMOISEAU: Memory, Relation, and the Creolized Imaginary 76

CHAPTER 4
EDWIDGE DANTICAT: Connecting the Political and Personal 100

CHAPTER 5
DANY LAFERRIÈRE: "I Write as I Live" 120

CONCLUSION 146

NOTES 151

WORKS CITED 153

INDEX 163

For Margaret
Richard, Sophie & Julien
Bev

ACKNOWLEDGMENTS

This book would not have been possible without the generous support of many people. First of all, I can't thank my family enough, in particular Margaret and Rod, Richard, Sophie and Julien, and Alex. They are, quite simply, my inspiration for everything. Other members of my immediate family, including John, as well as close friends Gill, David, Pam, Nicole, and Lillian, are equally precious, and I thank them too.

    I am fortunate to have had many inspiring students over the years who have made my job an absolute pleasure. Special mention should be made of Stephanie Harrison, Kelly Drummond-Hay, Alison Storey, and Agnes Pallagi, who have become friends as well as wonderfully rewarding students. They have taught me as much as I have taught them. My colleagues in French studies and the School of Humanities at the University of Western Australia are exceptional and have been supportive and collegial companions in challenging times. I must single out Beverley Noakes, who has been a beacon to me in so many ways. Not only did she introduce me to francophone Caribbean literature, she has also been a role model of gentle and positive guidance, first as a PhD supervisor and now as a treasured friend. Bev embodies the very best of what an academic and a person can be—intelligent, generous, and engaging.

    I would also like to thank the staff at the University Press of Mississippi, in particular acquisitions editor Vijay Shah and editorial assistant Lisa McMurtray. I would like to acknowledge the constructive and generous comments given by the anonymous reviewer to my work and to Norman Ware for his meticulous and insightful copy editing. All have helped make the process of publishing this book effective and efficient. I also wish to gratefully thank the editors of the journals and edited collections who have granted permission to reprint portions of my work from the following publications:

UTSe Press, Sydney, for "The Cook and the Writer: Maryse Condé's Journey of Self-Discovery," *Portal: Journal of International Studies* 10, no. 2 (2013). DOI:http://dx.doi.org/10.5130/portal.v10i2.3023.

Liverpool University Press, for "Narrating Trauma: Distance and Proximity in the Haitian Earthquake of 2010," *Australian Journal of French Studies* 53, nos. 1–2 (2016): 67–78.

The University of Wales Press for "Restarting the Stopped Clock of Time: Rethinking Mobility in Edwidge Danticat's Non-Fiction," in *Exiles, Vagabonds and Travellers: Rethinking Mobility in Francophone Women's Writing*, ed. Kate Averis and Isabel Hollis (Cardiff: University of Wales Press, 2016).

"Memory and Relation in Gisèle Pineau's *Mes quatre femmes*," *French Review* 86, no. 1 (2012): 136–46.

"Transgenerational Trauma in Gisèle Pineau's *Chair Piment* and *Mes quatre femmes*," *International Journal of Francophone Studies* 13, no. 1 (2010): 23–38.

Finally, I would like to thank the Caribbean writers who have been so generous in offering me their time and interest over many years, in particular Maryse Condé, Gisèle Pineau, Patrick Chamoiseau, Raphaël Confiant, Édouard Glissant, Dany Laferrière, Rodney Saint-Éloi, and Anthony Phelps. Their work and passions continue to inspire me.

A note on the text and translations: For clarity of reading, existing translations have been used where possible. If works are untranslated, translations into English follow immediately after the original citation in French. Unless otherwise indicated, these translations are my own.

The capitalized word "History" is used to emphasize the grand narratives of the historical process and the significant external events that shape people's lives. By contrast, the lowercased word "histories" focuses attention on the individual lives of "ordinary" people. A key feature of this book is to explore the intersection between the two.

CONNECTING HISTORIES

INTRODUCTION

History, Memory, and Trauma in the Francophone Caribbean

The francophone Caribbean is a veritable treasure trove of literary gems. Distinguished by innovative and elegant writing and its thought-provoking ways of engaging with questions of identity, this exciting body of work demands attention. A particularly striking feature of contemporary francophone Caribbean literature is the way in which its authors treat the traumatic legacies of historical and personal trauma that pervade the Caribbean experience, enunciating instead a path toward reconciliation, healing, and connection with the world and others. The creation of what I have termed "personal narratives"—a broad definition that encompasses autobiography, autofiction, travel writing, and reflective essay—is characteristic of many Caribbean writers, offering poignant illustrations of how the master narratives of History imprint themselves upon individual lives. Through their personal writings, the five authors whom I have selected for this study—Maryse Condé, Gisèle Pineau, Patrick Chamoiseau, Edwidge Danticat, and Dany Laferrière—offer compelling insights into confronting, coming to terms with, and reconciling with the past. In diverse ways but all pivoting on the notion of "connecting histories," these contemporary authors, from Martinique, Guadeloupe, and Haiti, intertwine their personal memories with reflections on the histories of their homelands and on the European and North American countries they adopt through choice or necessity. To date, no study has looked in detail at the diverse examples of personal narratives from the francophone Caribbean and what they can reveal about the intricate process of interrogating the past.

Each of the five writers has a different relationship with the Caribbean, nuancing the questions of history, memory, and identity that run like a thread through their work. Maryse Condé was born in Guadeloupe but has not lived there permanently since her youth; Gisèle Pineau was born in Paris but retains a passionate attachment to her parents' Guadeloupean birthplace and has chosen to live in adulthood between France and the Caribbean; Patrick Chamoiseau was born in Martinique and, apart from a period in France, where he undertook his tertiary studies and spent his early working years, remains a resident of Fort-de-France; Edwidge Danticat lived in Haiti for the first twelve years of her life before permanently immigrating to the United States; while Dany Laferrière was born in Haiti but was forced into exile in North America at the age of twenty-three. Each of these writers has also carved out a successful nonwriting career in addition to a literary role, displaying an acute sense of collective responsibility and awareness that exists alongside their individual creative endeavors: Condé was an academic until her retirement in 2002, Pineau was a psychiatric nurse, Chamoiseau works as a social worker with troubled youth in Fort-de-France, Danticat has taught creative writing and is a passionate advocate of various Haitian and human rights issues, while Laferrière has an extensive background in journalism and film.

Loss, Lack, and Discontinuity

Many studies—including those by Caribbean writers themselves—have emphasized themes of lack, rupture, and discontinuity in relation to Caribbean history. "Discovered" by Christopher Columbus in 1492 and colonized by the French in the seventeenth century, Martinique, Guadeloupe, and Haiti have all experienced the traumas of slavery, colonization, and continuing problems of identity. While Haiti's history diverges from Martinique's and Guadeloupe's following its establishment as the first independent black republic in 1804, intellectuals from the three islands wrestle with issues of social, political, and cultural displacement as a result of their past and its ongoing influence on contemporary reality. Each bears witness to what Mary Gallagher has described as "a sense of loss, lack, or fracture, caused by the dislocation of the historical continuity" (*Soundings in French Caribbean Writing*, 11). Indeed, studies of the Caribbean often invoke images of brokenness, rupture, and emptiness.[1] For Martinique and Guadeloupe, this loss is primarily explained as a result of slavery and its persistent psychological influences, combined with an ongoing and problematic relationship with France. In the case of Haiti, the loss relates more closely to the political and natural disasters that have plagued the country since independence and left it in a state of crippling poverty. While it is impossible to deny the impact of these traumas, the present book aims to view the traumatic legacy through a paradigm characterized instead by connection and connectivity. Indeed, the term "connecting histories" of the title highlights the vibrancy of this process, which is always evolving, always shifting. It is both a conscious act by the writer to connect to different parts of their lives and cultures as well as an observation of the intertwining of History and histories. While a fundamental part of this exploration involves the dynamic relationship between past, present, and future, such connectivity can also be read through other aspects of "the past," including the personal and familial past, the cultural past, intertextuality and the literary past, the linguistic past, and the traumatic and collective past. Writing histories, then, becomes a vital way of coming to terms with the past and forging a more positive path toward the future.

Elaborating on the notion of writing as a nurturing and innovative site, Nick Nesbitt depicts the creative literary practices that emerged as a result of the Caribbean's experience of slavery and plantation life. He argues that "the plantation system drove memory underground, where it hid in its least-visible, subterranean forms" (*Voicing Memory*, 3) and draws attention to "the imaginative capacity of individuals to act within yet think beyond the historically preformed society that complexly determines them" (4). Nesbitt's positive reworking of what many critics have viewed as an inherently destructive historical experience is characteristic of the approach of the writers chosen for this volume. All of them engage with a traumatic past in some form or other and without denying its deep-seated impact, yet each enacts a process of reconciliation with their individual and collective histories. This attention to empowerment and autonomy reframes the past as a place for renewal despite the persistent influence of deep-seated trauma. Emphasizing the fundamental role of writers in this reappraisal, Nesbitt describes francophone Caribbean writing as "aris[ing] from and . . . determined by historical, material conditions, and yet . . . refus[ing] to accept the present state of things as inevitable, generating a utopian vision informed by the historical past" (*Voicing Memory*, 34), or, put another way, "while the various genres of Antillean writing are manifold . . . the unifying characteristic of the outstanding texts from this tradition is their status as works of *critique*—as writings, that is, that cry out in subordination and aversion to the state of their world . . . and that seek to articulate the promise that another world is possible" (Nesbitt, *Caribbean Critique*, xi).

The redemptive possibilities of a new theoretical paradigm are evident in work by another famous theoretician of the Caribbean: Antonio Benítez-Rojo. In his groundbreaking 1992 publication *The Repeating Island: The Caribbean and the Postmodern Perspective*, Benítez-Rojo draws attention to the plural, rhizomatic nature of the Caribbean. He characterizes the Caribbean as a "meta-archipelago," a geographic feature without boundary or center that conjures up images of "unstable condensations, turbulences, whirlpools, clumps of bubbles... in short, a field of observation quite in tune with the objectives of Chaos" (2–3). However, Benítez-Rojo stresses that this chaos is not necessarily a negative phenomenon but, rather, offers a space for new and fruitful connections. Benítez-Rojo further likens the Caribbean to a fugue where all elements are necessary, even those that conflict, in order to create an intricate polyphonic composition (173) that refutes the notion of brokenness and discontinuity. In a place like the Caribbean where there are so many potentially dissonant influences—contrasting languages, cultures, and power relations—the image of the fugue allows for the possibility of positive intersection. This framework emphasizing plurality and interconnection sets the scene for an examination of history, memory, and trauma in the francophone Caribbean. Most significant in relation to this study is Édouard Glissant's belief in the "the Poetics of Relation, in which each and every identity is extended through a relationship with the Other" (*Poetics of Relation*, 11). It is particularly the employment of the term "poetics" in Glissant's assertions that proves invaluable when analyzing the diverse personal narratives chosen for this book. As Françoise Lionnet points out and the five writers featured herein demonstrate, writing itself becomes "a sheltering site, one that can nurture our differences" (5) and that can ultimately provide a means of envisioning a new future.

Édouard Glissant: Forging a Path toward Connection

Within the francophone Caribbean, poet, novelist, and philosopher Édouard Glissant is the most celebrated theoretician of history and memory. While Glissant's work is typically aimed at relationships on a cultural and geographical level rather than on a personal one, his insights can nonetheless be harnessed and extended for new purposes. Glissant's model emphasizes relationship, connection, and the way in which differences may enrich rather than endanger. Inspired by the rhizome, which gives a concrete image of relationship, interrelationship, origin, and belonging, Glissant's notion of

Relation provides a *point de départ* for understanding the five writers' interrogations of the past. Glissant's thought has evolved considerably from the time of his first publication in 1956, *Soleil de la conscience* (*Sun of Consciousness*), to his last published works before his death in 2011. His interrogations of the Martinican past in works such as *Le Discours antillais* (*Caribbean Discourse*) (1981) and *Poétique de la Relation* (*Poetics of Relation*) (1990) are indispensable to any discussion of historical trauma in the region. However, the focus of his analyses changes from seeing the Caribbean as bound to a past that is characterized by lack to one that favors interrelationship, connection, and looking toward the future. Several of his later publications, including *Une nouvelle région du monde* (2006), (with Patrick Chamoiseau) *Quand les murs tombent: l'identité nationale hors-la-loi?* (2007), and *Mémoires des esclavages: la fondation d'un centre national pour la mémoire des esclavages et de leurs abolitions* (2007), provide specific reflections on the notion of Relation that informs his approach to the past. According to Celia Britton, Glissant's works had a major change in tone in the 1990s, revealing a far more positive approach to creolization and the past. "This new position is encapsulated in the concept of the 'Tout-monde': the world envisaged as a multiplicity of communities all interacting and aware of each other's existence" (Britton, *Language and Literary Form*, 138).

The title of Glissant's 1990 book *Poetics of Relation* perhaps best encapsulates the development of his theorization about memory and the way in which he increasingly moves from an emphasis on a negative past to one that lays out paths of connection between past, present, and future. While early works such as *Le Quatrième siècle* (*The Fourth Century*), *La Case du commandeur* (*The Overseer's Cabin*), and, to some extent, *Le Discours antillais* privilege the Martinican experience of slavery, Glissant's subsequent books are more outward looking, drawing parallels between Martinique and the wider world. They also demonstrate a shift from binary thinking focusing on resistance and subjugation (encapsulated in the image of the slave and the Maroon) to a more holistic approach toward the legacies of the past. While Glissant maintains dichotomous pairing in his theorization of identity and memory, he nonetheless privileges a model that is focused on relationships rather than on rejection or acceptance of a dominant system. Historical commentators have noted that binary theorizations proliferate in the field of history and memory studies. As Ana Douglass and Thomas Vogler affirm: "Whether the focus of a given commentator is on personal memory, collective memory, or history, some form of binary opposition will be part of the discourse" (*Witness and Memory*, 15). As we will see in the course of this chapter, Glissant's model of Relation will arise as a form of challenge to this domination of oppositional frameworks. Rather than opposing two terms against each other, Glissant and his Caribbean counterparts strive toward a model that privileges relationship and connection.

According to Glissant, it is the Caribbean landscape that most effectively illustrates this "thought of Relation" in which the experience of slavery emerges "not merely [as] an encounter, a shock . . . , a *métissage*, but [as] a new and original dimension allowing each person to be there and elsewhere, rooted and open, lost in the mountains and free beneath the sea, in harmony and errantry" (*Poetics of Relation*, 34). Michael Dash locates the first expression of the notion of historical healing in Glissant's very early writing, asserting that his 1956 publication *Soleil de la conscience* draws on the Caribbean's archipelic shape as a symbol of its openness to a new way of interpreting history. "It was precisely the inability to restore historical continuities and absent origins that represented for Glissant the Caribbean's potential to establish new connections and envisage repeated crossings" ("Martinique Is (Not) a Polynesian Island," 126). The Caribbean space itself becomes for Glissant the point of departure for a model of history and memory that does not focus on a deterministic and linear historical continuum.

Glissant's developing notion of a relational approach to past and present infuses his later conceptualizations of identity. With an ongoing emphasis on the national and cultural, Glissant published a short pamphlet with Patrick Chamoiseau in 2007, entitled *Quand les murs tombent: l'identité nationale hors-la-loi?*, in which they elaborate the notion of an identity unbound by national borders and emphasize instead the interconnectedness of all peoples. Central to this conception of identity is the distinction between a "fixité identitaire" (fixed identity) (1)—such as that advanced by Aimé Césaire—and an identity that exists in relation to others (9). They align the former with colonizing powers who attempt to impose their values on others to preserve a sense of national identity and the latter as a positive and healthy identity oriented toward others. Embedded within Chamoiseau and Glissant's argument is the idea that "[s]*apiens* est par définition un migrant, émigrant, immigrant" (*human beings* are by definition migrants, emigrants, immigrants) (7), which emphasizes the idea of continual movement rather than a fixed notion of time, space, and being. In this schema, it becomes impossible for people to maintain immutable identities; rather, they are subject to processes of creolization that affect everyone. Identities—and, by extension, histories—are dislocated from linear processes of history or chronology and instead are flexible, fluctuating entities that drift in and out of contact with others.

To some extent, *Quand les murs tombent* provides the literary expression of Glissant's Institut du Tout-Monde, which he founded in 2006. According to its website, the institute was created with the aesthetic and philosophical purpose of forming "un lieu rhizome de Relation et d'échanges, une plate-forme où se rencontrent les imaginaires et les écritures du monde" (a rhizomatic place of Relation and exchanges, a platform where the imaginations and the writings of the world meet), where creolization flourishes and is embraced and where researchers "relient, relayent, relatent les espaces des pensées et du tremblement du monde" (relink, relay, and relate the thought spaces and the trembling of the earth).[2] In contrast to such positive images of creolization, Chamoiseau and Glissant in *Quand les murs tombent* argue that the very notion of identity has traditionally served to erect walls between people—emphasizing differences that threaten rather than creating a rich melting pot of peoples (8). The idea of national walls is paralleled with the notion of single-rooted identity that is fearful of difference, while Chamoiseau and Glissant's concept of relational identity emphasizes the myriad influences that construct one's identity and situates them in relationship with other identities rather than in opposition to them. Chamoiseau and Glissant's concept of identity requires recognition of the creolized nature of the world and the fact that it is "l'inaptitude à vivre le contact et l'échange qui crée le mur identitaire et dénature l'identité" (the inability to live with contact and exchange that creates identity walls and distorts identity) (10). Real diversity can only be found in the imagination, modeling a way of perceiving the world that embodies the spirit of Relation: "la façon de se penser, de penser le monde, de se penser dans le monde, d'organiser ses principes d'existence et de choisir son sol natal. Des imaginaires semblables peuvent s'accommoder de peaux, de langues et de dieux différents" (the way of thinking of oneself, of thinking the world, of thinking of oneself in the world, organizing one's principles of existence and choosing one's native soil. The same skin can have different imaginations. Similar imaginations can have different skins, languages, and gods) (15–16). Equally, the imagination can accommodate the highs and lows of history. These statements also signal the decisive roles writers may play in constructing a memory and identity.

In the closing pages of *Quand les murs tombent*, Chamoiseau and Glissant explicitly link their concept of relational identity to memory, arguing that history needs to be laid out flat, or started afresh, for those involved in slaveries, genocides, and holocausts—not so that some can repent and others remain memorialized as victims, but so that memories can be openly heard and joined together (24–25). Glissant and Chamoiseau explore the notion of interrelation on a historical level by advocating the need to draw together victims of trauma in a day of international commemoration such as that obtained in France on May 10 each year, not as a way to dwell on the past but as a way to understand and move forward in a gesture of Relation. Glissant had previously explored this idea of the interconnectedness and openness of all peoples in his 2006 publication *Une nouvelle région du monde*, asserting: "Chacun de nous a besoin de la mémoire de l'autre . . . et si nous voulons partager la beauté du monde, si nous voulons être solidaires de ses souffrances, nous devons apprendre à nous souvenir ensemble" (We each need the memory of the other . . . and if we want to share the beauty of the world, if we want to show solidarity in its suffering, we have to learn to remember together) (161). Once again finding inspiration in the Caribbean landscape to convey his thought, Glissant argues: "Il nous faut recompenser la trame archipélique et continentale de nos mémoires et la rhizomer sur toute l'expansion de nos histoires et sur le devenir de nos géographies" (We must recompose the archipelic and continental framework of our memories and "rhizome" it over the whole expansion of our histories and over the evolution of our geographies) (162). With the rhizome suggesting the notion of new buds sprouting from a network of interconnected roots and the archipelago embodying openness to the sea and other lands, Glissant emphasizes the bonds between peoples, cultures, histories, and memories. These evocative environmental images that are so recurrent in Glissant's works are summed up in his assertion that "[o]ur landscape is its own monument" (*Caribbean Discourse* 11).

Glissant elaborates his theory of memory in another 2007 publication, *Mémoires des esclavages*, in which he explores issues relating to the construction of a national memorial center in Paris. Glissant expands on the binary organization of identity outlined in *Quand les murs tombent* with what he terms "mémoire de la tribu" (memory of the tribe) and "mémoire de la collectivité Terre" (memory of the Earth collectivity) (164–65). Glissant characterizes the former as those memories "fondées sur une expérience commune d'un passé . . . et qui déclenchera chez les individus des réactions différentes" (founded on a common experience of the past . . . which unleashes different reactions in individuals) (164). By contrast, memories of the Earth collectivity "rapproche les membres d'une collectivité ou d'une nation dans leur commun rapport à l'autre, considéré à son tour non pas comme communauté ou nation, mais comme élément de la globalité Terre" (resemble all that brings together the members of a collectivity or a nation in their common relationship to the other, but which are to be considered not as a community or nation, but as an element of global Earth) (165). Linking these categories of memory to his earlier theoretical works, Glissant likens tribal memory to continental thought, which has little consideration for the Other, while memory of the Earth collectivity is archipelic, inventing "à chaque moment les effets de la Relation" (at each moment the effects of Relation) (166). Glissant goes on to argue that the memory of the Earth collectivity holds the key to understanding slavery. Memory of the Earth collectivity, with its capacity to transcend national borders and promote fruitful encounters between peoples, provides the conceptual framework necessary to encompass historical phenomena specific to particular societies, but also to draw together the experiences of diverse nations. Through the dialectical contrast of these two types of memory making, Glissant is able to arrive at what he terms "la mémoire délivrée" (delivered memory) (176), a memory space that is inclusive, grounded in the present, and oriented toward the future.

Like Césaire before him, Glissant has always perceived the poetic and political as intertwined. In an interview with Lise Gauvin, Glissant explicitly links poetics and politics: "[L]a poésie est jusqu'ici le seul art qui peut aller réellement derrière les apparences. Je crois que c'est là une de ses vocations. C'est la volonté de défaire les genres, cette partition qui a été si profitable, si fructueuse dans le cas des littératures occidentales" (Poetry is up until now the only art that can really go behind appearances. I think that is its primary vocation. It's the willingness to undo genres, this partition that has been so profitable, so fruitful in the case of Western literatures) (Glissant, *L'Imaginaire des langues*, 29). For Glissant and his literary compatriots, it is the *imaginaire* (imagination) that is paramount, and this belief lies at the heart of their political and poetic projects. The poet is charged with the responsibility to find "des imaginaires ouverts pour toutes sortes d'avenirs de la créolisation" (imaginations open to all sorts of futures of creolization) (*L'Imaginaire des langues*, 33). Both paths lead to the idea that rigid and reductive ways of viewing the world are no longer possible: "[I]l n'y a donc pas de pensée de système, pas d'idéologie" (There is therefore no system of thought, no ideology) (55). Glissant's thought provides a dual path to reconciliation with the past: first, the need to resituate trauma, whether social or individual, within a network of Relation that reduces the impact of its power; and second, the means of doing it, which is by adapting a mode that is itself symbolic of Relation—in this case, literature.

History, Memory, and Reconciliation: Reappraising the Role of the Past

Alongside Glissant's theorizations, other theories developed outside the Caribbean have added to our understanding of individual and collective memory and its role in shaping contemporary identity. Those working in the realm of the Holocaust have elucidated an understanding of trauma and its transgenerational effects, which are particularly useful in the context of this book. These and other theorists of memory offer important insights for placing the concepts of past, present, and future in a network formation rather than a linear relationship that moves deterministically forward. Such thinkers also illustrate the slipperiness of using the terms "history" and "memory" as well as associated terms such as "redemption" and "forgiveness," which are key to reappraising history and trauma in the present. This next section of the discussion will focus on the employment of theoretical terms common to the practice of historiography, the necessarily constructed nature of the historical project, and the way in which the flexibility inherent in these processes can in fact help to reorient the transgenerational impact of trauma.

The theoretical terrain related to memory studies is vast. While it is impossible to do justice to the depth of scholarship that surrounds this field in the present study, it is vital to have some understanding of these issues in order to situate the Caribbean writers in an intellectual context. A key starting point is the relationship between history and memory, and, as a consequence, the complex interplay that exists between past, present, and future. Many critics have pointed to the highly contested nature of these theoretical terms, although they are often employed as if they were unproblematic and transparent. Ana Douglass and Thomas A. Vogler, editors of *Witness and Memory: The Discourse of Trauma*, cite as an example the multiple variations of the term "memory" that includes "memory, counter-memory, common memory, deep memory, post-memory, anti-memory, repressed memory, social memory, socially-constructed memory, public memory, collective memory, memorial practice, memorial consciousness, real memory, mythic memory, memory talk, memory industry, [and] politics of memory" (14–15). Furthermore, the very terms "history" and "memory" are indistinct; they may mean the same thing for one theoretician but vastly different things for another (2).

Paula Hamilton, in her coedited volume *Memory and History in Twentieth-Century Australia*, draws attention to a number of fundamental questions relating to the distinction between history and memory, particularly the notion that "[c]ontemporary societies seem obsessed by remembering" ("The Knife Edge," 10). In the francophone Caribbean context, this "need to remember" came to the fore in debates such as those that raged throughout France and the francophone Caribbean in 2005. Set against a backdrop of a number of significant commemorative dates such as the 500th anniversary of the new world's "discovery" by Christopher Columbus (1992), the 150th anniversary of the abolition of slavery in Martinique and Guadeloupe (1998), the 200th anniversary of the Haitian declaration of independence (2004), and the sixty-year anniversary of Martinique and Guadeloupe becoming overseas departments of France (2006), the role of history's legacies in the present took center stage. When Article 4 of the February 23, 2005, law on French colonialism declared the "positive role" of colonization, the public response was so outraged that President Jacques Chirac was forced to abolish the controversial article and reassess the French government's attitude to its colonial past, including its involvement in the slave trade. Although the French government adopted the Christiane Taubira law in May 2001, which acknowledges slavery as a crime against humanity, 2005 and 2006 saw the creation of a number of significant forums for remembering France's shameful role in slavery. Two such steps were the establishment of the Comité pour la Mémoire de l'Esclavage,[3] initially chaired by Maryse Condé, later by Françoise Vergès, and, since 2013, by Myriam Cottias; and Chirac's appointment of Glissant as the founder of a national center devoted to slavery. While the latter project has not been brought to fruition, the former has an important role in preserving and representing historical memory, underlining the importance of writers in contributing to public memory. The deaths of Césaire in 2008 and Glissant in 2011 have further underscored the relationship between writers, their role in shaping cultural identity, and how to memorialize them appropriately.

A dominant theme in the writings of many historians is the distinction they make between "history" and "memory." For some, these terms are interchangeable; for others, the former corresponds to an objective notion of the past while the latter belongs to the subjective realm. A similar binary opposition is frequently formed between the master narratives of History and the myriad histories of "the people." Jacques Le Goff, *Annales* historian and important contributor to medieval thought, offers useful insights into the history/memory equation, asserting that "history" and "memory" are not neutral terms but are equally subject to manipulation and construction by its practitioners (*History and Memory*, xi) and that the future is indispensable in any consideration of past and present (2). In contrast to some theorists who argue the "authenticity" of history over memory or vice versa, Le Goff emphasizes instead a positive relationship between the two whereby "the discipline of history nourishes memory" (xi), and indeed, that "the interest of the past is that it illuminates the present" (xx). Other historians have taken a more negative stance toward the question of history, highlighting the notion of disconnection rather than connection. Michel de Certeau, for example, argues that the practice of history ruthlessly separates past and present and "everywhere it repeats the initial act of division" (3). He asserts, moreover, that "[b]reakage is ... the postulate of interpretation" (4), a position reflected in his text *The Writing of History*, which abounds with images of "shards," "rifts," "crannies," and "lapses." Hamilton has also observed the frequency of terms relating to brokenness, asserting that much historical debate is written "in the language of loss or mourning: words like rupture, fissure, fracture, underline assumptions about the loss of continuity that the existence of a previously coherent somehow organic memory presumes" (11). Even Glissant, despite his later stance of positive Relation, is most famously recognized for his declaration that the French Caribbean is "a site of a history characterized by ruptures and that began with a brutal dislocation, the slave trade" (*Caribbean Discourse*, 61). As the proceeding chapters will demonstrate, the five Caribbean writers chosen for this study all refute the notion of disconnection in their writing, favoring instead an approach of connecting histories and relationship.

French philosopher Paul Ricoeur, in *Memory, History, Forgetting*, introduces a different element into the history/memory debate, asserting that forgiveness "constitutes the horizon common to memory, history, and forgetting" (457). Ricoeur's volume is exhaustive, but it is his emphasis on forgiveness and resurrection of the past that is most useful in relation to this study. He argues that "events like the Holocaust and the great crimes of the twentieth century, situated at the limits of representation, stand in the name of all the events that have left their traumatic imprint on hearts and bodies; they protest that they were and as such they demand being said, recounted, understood" (498). However, rather than emphasizing the devastating consequences of trauma, Ricoeur argues that the "work of memory would have attained its aim if the reconstruction of the past were to succeed in giving rise to a sort of resurrection of the past" (499).

Ricoeur's religious imagery resonates in the work of more contemporary theorists such as Mireille Rosello, who has devoted an entire book to the search for the "reparative" in narrative. Rosello draws a distinction between repentance and the "reparative," with the former constituting "the name that I give to the kind of memory that I do not value" (6) while the latter "can begin only once a certain amount of working through trauma has already taken place" (3). Françoise Vergès gives a different angle to the need to work through historical traumas, arguing that liberation in the present can only be achieved through a rigorous examination of the past. She cites specifically the case of the descendants of slaves who are now French citizens in Martinique and Guadeloupe and who are demanding a reappraisal of their past: "Ils ne veulent plus être esclaves de l'esclavage, qui fut imposé à leurs ancêtres. Ils ne veulent pas être enfermés dans le passé, mais sont convaincus que sans un examen et un tri de l'héritage, ce passé restera un passif, une assignation à résidence" (They no longer want to be slaves to the slavery, which was imposed on their ancestors. They no longer want to be enclosed in the past, but they are convinced that without an examination and a sorting out of this heritage this past will remain passive, a house arrest) (23). All of these thinkers stress the importance of the past in order to illuminate the present and future. As this book progresses, we will see that the Caribbean writers' engagement with their histories allows them to carry out this very examination but in a way that is about connecting, thereby enacting a powerful path toward reconciliation and liberation.

Given that the focus of this book is the personal narratives of writers and their engagement with history, it is useful to consider the role historians play in selecting, writing, and memorializing the past. Historians are increasingly acknowledging their active role in writing their vision of the past, which offers important potential for reclaiming history and rewriting the future. Certeau, for example, asserts that history is not a seamless process of weaving tales of the past but an occupation that involves the "making of histories" that are "at once critical and fictive . . . legitimized through power and drawn from it" (8). Certeau's assertion that "the past is the fiction of the present" (10) points to the definitive role of the historian who has the ability to influence how a society sees itself through her or his interpretations. Correspondingly, writers have an important role in how they portray the past, present, and future to their reading audience. Rosello argues in her book that "the present is the choice of the story that we make of the past" (18), while Susannah Radstone asserts that memory "is always mediated" (135). These assertions highlighting the constructed nature of history emphasize the decisive role of the historian or writer in deciding what constitutes "the past." Hamilton characterizes this approach as "a return to the storytelling function in history, a celebration of the imaginative elements in historical reconstruction, a greater awareness of history writing as a literary practice" (25). This recasting of the historical role itself allows greater flexibility for reinterpreting the past's influence and freeing oneself from its traumatic burdens. No longer an immutable entity, the past can be reappraised in order to promote healing and reconciliation.

Trauma and Its Transgenerational Effects

Any study of history and memory in the Caribbean context necessarily involves a consideration of trauma. A pioneering theorist of trauma studies, Cathy Caruth, defines trauma in *Unclaimed Experience: Trauma, Narrative, and History* as "an overwhelming experience of sudden or catastrophic events in which the response to the event occurs in the often delayed, uncontrolled repetitive appearance of hallucinations and other intrusive phenomena" (11). The intensity of trauma is such that it cannot always be expressed in the present moment but has a delayed effect such as that in post-traumatic stress disorder (PTSD). PTSD affects its victims in a manner whereby the "experience of the trauma, fixed or frozen in time, refuses to be represented *as* past, but is perpetually reexperienced in a painful, dissociated, traumatic present" (Leys, 2). Caruth's assertion that "trauma is not locatable in the simple violent or original event in an individual's past, but rather in the way that its very unassimilated nature—the way it was precisely *not known* in the first instance—returns to haunt the survivor later on" (4) is key to understanding the powerful influence of the traumatic past on one's present circumstances. Douglass and Vogler argue that the "traumatic event bears a striking similarity to the always absent signified or referent of post-structuralist discourse, an object that can by definition only be constructed retroactively, never observed directly" (*Witness and Memory*, 5). They declare, moreover, that trauma may also manifest itself in a secondary manner in conditions they characterize as "onlooker trauma," "secondary PTSD," and "transgenerational trauma" (10). These experiences of trauma that occur at a distance are relevant to this study, as many of the events described by the authors are not ones they have experienced directly. Interestingly, though, Laferrière and Danticat have a more immediate experience of some aspects of Haitian history as they actually bear witness to certain definitive periods such as the Duvaliers' dictatorships and the devastating earthquake of 2010. By contrast, Condé, Pineau, and Chamoiseau relate stories that are more concerned with the psychological effects of slavery that they experience transgenerationally or with colonization that they experience in a more direct manner.

The concept of transgenerational trauma is particularly useful in relation to Martinique and Guadeloupe, which are noted for the persistent psychological effects of slavery and colonization on their people. However, it also provides valuable conceptual tools when looking at Haiti, whose people are struggling with contemporary traumas that demand attention. Theories of transgenerational trauma may be beneficial when thinking about how these current crises will be experienced by future generations. Nicolas Abraham outlined the phenomenon in his 1975 publication "Notes on the Phantom" after studying the passing on of secrets by one generation to another. Nicholas Rand, editor of Abraham and Maria Torok's book *The Shell and the Kernel: Renewals in Psychoanalysis*, characterizes this phantom figure of memory as "a function of the individual life experiences of the person who transmits it to his or her descendants" and argues that it concerns particularly "the interpersonal and transgenerational consequence of silence" (Abraham and Torok, 169). According to Abraham, "what haunts are not the dead, but the gaps left within us by the secrets of others" (171). This notion of gaps and secrets is particularly appropriate when examining Condé's and Pineau's relationships to their cultural and personal pasts. Abraham's phantom emerges as the result of a predecessor's secret on an individual in which certain symptoms displayed by one person are in fact a response to the trauma of another. Abraham draws parallels between the phantom and Freud's description of the death instinct in that it has no energy of its own; it works in silence, gives rise to endless repetition, and eludes rationalization (175). His essay abounds with imagery of haunting, silence, gaps, and the unspeakable nature of individual secrets, all of which point to the potent yet often unconscious nature of transgenerational haunting. As we will see in the course of this book, part of the writers' role in engaging with their personal and cultural past is to bring these silences into the spoken or written realms and in this way put a stop to their transgenerational effects. Moreover, it becomes a way of introducing points of connection where previously there were gaps.

Marianne Hirsch, who has worked on the Holocaust, refashions the concept of transgenerational trauma into what she terms "postmemory." According to Hirsch, postmemory is "a *structure* of inter- and trans-generational transmission of traumatic knowledge and experience. It is a *consequence* of traumatic recall but (unlike post-traumatic stress disorder) at a generational remove" (106). Acknowledging the transgenerational consequences of cultural trauma, Ron Eyerman argues that representation plays a key role in how such trauma is continually experienced and reexperienced (12). Trauma is often situated outside of representation, with its victims or survivors "reliv[ing] the original experience through a body memory yet struggl[ing] to find words for an experience that exceeds representation" (Griffiths, 1). For all persons, this struggle to find a language in which to express their trauma is essential to healing; the process becomes even more complex when "this struggle passes down within families" (Griffiths, 70). Pointing to the need to create a "discourse of witness" in which trauma is explicitly acknowledged, Douglass and Vogler argue that witnessing may come at a generational remove (*Witness and Memory*, 3). The personal narratives in this volume can be considered part of the process of bearing witness to Caribbean cultural trauma and therefore contributing to psychological and cultural healing. All the writers in this study find solace in the restorative power of words both for themselves and for their countries of origin more generally.

Hirsch's underlining of the importance of narrative—both constructing one's own narrative and having it heard and affirmed by another—emerges as a vital means of surviving trauma and reclaiming one's past. Michael Lambek and Paul Antze highlight the intimate relationship between experience and narrative where people "emerge from and as the products of their stories about themselves as much as their stories emerge from their lives" (xviii). Numerous psychoanalysts have pointed to the liberating possibilities of narrating—whether it be through talking or writing. Caruth expresses this ideal of reciprocal dialog as "the way in which one's own trauma is tied up with the trauma of another, the way in which trauma may lead . . . to the encounter with another" (8). Susan Brison asserts that "narrating memories to others (who are strong enough and empathetic enough to be able to listen) empowers survivors to gain more control over the traces left by trauma" (40), while Rand expresses it differently again: "[W]e must be able to remember the past, recall what was taken from us, and understand and grieve over what we have lost to trauma, and so find and renew ourselves" (13). Nicola King reinforces this notion of renewal rather than returning to an original state of purity in her declaration that reading "the texts of memory shows that 'remembering the self' is not a case of restoring an original identity, but a continuous process of '*re*-membering,' of putting together moment by moment, of provisional and partial reconstruction" (175). It is the abandonment of the dream to return to an untouched Eden that marks an important point of departure when reframing a traumatic past. This psychological shift frees the sufferer of trauma to look forward and no longer to be bound by the burdens of the past. It forces a chink in the chain of historical determinism and introduces the vital third element into the past/present equation—that of the future. Ultimately, then, trauma can be positive: "a way of inserting a radical, often transformative break in the flow of a life narrative" (Lambek and Antze, xvii). The five Caribbean writers explore this concept at both a social and an individual level through their personal engagements with the past.

In *Writing History, Writing Trauma*, Dominick LaCapra draws on Freudian psychoanalysis to characterize "working through" as an articulatory practice in which "one is able to distinguish between past and present and to recall in memory that something happened to one (or one's people) back then while realizing that one is living here and now with openings to the future" (22). LaCapra argues that empathy and empathic unsettlement "involves a kind of virtual experience through which one puts oneself in the other's position while recognizing the difference of that position and hence not taking the other's place" (78). This attention to the importance of the past without becoming a prisoner of it is essential in reappraising the impact of trauma in the present. Ricoeur terms this process "memory-as-care," in which "we hold ourselves open to the past, we remain concerned about it" (505), without being wholly defined by it. Theorists of memory bring to light the close relationship that exists between memory and identity, a trend that is evident in all the books under discussion but that is treated differently by each of the five authors. Lambek and Antze highlight that memory is vital to identity construction, both in stabilizing our identity in continuity or threatening to disrupt it (xvi). Furthermore, they emphasize that memory making is an intensely physical activity drawing on a person's effort and energy as he or she engages in the "ceaseless activity of remembering and forgetting, assimilating and discarding" (xxiv). King coins the term "rememory" as a way to stress "the afterwardsness of memory . . . the fact that memory is always a representation . . . 're-remembering,' a remembering *after* a forgetting" (158). Presence and absence reveal themselves to be equally potent in these processes of identity construction as well as more generally to the way in which a society is represented. History, memory, and trauma, with all the richness these terms connote, form a vital backdrop to the discussion of the selected works in this book.

The Question of Genre

Now that the theoretical scene is set, it is important also to consider the genre of the texts chosen for this study, which fall broadly under the banner of autobiography and autofiction. However, just as it is impossible to reduce Caribbean experience to a single, universalizing *identité-unique*, so too the books under discussion do not neatly conform to a straightforward definition of autobiography or autofiction. Critics such as Maeve McCusker and Louise Hardwick point out that the genre of autobiography is a relatively recent phenomenon in the francophone Caribbean (McCusker, "Troubler l'ordre de l'oubli," 439; Hardwick, *Childhood*, 1–2), having been dominated instead by a more collective approach to autobiography and summarized in the concept of Glissant's *roman du nous*. As we have seen, many studies of the Caribbean have emphasized lack, rupture, and discontinuity when appraising the effects of history on the present, and a more collective approach to telling individual stories is one method the region's authors have employed to create coherence in these disparate experiences. Mary Gallagher observes that the link between the personal and the collective is particularly noteworthy in societies such as the francophone Caribbean, where "a searing awareness of a deficit in collective memory lies at the heart of the literary endeavour of many French Caribbean writers" (*Soundings in French Caribbean Writing* 88). According to Gallagher, this trend is evident in the predominance of first-person life narratives among this group of authors, which seem to go "some way towards suturing the torn and alienated collective self-image" (90). Renée Larrier gives another dimension to this need for a record of collective memory, arguing that "Caribbean autofiction is invested in remembering and recording history and in challenging society's perception of Caribbean people. Consequently, these texts play an advocacy role as do some of the authors in real life" (24). As established at the outset of this chapter, all five authors in this study practice a profession alongside their writing, and each one is devoted to communicating and agitating for a deeper and more nuanced understanding of their countries' past and present.

In her astute study on childhood narratives in the francophone Caribbean, Hardwick asserts that the genre of autobiography is still heavily influenced theoretically by French thinkers Philippe Lejeune and Serge Doubrovsky, both of whom emphasize the problematic relationship between "truth" and "reality" (Hardwick, *Childhood*, 6–8). Some Caribbean authors, such as Maryse Condé and Dany Laferrière, face this uneasy tension with humor and relish, the former admitting of her memoir of her maternal grandmother: "[H]ere is the portrait I have managed to trace, whose impartiality or even exactitude I cannot fully guarantee (*Victoire*, 4); while the latter declares in interview with Paola Ghinelli: "Naturellement je ne dirai pas la vérité" (Naturally I will not tell the truth) (Ghinelli, 100). Pineau and Chamoiseau take a more serious approach to filling the gaps in Caribbean history, which demonstrate their commitment to providing histories for the present and future. Of her 1998 publication (with Marie Abraham), *Femmes des Antilles: traces et voix*, published on the occasion of the 150th anniversary of the abolition of slavery in Martinique and Guadeloupe, Pineau writes of the urgent need to record her country's past by telling the stories (real or imagined) of individual women: "[C]es femmes sortent de l'ombre et marchent dans les traces ouvertes de la grande Histoire. . . . Et leurs voix s'élèvent de l'abîme, croisent et rencontrent enfin celles des Antillaises d'aujourd'hui. Elles racontent hier et nouent au grand jour les fils qui les lient à ces femmes du présent" (These women are coming out of the shadows and walking in the open paths of History. . . . And their voices are rising out of the abyss, crossing and finally meeting those of today's Caribbean women. They are recounting yesterday and bring to light the threads that tie them to the women of the present) (13). In this conception, the blurry division between truth and fiction and individual and collective is in fact essential to the vital process of remembrance and reconciliation. Nesbitt makes a similar observation of Condé's historical/imaginative approach in her 1977 publication *La Civilisation du bossale: réflexions sur la littérature orale de la Guadeloupe et de la Martinique*, which he declares is "a historically informed, imaginative reconstruction of undocumented events lost to the past" (Nesbitt, *Caribbean Critique*, 123).

Far from shying away from their lack of historical accuracy, Hardwick declares that Caribbean writers shine the spotlight on the impossibility of objective "truth" in their personal memoirs. "The narrative process becomes a process of memory retrieval, which often draws attention to its own artifice and shortcomings through acknowledgements of significant memory lapses or the ludic manipulation of the truth" (Hardwick, *Childhood*, 16). The authors in this study employ different techniques with which to highlight this process: Condé repeatedly emphasizes her need to invent "facts" when she cannot remember them; Pineau's narratives are nonlinear and highly complex literary constructions; Chamoiseau uses frequent authorial intrusions and a deliberate blurring of narrator and author; Danticat likens her work to a braiding or collage; and Laferrière adopts a deliberately provocative stance in much of his literature. While an author like Chamoiseau, following in the footsteps of Glissant, asserts a more explicitly communal aspect to his childhood memoirs, an observation Nesbitt makes about Condé's more individual approach is applicable to all five writers: "Her focus is not the objective determinations in society, whether historical, economic, or political, that limit the freedom of Antillean subjects . . . , but rather to trace the effects of this macro-structural dependency and alienation as it manifests itself in the figures and dispositions of Antillean subjective experience" (*Caribbean Critique*, 127). To a greater or lesser degree, then, the broad genre of autobiography and autofiction provides these writers with a unique medium for exploring many of the distinct tensions that arise in a society whose collective history was denied and who needs its individual voices to emerge for the future.

In her recent examination of Glissant, *Language and Literary Form in French Caribbean Writing*, Britton adds a different dimension to this debate, observing that the Martinican himself long refused to be categorized into a particular literary genre defined by rigid rules. According to Britton, this approach is encapsulated in Gilles Deleuze and Félix Guattari's image of the rhizome, where "anything can and should be connected to anything else, and this includes the different types of discourse that traditionally allows us to categorize different literary genres" (128). Writing of Glissant's *Tout-monde*, she argues that "Glissant is doing something more radical than simply subsuming real-life experiences into a fictional framework. Rather, this is a deliberate interrogation of the relationship between fiction and the real, and its effect is to open the text out onto the real in a way that is quite unusual" (130). Once again, this idea of connecting and connection becomes important, drawing together elements that are usually placed in opposition to each other in a new and dynamic way. Thus, binary opposites such as individual/collective, subjective/objective, History/story, autobiography/History no longer exist as points of tension but are recast in a network relationship where each one is important to create a coherent entity.

It is in this spirit, then, that we will proceed to close readings of five important writers from the francophone Caribbean and the interrogation of the past through their personal narratives. Chapter 1 will examine the way in which Maryse Condé's increasing ability to view her life in a more holistic manner arises as a result of diverse explorations into her past; chapter 2 reveals Gisèle Pineau's quest to unite her personal and collective histories by drawing together the bonds that link people rather than those that divide them, stressing in particular the way in which writing acts as a form of therapy; chapter 3 focuses on Patrick Chamoiseau's three-volume study of his childhood to underline the importance of Creole culture as a model of positive creolization, revealing his close adherence to Glissant's model of Relation; chapter 4 looks at Dany Laferrière's reflective and eyewitness accounts of key events in Haitian history and the way these condition his view of identity and belonging; and, finally, chapter 5 analyzes Edwidge Danticat's firm belief in literary advocacy as a way to promote a humanitarian approach to life. Through interviews and their literary works, the voices of these talented writers emerge with clarity, providing a compelling demonstration of how they explore notions of past, present, and future.

Chapter 1

MARYSE CONDÉ
Filling in the Gaps of "Herstory"

Maryse Condé's contribution to francophone Caribbean writing, postcolonial thought, and literature in general is enormous. Her famously defended stance of independence and irreverence stands alongside a literary oeuvre distinguished by its great variety of settings, genre, and style. As a consequence, there are many angles from which one could approach Condé's work. This chapter will focus on the ways in which her autofictional narratives engage with questions of history and memory, particularly the notion that self-knowledge achieved by filling in the gaps of her personal history is a means to reconcile with the past. The term "herstory" is perhaps more appropriate in this context given Condé's attention to understanding her female lineage and her own roles as mother, lover, and writer. The discussion will center on what Edgard Sankara has termed Condé's "acknowledged autobiographies" (146), that is, *Le Coeur à rire et à pleurer: contes vrais de mon enfance* (*Tales from the Heart: True Stories from My Childhood*) (1999); *Victoire, les saveurs et les mots* (*Victoire: My Mother's Mother*) (2006); and *La Vie sans fards* (2012). These three narratives have been chosen for their illuminating demonstration of the continuous interchange that exists between the personal and the historical as well as Condé's emphasis on the importance of connecting histories within one's own family and with her literary forebears. As the title *La Vie sans fards* suggests, the sense of liberation she achieves as a result of knowing herself, "warts and all," ultimately leads her to a place where she is able to relate to the Other—both within herself and externally—without fear of self-erasure.

A brief biographical sketch will set the scene for an examination of Condé's work and its relationship to her familial and collective past. Condé was born in Guadeloupe in 1937 to black, middle-class, and upwardly mobile parents. The lofty values and language of France were conveyed to her from a young age through her parents' passion for the "motherland" and regular trips to the Metropole. Condé completed her tertiary studies in France and spent more than ten years in Africa with her first husband, Mamadou Condé, with whom she had little in common, although the marriage had benefits on both sides. *La Vie sans fards* details the emotional and cultural struggles Condé underwent in Africa, which laid the foundation for many of her published works. This book also explores the origins of Condé's intellectual discovery of francophone literature, providing an almost literary history of some of Africa's and the Caribbean's most important writers. During this formative period, Condé was to experience firsthand the complex cultural dilemmas that arose for a Guadeloupean woman living and working in Africa. This situation was further complicated on an intellectual level by Aimé Césaire's notion that a positive relationship with Africa was the key to a "successful" Caribbean identity. While the marriage to Mamadou Condé ultimately dissolved, Condé met her second husband in Africa, Englishman Richard Philcox, and they eventually embarked upon a life divided between Guadeloupe, the United States, and, since her retirement from Columbia University in 2002, Paris. They now move between Paris and Gordes, France, where Condé continues to write and Philcox to translate. While Condé's physical inhabitations clearly demonstrate multiple cultural and linguistic migrations, her working life has followed an equally nonconventional path. Far from being confined to a singular role as a "Caribbean novelist," Condé has crossed many genres within her craft (including fiction, theater, autofiction, books for young adults, and essays) as well as occupying a decisive role within the academy as an academic at a number of American universities. Her rich life experience spanning a vast variety of countries, cultures, and languages distinguishes her as a particularly worldly writer who is renowned for her refusal to be placed in a fixed category.

Many critics have remarked upon the staunchly defended independence that is characteristic of Maryse Condé, who "aime à répéter que je n'écris ni en français ni en créole. Mais en Maryse Condé" (likes to repeat that I write in neither French nor Creole. But in Maryse Condé) (Le Bris and Rouaud, 205). Indeed, Condé has consistently asserted her individuality in both written and oral form. In a 2006 interview, she argues that "I've never had this sense of collectivity, of the importance of the Creole language, of common origins.... I've always been a little different" (Hardwick, "J'ai toujours été une personne un peu à part," 118). In a 2008 monograph focusing on Condé's contribution to postcolonial theory, Dawn Fulton asserts that "Condé's talent for dismantling myths, averting expectations, and provoking discomfort has become her hallmark, receiving more consistent critical attention than any other aspect of her work or career" (5), while critic Lydie Moudileno comments that "insolence has become the dominant paradigm in the characterization both of the person and the fiction" (135). Edgard Sankara equally observes that there is a certain amount of "play acting" that goes along with this attitude of independence (158), while Eva Sansavior observes that "Condé's shifting positions within her interviews serve to enact a model of open-ended individual subjectivity that is constructed at the intersection of fiction and the real world" (32) and "can be viewed as sites of performance" (33). The result of this constant instance on the individuality of her identity also leads her to embrace new possibilities for her literary characters. According to Typhaine Leservot, Condé "avoids the ghettoization of her Caribbean world within the confines of its French heritage and opens it instead to the rest of the Americas" (47). In this way, Condé adds a wider significance to her works where geographical, cultural, and linguistic specificity is no longer of primordial importance. Ronnie Scharfman argues that, as a result, Condé's characters "embody the rich sophistication of cosmopolitanism, the invention and imagination of community founded on creative criteria and the sheer exhilaration of liberty of movement, traversing languages, borders, and cultures" ("Criss-Crossing the Mangrove," 202–3). As this chapter will demonstrate, this approach that privileges the individual over the group and that defines both Condé and her work is an essential component of her engagement with history and memory.

Condé and Caribbean Identity

Before proceeding to an analysis of Condé's autofictional works, it is fruitful first to situate her views on Caribbean identity, literature, and history, as these inform the production of her ideas. Condé's appreciation of the complexities of identity—both from a global and a local point of view—is a topic that she has discussed in a number of contexts over many years. In 1991, in her interviews with Françoise Pfaff, Condé underlines the multiplicity of Caribbean identity, arguing that it cannot be simply reproduced like a recipe for cooking but, rather, that there are several ways to be Caribbean

(Pfaff 113). In her 1995 contribution to the edited collection *Penser la créolité*, Condé defines the contemporary Caribbean as a place "sans contours définis, poreux à tous les bruits lointains, traversé par toutes les influences, même les plus contradictoires" (without definite contours, porous to all distant noises, traversed by all influences, even the most contradictory) ("Chercher nos vérités" 309). This idea of the openness of the Caribbean space to multiple influences resonates with the conception of contemporary historians, including Glissant, that identity, history, and memory cannot be rigidly fixed. The year 1995 emerges as a particularly significant period for Condé as she locates it as a time when the forces of globalization take over and the importance of national borders diminish. Condé's reflections post-1995 demonstrate her increasing awareness of these globalizing influences, a position she articulates in novels such as *Desirada*. These personal tales form a complement to the more cerebral works produced by Chamoiseau and Glissant on the subject, such as their jointly authored *Quand les murs tombent: l'identité nationale hors-la-loi?*

In 2005, Condé made an address at the Alliance Française in Perth, Australia, entitled "Maryse Condé: Itinerary of a Caribbean Writer," in which she reflected on her personal and literary journey. Condé divided her talk into four parts that she believed mirror the transformations in her literary life: (1) Peau noire, masques blancs (Black skin, white masks); (2) What is Africa to me?; (3) Cahier d'un retour au pays natal (Notebook of a return to the native land); and (4) Imagine there is no country. The suggestive literary and cultural allusions of these four titles make it possible to group Condé's prolific output and to map her development as a writer. In 2014, Condé published, in English, *The Journey of a Caribbean Writer*, which draws together essays and lectures from different periods of her career and which summarizes her principal reflections on various contemporary issues such as race, language, and literature. This publication seems to be part of a wider stage of retrospection with other recent autobiographical books such as *La Vie sans fards* and *Mets et merveilles* (2015). The first phase of Condé's literary development details her grapple with the contradictions of being an educated, impeccably French speaking girl growing up in Guadeloupe. The second phase relates to the considerable time she spent in Africa, detailed in works such as *Hérémakhonon* (1976) and the two volumes of *Ségou* (1984 and 1985), which highlight some of the challenges faced by a Guadeloupean woman living in Africa. "Cahier d'un retour au pays natal," a reference to Césaire's famous poem of the same name, marks Condé's return to her Caribbean roots and a reexamination of Creole cultural traditions such as the *veillée* (wake). *Traversée de la mangrove*

(Crossing the Mangrove) (1989) is perhaps the best example of the literary incarnation of Condé's rediscovery of her country after many years away. However, this period also poses new questions about how Condé fits into her island homeland, particularly in relation to the French-Creole language question. Condé explores many of these issues in an extended interview with Vèvè Clark. Finally, Condé details the unexpected freedom she found in the United States, a place that allowed her to exist as a nomadic writer unburdened by national or cultural baggage. She asserts that her eleventh novel, *Desirada* (1997), ushers in this new phase in her writing. In a 2003 interview, Condé asserts that one overarching question drives her entire literary project, serving both to unify her eclectic body of work and to allow diverse transformations to take place: "how to find one's place in the dominant world, how to maintain one's voice, how to be oneself in this world that asks you to conform" (Alexander et al., 12). This quest for selfhood is central in shaping her approach to history and memory.

In 2007, Condé further reflects on her vision of Caribbean identity through her contribution to the collection *Pour une littérature-monde* ("Liaison dangereuse"). Michel Le Bris coined the term *littérature-monde* in 1992 in a collective volume entitled *Pour une littérature voyageuse* (Borer, Bouvier, and Chaillou). Le Bris and others developed this concept following the Étonnants Voyageurs writers' festival, which focused on reinvigorating French literature after decades of being subject to the changing ideological demands of twentieth-century intellectual thought. According to Le Bris, this festival was born out of "un gigantesque ras-le-bol devant l'état de la littérature française, devenue sourde et aveugle . . . à la course du monde, à force de se croire la seule, l'unique, l'ultime référence, à jamais admirable, modèle livré à l'humanité" (a widespread discontent about the state of French literature, which had become deaf and blind . . . to the movement of the world, as a result of thinking itself the only, the unique and ultimate reference, the always admirable model, bequeathed to humanity) (25). For these thinkers, the concept of *littérature-monde* would constitute, by contrast, a more outward-looking, global literature that was not fixated upon metropolitan France or the French language, more akin to the anglophone concept of "world literature." *Littérature-monde* proposes an approach to literature that displaces the predominance of France and French and instead constitutes a body of writing that just happens to be in the French language. Many of these ideas fit in with Condé's conception of her role as a writer unhindered by geographical, cultural, and linguistic specificities and thereby her ability to resist immutable categories of identification in her work and person.

Condé chooses language as the subject of her contribution to *Pour une littérature-monde*, "Liaison dangereuse." From the outset, Condé adopts a position of empowerment in relation to her country's cultural legacies. Rather than portraying herself as the passive victim of colonial linguistic dominance, Condé is instead an active player in her self-expression, a position she reasserts in an interview with Paola Ghinelli. "La langue française, je l'aime. C'est un élément qui m'est venu de la colonisation, d'accord, mais que je me suis mise à aimer et que j'ai intégré en moi pour en faire une autre langue, qui est la langue Maryse Condé" (I like the French language. It's an element that came to me from colonization, yes, but I started to love it and I integrated it into myself to make another language, which is the language of Maryse Condé) (Ghinelli 44). In Condé's understanding, both French and Creole must surrender to her self-determining will. While she does not deny the historical significance attached to both languages, she succeeds in displacing the French-Creole dichotomy by introducing a third possibility— that of "Maryse Condé"—which privileges the notion of interrelationship and connection rather than rigidly defined and oppositional elements.

This introduction of a third element resonates in a more personal way with the idea of historians such as Michel de Certeau, who explores history and memory in a continuum that also includes the present and future. While Creole offered certain subversive possibilities for the slaves, it was firmly devalued by those wanting to advance in society. However, Condé notes that as a result of *créoliste* writers reappropriating the Creole language and linking it to "authentic" French Caribbean culture, they simultaneously managed to exclude those, like Condé, who grew up speaking French at home. In a demonstration of the way in which Condé rewrites "the colonial/postcolonial relationship itself" (Mardorossian, 8), she reclaims the colonizer's language for herself: "Il a été forgé pour moi seule. Pour ma dilection personnelle" (It was created for me alone. For my personal delectation) ("Liaison dangereuse," 215). Her problematization of the concept of the "mother tongue" is an issue that becomes important in her autofictional works, where it served to exclude people within her own family as well as at a more general social level.

Condé's attitude toward language is part of a process she has referred to as "cultural cannibalism." In a literal declaration of her ingestion of certain cultural norms and their transformation into something new, Condé asserted in a 2005 interview: "J'ai avalé toute une série de réalités et je suis le résultat de ces mélanges" (I swallowed a whole series of realities and I am the result of these mixes) (Ghinelli 43). Nick Nesbitt emphasizes the positive attributes of this engagement with colonialist norms, arguing that "cultural cannibalism invokes a mode of relating to the world that refuses destructive confrontation... cultural cannibalism renews rather than destroys the culture it absorbs and transforms" ("Stepping Outside the Magic Circle," 400). Condé's cultural cannibalism is particularly bound up in writing where she strives to imprint her own unique stamp on every work that she produces. Moreover, the freedom that this creative medium offers her proves central to her reconciliation with the past on a personal and political level.

Condé reveals that part of the process of reconciliation with the past is the need to redefine categories of identity. In the introduction to her book *Reclaiming Difference: Caribbean Women Rewrite Postcolonialism*, Carine Mardorossian asserts that the defining element of postcolonial women writers is their rejection of simplistic categories of identification such as race, gender, and class. Instead, they present a more nuanced vision of identity, privileging the way in which such differences "come into being *through* rather than *prior to* their interrelationships" (3). Alluding to Glissant's notion of Relation, and Chamoiseau and Glissant's jointly authored publications on identity such as *Quand les murs tombent: l'identité nationale hors-la-loi?*, Mardorossian draws attention to the way in which difference "binds rather than blinds, connects rather than isolates, and enriches rather than threatens" (6). Condé's personal narratives reinforce the redemptive possibilities of this relational model as well as its fruitful application in history and literature. By refusing to privilege received notions, Condé's approach liberates her to posit new interpretations of the past—whether they are personal or historical.

According to Nesbitt, Condé achieves this end in the interconnected way she approaches history. "Her goal is not to depict in broad objective strokes the history of the Antilles or Antillean literature, but rather to produce something like a multi-faceted study of singular human experiences" ("Stepping Outside the Magic Circle," 393). For Nesbitt, this historical practice constitutes more than just a literary approach to the past; it is also a means to act politically by writing the forgotten players of history into an acknowledged existence. As we will see in this chapter, one way in which Condé achieves this aim is by filling in the gaps of her own personal history. Moreover, in contrast to her *créoliste* counterparts such as Chamoiseau and Raphaël Confiant, whom Condé considers as dangerously fixated on the past, she injects a sense of perpetual movement into her work. Her books frequently move between past and present; they change genre and switch tone. Indeed, there is nothing fixed or reductive in her work. Condé explicitly asserts that the inevitable intersection between what she terms as "le passé individuel" (the individual past) and "le passé historique" (the historical past) is a space where "tout cela se confond tellement" (everything is so mixed up) (Ghinelli 37). Scharfman praises Condé's questioning of history, arguing that her work holds in tension the dilemma of "unburden[ing] ourselves of our past without falling prey to the illusion that we can turn our backs on it" ("A Fugue of Legacies," 463). Just as Condé displaces the primacy of categories of identity such as race, gender, and class, so too does she open up questions of time, history, and memory for renewed consideration.

As a writer who is frequently heralded for her postcolonial insights, Condé nonetheless questions other key concepts in the field such as "homeland," "exile," and "origin," in keeping with her provocative nature. These hallmarks of postcolonial criticism are often presented as immutable categories of identification, but Condé rejects an oversimplification of these terms. Early in her career, Condé asserts: "Je pensais que chacun avait un lieu d'origine et quand on le quittait on devenait un exilé, mais au fur et à mesure je me suis rendue compte que même le lieu d'origine voyage avec vous.... Au fur et à mesure je suis donc arrivée à ne plus croire à l'exil" (I used to think that everyone had a place of origin and when we left it one would become an exile, but gradually I realized that even one's place of origin travels with you ... Gradually I managed to no longer believe in exile) (Ghinelli 34–35). In contrast to many postcolonial critics who posit "exile" as central to their theories of home and belonging, Condé refuses to generalize about the experience of leaving one's homeland. Echoing her approach to language, which she fashions for her own designs, Condé highlights that one can exercise the same "cultural cannibalism" in relation to one's country of origin: "[P]etit à petit je découvre que le monde est à moi puisque, à cause de l'histoire même de mon peuple, je peux être partout chez moi" (Little by little, I discovered that the world is mine since, because of my people's very history, I can be at home everywhere) (Ghinelli 35). Her questioning of these various theoretical concepts allows her to embrace the idea of an evolving world where it is impossible to freeze things in time. This forward-facing approach and consistent refusal to be constrained is what allows Condé to embrace her writing life with such originality and to put forward a notion of history and memory that is characterized by connection and movement.

In her personal narratives, Condé explores these questions by filling in the gaps of her own history through a combination of "hard facts" and imagination. Her bricolage-like approach mirrors the techniques adopted by Gisèle

Pineau and Edwidge Danticat in their autobiographical explorations. As in all her work, Condé announces an attitude of creative freedom and irreverence when reflecting on the genre of autobiography: "[A]ll books are autobiographical! I would term it autofiction, rather" (Alexander et al., 11). Condé explicitly rejects the notion that fiction can be pure invention while autobiography is self-proclaimed "truth." As she states in an interview with Bénédicte Boisseron, "Let's say that the difference lies in that, with autobiography, one relies on controllable facts while with intimacy, there is a lot of autobiography and also a lot of imaginary facts" (Boisseron, "Intimité: entretien avec Maryse Condé," 144). Regarding her first foray into autobiographical reflection, *Le Coeur à rire et à pleurer*, she asserts: "when I say *contes vrais*—'true tales'—it means that it is true, but with the distance of age, the gap of time, and so on, it has become a kind of fiction" (Lewis 102). Moreover, as critics such as Hardwick have pointed out, there are certain glaring untruths in this first autofictional work; for example, the names of Condé's siblings change from those she states in her interview with Vèvè Clark (Hardwick, "J'ai toujours été une personne un peu à part," 111; Clark, 90). Regarding *Victoire: My Mother's Mother*, Condé is particularly open in her admissions about the ambiguities of "truth" versus "fiction" when she imagines and invents her grandmother's life as much as she tries to recount the "true" facts of her existence.

Her 2012 publication *La Vie sans fards* is Condé's most serious attempt at rejecting artifice in favor of the "truth." Condé consistently refuses binary opposites and poses instead an overlapping network of interrelationship in all three books. Two important themes stand out in these works: Condé's need to situate herself in relation to her female relatives and the self-understanding she gains from placing her writing life in relation to the literary influences around her. As the following analyses of Condé's principal autofictional narratives reveal, she puts the notion of autobiography itself into a network formation where "truth" and "invention," "fact" and "fiction," intermingle with the aim of helping Condé to understand herself and her craft against the backdrop of francophone Caribbean history.

Le Coeur à rire et à pleurer: contes vrais de mon enfance

In 1999, Condé published her first extended autobiographical reflection entitled *Le Coeur à rire et à pleurer: contes vrais de mon enfance*, translated into English by Richard Philcox as *Tales from the Heart: True Stories from my Childhood*. While this book is centered on Condé's childhood in Guadeloupe, it also offers insights into her growing awareness of the way in which the personal and historical are intertwined. From the very first page of the inaugural chapter, entitled "Family Portrait," Condé links her family life to the larger historical context of her island. She remarks that, for her parents, World War II represented the darkest period in their lives because it restricted the family's regular trips to France. Condé's discussion of language in "Liaison dangereuse" reveals that France and French were decisive elements in her childhood, as her parents were passionately attached to the Metropole and all that it represented. "For them France was in no way the seat of colonial power. It was truly the Mother Country and Paris, the City of Light that lit up their lives" (*Tales from the Heart*, 3). However, as Condé grows and develops as an individual, she becomes increasingly conscious of the gaps that exist between the idealized vision of France that her parents present to her and outsiders' perception of the Boucolon family as exceptional blacks because they can speak French. The ability to speak French or not proves even more crucial in *Victoire: My Mother's Mother*, as language becomes one of the principal grounds for Victoire's exclusion from bourgeois society.

In a memorable and illustrative scene from *Tales from the Heart*, Condé portrays the potency of language when a white waiter in Paris compliments the Boucolon family on their French. While her father merely replies that of course they are as French as the French, her mother refuses to accept this condescending attitude, asserting instead that they are even *more* French: "We're more educated. We have better manners. We read more" (4). For the young Condé, this experience provokes her first questioning of her identity, further deepened when her older brother, Sandrino, declares that their parents are "a pair of alienated individuals" (6). The split that Condé senses between her parents' perception of themselves as exceptional individuals, coupled with the attitude of superiority adopted by the Parisian waiter, marks the beginning of her refusal to be defined by others. It also brings to mind the psychological dilemmas described by Frantz Fanon in *Peau noire, masques blancs* (*Black Skin, White Masks*). While still not fully understanding the concept of alienation, the young Condé eventually comes to the conclusion that an alienated person must be someone who "is trying to be what he can't because he does not like what he is" (*Tales from the Heart*, 7). According to her memoir, she becomes permanently altered by this revelation and transforms overnight from a model of obedience into an obstinate child. We see here the seed of an important characteristic of the adult Condé: her desire to achieve complete freedom of self and her rejection of "playing the game."

As Condé explores different facets of her childhood memories through a series of interconnected chapters, it becomes clear that the disjuncture between the "French" and "Creole" worlds affects her profoundly. In "The Bluest Eye," for example, a title Condé borrows from Toni Morrison's novel of the same name, Condé recalls an early "love affair" with the young Gilbert, who writes her a love letter complimenting her on her beautiful blue eyes. Condé is outraged by his audacity in describing her in this way when her eyes are dark brown. At the same time, however, Condé acknowledges that her cultural references are French, too, and these have a profound influence on her development as an individual. While Condé speaks of "cannibalizing" such cultural traditions later in her life, as a child they provoke a questioning of who she is. The process we have witnessed as Condé moves from defining herself in opposition to the "French" or "Creole" worlds to one where she is in interrelationship with these elements is indicative of her maturing vision of identity. Her coining of the concept of writing in "Maryse Condé" as an adult allows her to exceed the limitations of expressing herself too well in French (as postcolonialists would accuse her of) or not well enough in Creole (as *créolistes* would complain). Her three autofictional narratives reveal that the language question is a constant challenge in her life, until she ultimately arrives at a place in *La Vie sans fards* where she does not care what others think and expresses herself in her own unique way.

One of the most powerful chapters in *Tales from the Heart*, "History Lesson," centers around Condé's discussion of the master-slave dialectic. This story also underlines the importance of history in understanding one's present and future. In the book, Condé remarks upon the constant anxiety that infused her childhood because of her parents' desire for upward mobility through assimilation with the French. As a result of their determination to maintain the appearance of French respectability, any behavior or outburst in Creole was to be repressed. Condé gives the example of not being able to eat grilled peanuts or coconut candies in the street while she accompanies her parents on their evening walk because respectable people do not behave in this way. "Because of my parents' paranoia, my childhood was lived in a constant state of anxiety" (54). More disturbingly, however, we see the intelligent, outspoken Condé become bullied by a young white girl whom she meets in the course of one of these evening promenades. According to this young girl, Anne-Marie de Surville, who ironically addresses Condé in Creole: "I have to hit you because you're black" (56). When Condé questions her parents on this disturbing declaration, she receives evasive and incomplete answers. "I guessed that a secret was hidden at the bottom of my past, a painful, shameful secret that would have been wrong, even dangerous, to prise open" (57). Condé's assertion here is strongly suggestive of Nicolas Abraham's notion of the metaphorical tomb in which family secrets are buried, but never forgotten. While Condé later queries the reality of this episode, she nonetheless reveals some of the psychological consequences of the colonial burden on children. The conflicting worlds she uncovers between black and white, French and Creole, remain decisive factors in her development and constitute major themes in her literary works, which serve as a kind of retrospective "working through." This disturbing scene powerfully illustrates how History may intrude into an individual narrative.

Condé's organization of her book into a series of interconnected chapters that are positioned in relation to each other rather than as the unraveling of a continuous linear narrative is reflective of her approach to history. The physical structure of the book also draws attention to Condé's journey of self-discovery in which she seeks to understand different parts of herself, transforming memories that are defined in opposition—for example, Condé against her parents, French against Creole, childhood versus adulthood—to ones that are connected to each other and contribute to the evolution of the self-assured, adult persona of "Maryse Condé." Thus, as a mature narrator, Condé can splice together the linguistic and historical idiosyncrasies of her childhood to arrive at a point where these differing influences coexist in the character of Maryse Condé. For example, the conflict Condé perceives in her parents' blind obsession with France is moderated into a place where Condé the adult is able to profit from the advantages of France without abandoning the other influences of her childhood in Guadeloupe. Each chapter in the book forms part of Condé's overall attempt to know herself in an integrated way, a process that helps her to reconcile with some of the more troubling aspects of her past.

An aspect of Condé's life that remains a source of conflict is the relationship between herself and her mother, Jeanne Boucoulon. Condé foreshadows the importance of mothering and the female line in *Tales from the Heart*, dedicating it to Jeanne and recalling one of her mother's birthdays as the day she decided to become a writer. Condé cites this scene in numerous publications, which is also noteworthy for the indistinct nature of time. Condé had prepared a play for her mother, which had brought Jeanne to tears for its unfavorable portrayal of her. Recalling this revelation in an interview, Condé emphasizes the empowerment she felt in defining herself against her mother: "The feeling of power that I felt that afternoon from making my mother cry ... is what I have to admit I have been searching for, book after book. To take the wind out of people's sails! To lay bare their skeletons! To denounce all the hypocrites, the zealots, the self-righteous! To smash apart clichés and lies!" ("How to Become a So-Called Caribbean Writer," 674). While proving motivating for Condé, this attitude presents itself in clear opposition to the notion of interconnection and relationship. By taking pleasure in the act of making her mother cry and freezing her mother into a stereotype of emotional detachment in her desire for upward mobility, Condé initially casts the mother-daughter relationship as an immutable negative in her life. However, while this stance provides some sense of certainty to Condé as she defines herself in her difference from her mother, her later reflections reveal the limitations of this approach. Indeed, as she reflects back on her life, she realizes that it is more empowering to view her mother in connection to herself, rather than in opposition.

Before Condé comes to the realization that her relationship with her mother must be reevaluated if she is to move forward, the search for the maternal occurs as a haunting and recurrent theme in her work. "I lost my mother early on. I address this a great deal: the absence of a mother, the challenge of forming oneself, of educating oneself without a mother" (Alexander et al., 13). Condé speaks here of the physical loss of her mother, who died when Condé was a young woman, yet she is also referring to the absence of her mother as a nurturing figure when she was alive. The toxic relationship between the two women resembles a trauma in which the repeated search for the mother in Condé's writing enacts Caruth's assertion that the traumatic experience is often experienced as a repeated and uncontrolled intrusion into one's imagination. Due to her negative characterization of Jeanne when she was a child and young adult, Condé attempts to negate her influence when it is in fact impossible to do so. The same process is at work in *Victoire: My Mother's Mother*, where Condé depicts Jeanne's rejection of her own mother, Victoire, in order to define herself. In both cases, the complexities of the mother-daughter relationship demand attention, and the two books reveal daughters in search of a reunion with the mother. *La Vie sans fards* adds a further layer to this journey when Condé interrogates her own role as a mother. By assessing her relationship with her four children, she stresses the vital place genealogy has in conditioning one's self-identity. Moreover, she highlights the need to fill in the gaps of history—or "herstory"—in order to know oneself fully and move positively toward the future. We see a similar process at work in

Pineau's writing, in which she traces a female genealogy at a collective level in *Femmes des Antilles* and a personal level in *Exile According to Julia* and *Mes quatre femmes*. As Condé states in an interview with Noëlle Carruggi:

> Chez nous aux Antilles toutes les généalogies doivent passer par les femmes. Il faut qu'on ait un rapport particulier avec les femmes de sa famille. Moi je n'ai pas eu ce rapport ... j'ai toujours eu l'impression que j'étais un peu une sorte d'électron libre, lâché comme ça dans l'azur. Donc, pour arriver à me rattacher à cette société antillaise, à ce monde guadeloupéen auquel j'appartiens en principe, il m'a fallu voir, recréer toute cette généalogie féminine que je ne connaissais pas.
>
> (In the French Caribbean, all genealogy passes by women. One has to have a particular rapport with the women in one's family. I didn't have this relationship.... I always had the impression that I was a bit like a free electron, let out like that in the blue. So, in order to reattach myself to this Caribbean society, to this Guadeloupean world to which I belong in theory, it was necessary for me to recreate this female genealogy that I didn't know.) (Carruggi, "Écrire en Maryse Condé," 210)

In this characterization, it is as if Condé needs to establish the mother figure at the center of her psyche before she is able to make the connections necessary to heal other layers in her character. As the following sections will reveal—and which is also suggested in the birthday scene—two elements are vital to her journey of self-discovery: integration of the mother and writing.

Victoire, les saveurs et les mots

In an even more explicit way than *Tales from the Heart*, *Victoire, les saveurs et les mots* (*Victoire: My Mother's Mother*) details Condé's search for self-understanding through the female line coupled with her belief in the empowering possibilities of expressing oneself creatively. The life of Condé's maternal grandmother, Victoire Quidal, is the focus of this book, but Condé also attempts to better understand her own mother, who, as we have seen, existed primarily as a negative figure in her early life. As she asserts in "Liaison dangereuse," "I tried to explain the complex relationships with my mother and grandmother, all this life before mine that influenced my behavior" (213). Like *Tales from the Heart*, Condé underscores the importance of francophone Caribbean history in this narrative, particularly its secretive nature, which resembles Abraham's entombed secrets. Condé recalls that "nobody in my family told me anything about slavery or the slave trade, those initiatory voyages that founded our Caribbean destiny. I had to negotiate on my own the weight of this terrible past" (*Victoire*, 84). Alongside the fractured family structures that were characteristic of many postslave societies, Condé becomes aware of the sacrifices her grandmother made for her daughter and consequently for her descendants. The historical thread is an element woven into many Caribbean women writers' stories, which act in a similar way to the revered Caribbean grandmother passing stories down the line. As a result of Victoire's commitment to her daughter's future, Jeanne becomes one of the first black schoolteachers in Guadeloupe, which enables her to advance socially in a way that was denied an illiterate domestic servant like Victoire. While Victoire herself was unable to realize any possibility of social progression, her unrelenting push of Jeanne to achieve an education and a career—even when this meant denying her daughter emotionally—demonstrates an awareness of the importance of looking outward and upward in an era that was often characterized by parochial thinking.

Images of brokenness and disconnection, emphasized by the early theorizations of historians such as Michel de Certeau and Édouard Glissant about the Caribbean, are evident on a more personal level in Condé's reminiscences of her early life. Like many others at the time, including Condé's father himself, Jeanne grew up fatherless. Condé recalls that her mother never revealed her grandfather's name to her nor the circumstances of her birth, while her father, Auguste Boucolon, dreamed up exotic explanations for his own father's absence. "I think he recreated [the truth] at will, taking pleasure in pronouncing the syllables that made him dream: Paramaribo, Sumatra. Thanks to him I understood from the time I was small that identities were created" (*Victoire*, 16). Alongside this backdrop of paternal absence, Condé reveals certain destructive traits that flourish in her female line. She demonstrates that Victoire's suffering as a result of her social limitations leads to her emotional torturing of others, a behavioral attitude that is passed down to daughter and granddaughter in a pattern of transgenerational emotional suffering. In *Victoire*, Condé ponders the effect this psychological inheritance has on her life despite the fact that she never knew her grandmother personally: "I often wonder what my relationship with myself, my vision of my country, the Caribbean and the world in general, indeed what my writing of these things would express, if I had jumped on the knees of an expansive and jolly grandmother ... whispering in my ear a honeyed myth of the past" (17). *Victoire* expands the portrait Condé gives of her family in *Tales from the Heart*, situating the way in which historical circumstances condition the development of individual families. As a result of Victoire's and Jeanne's struggles with the legacies of slavery and colonialism, Condé's own life is irrevocably changed. Her focus and circumstances may be different from those of her female ancestors, but as her battles with language and alienation show, the francophone Caribbean past continues to profoundly influence her life experiences. Nesbitt characterizes this approach as "an individual experience of French Caribbean history, saturated with affectivity" ("Le sujet de l'histoire," 115). His assertion highlights Condé's commitment to displaying the imprint of the historical on the personal.

A major focus of *Victoire* is the parallels Condé draws between her own occupation as a writer and Victoire's as a cook. Both of these means of self-expression serve to empower their creators by allowing them to bring about changes in their own lives and those of others as well as constituting the bonds of connection that allow Condé to understand her life more fully. Condé demonstrates that creative activity allows one to reimagine one's life's circumstances, reconfiguring previously negative situations into new and more positive arrangements. In contrast to her mother and daughter, Jeanne emerges as lacking, as she does not dedicate herself to a comparable artistic activity. While she does find an intellectual outlet in her teaching career, Condé reveals that the rewards of personal satisfaction are not the same for her, as this activity is linked to the painful process of social progression. Teaching gives Jeanne the entry card to join the burgeoning black bourgeoisie in Guadeloupe, but it is a milieu that requires Jeanne to repress the Creole side of her character and consistently present herself as more "French" than the French. The psychological cost of maintaining this side of her character is evident in the ire she displays toward the arrogant Parisian waiter in *Tales from the Heart*. Moreover, the rules as to what constitutes "French" consistently change, so it appears that Jeanne can never rest comfortably in her own identity. By contrast, Condé shows that a creative outlet helps you to understand yourself, situate yourself in relationship with rather than in opposition to others, and thereby take control of your life. While Victoire is not the director of her affairs in one sense, Condé shows that her efforts to release her descendants from poverty through her dogged commitment to Jeanne's education are part of a progressive process of liberation that travels down the female line.

Early in the book, Condé underlines both distance and proximity in her description of her female ancestors. When Jeanne reveals that Victoire was a cook, the young Condé distances herself from her mother and also places an obstacle between her mother and her grandmother: "I couldn't believe it. My mother, the daughter of a cook! My mother, who had no palate and was notoriously incapable of boiling an egg" (2). By contrast, Condé draws parallels between Victoire and herself. "Most of her days [Victoire] spent locked up in the temple of her kitchen, a small shack behind the house, set slightly back from the washhouse. Not saying a word, head bent, absorbed over her kitchen range like a writer hunched over her computer" (59). As the narrative progresses, Condé reveals that cooking is key to Victoire's social advancement for her daughter and, consequently, for Condé herself. Victoire suffers throughout her life from poverty and prejudice, but culinary creation gives her the means of transforming her destiny. Cooking is a way for Victoire to express her creativity in the same way Condé expresses hers through writing. Most importantly, both creative outlets allow their creators to gain a sense of sovereignty over their lives and to inject elements of optimism in situations of hardship. For Victoire, this activity is closely linked to asserting herself in a space where she has very little social or political control; for Condé, it is more an opportunity for her to express herself in complete freedom. *Victoire* also underlines the intricate relationship that exists between the ability to express oneself and one's attitude to life. For example, when Victoire is no longer able to set foot in the kitchen, Condé laments the feeling of uselessness that must assail her, just as she would feel if she were banned from her computer (116). When Victoire loses her purpose in life, it is because she cannot cook, in the same way that the gift of writing may desert one if one loses the will to live (171). The parallels Condé draws between herself and her grandmother through their shared creative prowess prove empowering on both a material and a personal level as well as creating a positive connection between the two women that forms a contrast to Condé's earlier impressions of Victoire as a psychologically manipulative grandmother.

Condé's narrative reveals that, in contrast to her mother and daughter, Jeanne's lack of a creative outlet results in an attitude that can only react against something, rather than be expressed in a more positive way. Jeanne's discontent toward life is frequently articulated in relation to her mother's cooking, such that rejecting her food becomes a way of rebelling against her mother. Her reaction seems to incite an either/or option of relating to the world. When she is angry at Victoire for deserting her in order to follow a man to Martinique, Jeanne loses a significant amount of weight "as a way of punishing her mother who placed so much importance in [food]" (96). As Victoire feels increasingly rejected by her daughter, she too expresses her emotions through food by "cooking to excess" (112). Victoire and Jeanne consistently play out their emotional battles through the indulgence in or rejection of food—to the point where Victoire feels so withdrawn from her daughter that she literally loses her taste for life. The conflicted relationship that they play out with food, which is Victoire's source of expression rather than Jeanne's, demonstrates both the connectivity and disconnectivity that mark Condé's ancestry. In the same way that Caribbean history is scarred by patterns of conflict, so too is this clashing between Condé, her mother, and her grandmother. While Condé is removed to a degree from the emotional turmoil of the battles she imagines in *Victoire*, she attempts to harness her own creative outlet of writing in order to bring connection back to her female line. This desire for reconciliation is evident from the outset, where Condé dedicates the book to her daughters and granddaughters. Creative expression, then, proves to be a tool of great potency for Condé.

On a different level, Condé uses her grandmother's culinary talents as a way to inscribe her tale in a larger historical narrative by recording the concrete traces she leaves behind her. Condé's work is like that of a historian piecing together information, although, in the absence of hard facts, she must equally imagine the details of her grandmother's life. Mary Jean Green goes to some length to detail the various historically verifiable facts in the book while also noting the presence of four prominent Guadeloupeans in the dedication—historian Raymond Boutin, writers Lucie Julia and Jean-Michel Renault, and especially historian Jean-Pierre Sainton. "Her project of reconstitution or reconstruction of her grandmother's life has also entailed a reconstruction of the Guadeloupe within which her grandmother had lived and died, a period stretching from the post-emancipation years of the 1880s to her death in 1915" (Green, 301). Despite the difficult relationship that exists between mother and daughter, it is Jeanne who conserves many of the existent "traces of the past," as if she is trying to transpose Victoire's worth onto a level that is acceptable among the black bourgeois society that she joins as a result of her education. "Among the papers my mother kept was issue 51 of *l'Echo pointois*, where right in the middle of a laudatory article appears the menu for this christening banquet [for Boniface Walberg Jr.], lyrically composed like a poem" (*Victoire*, 70). Condé recalls hearing her mother constantly asserting: "My mother could neither read nor write, but without her I wouldn't be where I am today" (114). It is as if Jeanne is desperate to remember her mother in a meaningful way but struggles to do so in a society that denies the worth of an illiterate domestic who cannot speak French. Jeanne finds herself in a complex web of conflicting demands in which Victoire is the one who enables her promotion to bourgeois society, but at the same time Jeanne must relinquish attachment to her mother in order to accept this position. Jeanne's ambiguous, emotionally detached approach to life reflects her internal struggle as she fights to find a way to integrate these two very different worlds. In fact, it falls to her daughter to forge this reconciliatory network of relationship as if the distance afforded by one generation's remove is the only way to heal from the past.

Throughout the narrative, Condé attempts to create connections between her female relatives and to replace images of brokenness and dissonance with relationship. On a social level, Condé elevates Victoire to a place of significance, likening her culinary creations to a religious experience that dramatically challenges her exclusion from colonial society. Condé's reevaluation of Victoire's role provides a bonding link between three generations of conflicted female relationships. When Victoire is close to death, Condé imagines her grandmother preparing a final meal she labels "the Last Supper" as a way to leave a final imprint on her descendants' narrative. This lunch represents Victoire's "way of writing her last will and testament" (189), and in a rare moment of intimacy between mother and daughter, Jeanne records the menu of this significant day "on one of her exercise books that she carefully kept, scribbled with bits of her diary, memos, class timetables, and her children's height and weight" (189). Food ultimately becomes a way for Victoire to reach out to her daughter and for her daughter to reciprocate in a way that is meaningful for her. It is interesting that Jeanne chooses to record this culinary experience in written form, in some way forging a bond between all three generations in which the cook (Victoire) gradually becomes the writer (Condé). This book provides a powerful exploration of the empowering qualities of family connection and the redemptive possibilities of creative expression.

La Vie sans fards

Published in 2012, *La Vie sans fards* is a more introspective book than Condé's previous two memoirs, representing a striking example of her desire to express herself without fear of maintaining a particular self-image. When the book was published, Condé was seventy-five years old and no longer felt the need to justify herself in any way. In the opening lines of the book, she poses the dilemma that many face in how to present themselves to the world: "Pourquoi faut-il que toute tentative de se raconter aboutisse à un fatras de demi-vérités?" (Why is it that any attempt to talk about oneself ends up in a jumble of half-truths?) (11). The direct approach Condé adopts in this narrative encapsulates the sense of liberation she feels when she abandons literary embellishment for the sake of her truth. In *La Vie sans fards*, she describes her years spent in Africa, a period of her life when she struggled to resolve the competing influences of romantic and sexual love, motherhood, the quest for a cultural identity, and her beginnings as a writer. Often, she presents herself in less than idyllic terms, but the result is that Condé is able to embrace each curve in her life journey, allowing her to arrive at a position where she is comfortable with herself and unthreatened by the Other. Her long and varied life experiences serve to divest the self/other dichotomy of its power, creating instead a series of psychological and geographical positions among which she is able to move.

Africa is the focus of this book, and she describes in detail her migrations from Côte d'Ivoire to Guinea, Ghana, and Senegal as a young woman. She asserts that the book aims to unravel "la place considérable qu'a occupée l'Afrique dans mon existence et dans mon imaginaire" (the considerable place Africa occupied in my existence and in my imagination) (16), but it is also much more than that. It paints the portrait of a woman struggling to know herself: through her relationships with her mother, her children, and her lovers; the competing cultural influences of her "homelands" (Guadeloupe, France, and Africa); and the way in which writing comes to provide her with the ultimate freedom of expression, "cette joie que j'avais oubliée: celle de la liberté" (this joy that I had forgotten: that of freedom) (230). At the end of the book, we find that *La Vie sans fards* is also a kind of love letter to Condé's second husband, Richard Philcox, the man she credits with changing her life. Condé's African experiences act as a sort of laboratory test of the way in which one can view one's life, "[a]vec le recul que . . . donne la vieillesse" (with the distance of age) (286), in a relational manner.

The book is divided into three parts, and each chapter opens with a quotation from a different source—including Caribbean proverbs and quotations from popular and literary authors old and new—attesting to the cultural riches Condé acquires as part of her journey of self-discovery. As a retrospective book, *La Vie sans fards* seeks to spin many webs of connection, one of which is the interpenetration of her life and work. The story lays out how a number of her own books came to life, particularly *Hérémakhonon*, her first published novel and the one that most closely mirrors her African experiences. Three key themes emerge in this narrative, which prove fundamental in Condé's development as a writer: her role as a woman, her need to experience Africa firsthand in order to develop a sense of cultural identity, and her coming to literature, which becomes her lifeblood and longstanding passion. Moreover, the way in which Condé returns to her mother and her children's influence on her illustrates the importance of family to the construction of self. She refers repeatedly to Jeanne (54, 119, 157, 196) and again asserts that the writing of *Victoire: My Mother's Mother* was "l'ouvrage qui me fut le plus douloureux à écrire" (the book that was the most painful for me to write) (*La Vie*, 316). *La Vie sans fards* cements the genealogical journeys Condé undertakes in her first two autofictional narratives and underlines the importance of viewing one's family in a relational network. While *Tales from the Heart* and *Victoire* are focused more on her relationships with women, her latest work interrogates her role as a woman. All are driven by the desire to fill in the gaps of her family history.

La Vie sans fards depicts motherhood as a central feature of Condé's African years, an experience characterized by conflict, complexity, and deep love. It also provides potent examples of the way in which the political and personal are intertwined. In an early challenge to the moral standards of bourgeois society, Condé finds herself pregnant as a young woman in Paris and then abandoned by her Haitian lover, Jean Dominique, a prominent journalist and agronomist in Haiti who was later assassinated by the Jean-Claude Duvalier regime in 2000. This book is the first occasion when Condé reveals in a public way the father of her son Denis. Dominique inspired deep passion in Condé but also intense hatred, which she extended to the whole country of Haiti when he left her so abruptly. In fact it is another, later lover, Jacques, the illegitimate son of François Duvalier, who reignites her love of this island country. Condé's maternal experience with Dominique exemplifies the limitations for women in a society that did not yet tolerate single mothers and where contraception options were limited. Her later pregnancies, too, led her to feel as if she were a "victime du sort" (victim of fate) (78) rather than a driver of her own destiny.

The experience of motherhood itself is both positive and negative for Condé. While Denis's birth is always linked to the painful memories of Dominique's abandonment of her, the birth of her first daughter, Sylvie-Anne, with her first husband Mamadou Condé, provoked instead intense love: "Avec Sylvie-Anne, tout était différent. Tout était simple" (With

Sylvie-Anne, everything was different. Everything was simple) (58). And yet maternity is not an easy role for Condé as she struggles to strike the balance between her own needs and those of her children. As she asserts in *La Vie sans fards*: "Les lecteurs me demandent souvent pourquoi mes romans sont remplis de mères qui considèrent leurs enfants comme des poids trop lourds à porter, d'enfants qui souffrent d'être mal aimés et se replient sur eux-mêmes. C'est que je parle d'expérience" (Readers often ask me why my novels are filled with mothers who consider their children as burdens too heavy to carry, with children who suffer from not being loved enough and who turn inward. It is because I speak from experience) (29–30). It is only her progressive life experiences that allow Condé to find a relationship to motherhood that sits comfortably with her. In her case, it is by remaining committed to her children but not sacrificing her own aspirations and needs. Condé's journey highlights the individual nature of this common struggle for women, which remains a contemporary issue. By detailing her own path to maternal self-acceptance, she opens up the definition of motherhood to one that can only be understood in relation to one's individual circumstances and personality.

Condé's son Denis is particularly challenging for Condé, as it is his birth that topples her from the privileges of bourgeois society and leads her to a first marriage that is deeply unsatisfying. In fact, both parties in the relationship are searching for something other than love when they marry: "J'espérais grâce à ce mariage retrouver un rang dans la société. Condé avait hâte d'exhiber cette épousée universitaire de bonne famille qui parlait le français comme une vraie Parisienne" (I was hoping to find, thanks to this marriage, a status in society. Condé couldn't wait to show off this university-educated wife from a good family who could speak French like a real Parisian) (30). Once again, language proves to be fundamental to one's position in society, although in this case, the question is also mixed up with ethnicity and gender. The birth of Denis forces Condé to consider another aspect of exclusion in society when she reveals that he is homosexual (Boisseron, "Intimité: entretien avec Maryse Condé," 150). *La Vie sans fards* is the first book in which she writes in detail about her son, who loses his life at the age of forty-one to AIDS. In this book, she recalls his tendencies as a young boy to be "trop mou" (too soft) (116); she reveals that he is often accused of acting like a "petite fille" (little girl) (139). Condé's own discomfort with homosexuality—despite the fact that it is a feature in many of her novels—means that she has not been able to embrace Denis's existence in the same way as that of her three daughters until now. It is an example of the way in which maturity and reflection have led Condé to view her life in Relation and therefore to accommodate both its positive and negative aspects.

Alongside these personal journeys, Condé also details her quest for cultural understanding, which is central to her sense of identity. She situates herself clearly from the outset of the book as a young Guadeloupean woman trying to find her place in the world. In the introduction, she warns her readers not to forget "que je suis née dans un pays, à l'époque, sans musée, sans vraie salle de spectacle, où les seuls écrivains que nous fréquentions appartenaient à nos manuels scolaires et étaient originaires d'Ailleurs" (that I was born in a country, in a time when there was no museum, no real theater, where the only writers we knew belonged to our school books and came from Elsewhere) (14). Her geographical context thus established, Condé goes on in the first chapter to fix her cultural background: "L'arrogante Maryse Boucolon, l'héritière des 'Grands Nègres,' élevée dans le souverain mépris des inférieurs" (The arrogant Maryse Boucolon, heiress of upwardly mobile blacks, brought up in the sovereign contempt for inferiors) (20). Her sense of ill ease at her inherited bourgeois background recurs throughout her adult life, and *La Vie* details her trying on of different cultural costumes. While in Paris, she experiences the sense of racial alienation that Frantz Fanon describes in *Peau noire, masques blancs*: "Paris n'était pas comme pour ma mère la Ville-Lumière, la capitale du monde. C'est le lieu où j'avais brutalement découvert mon altérité" (Paris was not as it was for my mother the City of Light, the capital of the world. It is the place where I brutally discovered my otherness) (*La Vie*, 283). However, it is also in Paris that she discovers Aimé Césaire and Négritude, which provide her with a vital sense of identity, although she later—in opposition to her mother, who always strove to achieve this status—discovers its limitations.

Condé's connection to her Guadeloupean homeland is challenged in a different manner when her last surviving parent, her father, dies. Condé feels she has lost not only her father but also an enduring connection to her homeland, a situation that both terrifies and excites her: "Je n'étais pas seulement orpheline; j'étais apatride, une SDF sans terre d'origine, ni lieu d'appartenance. En même temps, cependant, j'éprouvai une impression de libération" (I was not only an orphan: I was also stateless, a homeless person without a homeland or a place to belong to. At the same time, however, I had an impression of freedom) (57). These conflicting experiences prove definitive in shaping Condé's sense of cultural identity, but it is the experience of living in Africa that is most crucial to the person she becomes.

The mystique of Africa, the place Césaire holds up as the key to Caribbean identity, proves equally enigmatic for Condé. Following her dissatisfaction with the supposed superiority of France and her diminishing connection to Guadeloupe, Condé moves to Africa in the hope of finding herself. However, instead of discovering the key to self-understanding, she lives through a period that is "riche surtout en souffrances" (especially rich in suffering) (300), during which she feels excluded, "toujours et partout qu'une spectatrice" (always and everywhere only a spectator) (55), and treated like "un non-être, une exclue de l'espèce humaine" (a nonbeing, someone excluded from the human species) (114). Paradoxically, however, Condé also finds that Africa is a place where diversity flourishes (202), "qu'il fallait accepter en bloc avec ses laideurs et ses trouvailles de splendeur" (that you had to accept as a whole with its ugliness and its splendors) (222). Despite the emotional depths to which she plunges in her extensive African journeys, Condé eventually arrives at a place where she is able to view these contrasting experiences in a more connected manner. In this way, both the good and the bad form part of her personal mosaic, and she is able to appreciate the African continent without the need to embellish it in her memory. As she says: "Accepter et même chérir" (Accepting and even cherishing) (222) her African years allows her to appreciate the necessity and importance of all her experiences, not just the positive ones.

Africa is also the site of Condé's birth as a writer. Her retrospective journey pays homage to her literary influences but also to the development of her own unique vision. It is through her years spent in different countries from the African continent that she discovers the rich traditions of francophone literature and feeds her passion for books, where she mixes with some of the most culturally and historically important figures of her time and where she gradually finds her own voice. The intertextual references, as well as being a way of connecting to the literary past, also reinforce Condé's stance of refusing boundaries of geography, culture, or gender, evident in the wide variety of books and authors mentioned. In *La Vie*, the breadth of the cultural and literary quotations she uses to open each chapter exemplifies the central role of literature in her life and the diversity of sources from which she draws. Just like her writing and her own life, her choice of influences refuse simple categorization and range from the Bible to Guadeloupean and children's proverbs to quotations from Victor Hugo and Paul Valéry to Sékou Touré and Aimé Césaire. Situating herself in a literary genealogy, therefore, becomes almost as important as finding her place in her female line.

Ultimately, the multitude of literary discoveries she makes—such as admiring her friend Roger Dorsinville's passion for writing, which was to overcome her, too, later in life (155), and alighting upon the surprising links she finds between writers as diverse as the Brontë sisters and those from the Caribbean (161)—gives her the confidence to embrace her role as "une provocatrice née" (a born provocateur) (270) and a woman who "ne fait rien comme tout le monde" (does nothing like the rest of us) (283). The empowering nature of writing allows Condé to situate her African trials in a connected and forward-moving journey, transforming hardships into "la matière de nombreuses fictions" (the subject of numerous fictions) (334) rather than an all-encompassing definition of who she is or is not. As she states in an interview with Barbara Lewis: "What matters to you is that you manage to find and discover who you are when you are writing. It is at the same time a kind of therapy, and a kind of liberation. Writing is not simply a pleasure—stories that you are telling to some reader. It is yourself, looking for yourself, finding yourself, and expressing who you are" (Lewis, 103). *La Vie sans fards* is a book which shows that Condé has achieved precisely that goal.

Édouard Glissant's model of Relation emphasizes multiplicity, mutual influence, and connection in order to produce a more harmonious and inclusive system of relationships. Condé's autobiographical narratives demonstrate the way in which people need to situate themselves in a connected network in order to understand both themselves and their country. In *Tales from the Heart*, Condé begins the journey by looking back at her country's past and the relationships that existed in her childhood home. In *Victoire*, this relational feat is achieved through her creative linking of Victoire's culinary art and her own literary craft as well as searching for an understanding of her female line and its relationship to history. Finally, in *La Vie sans fards*, Condé reflects back on her life with all the benefits of retrospection, arriving at a place where she is able to appreciate all the competing personal and political aspects of her existence. Her narratives do not deny the disconnections and ruptures that plague every person, but they also show that all are necessary if we are truly to create an integrated life journey. Condé effectively summarizes her position in an interview with Noëlle Carruggi: "[J]e suis arrivée à savoir que Maryse Condé n'est pas une Africaine, n'est pas une Américaine, n'est peut-être même pas Antillaise, Maryse Condé est simplement elle-même, un certain mélange, résultat d'une série d'expériences purement individuelles" (I have managed to learn that Maryse Condé is not an African, not an American, and maybe not even a Caribbean woman. Maryse Condé is simply herself, a certain mix, the result of a series of experiences that are purely individual) (Carruggi, 204). By filling in the gaps of her personal "herstory" and resituating her experiences in a network of connections, Condé achieves a sense of well-being in which past, present, and future coexist peacefully.

CHAPTER 2

GISÈLE PINEAU
Writing as Therapy

Guadeloupean writer Gisèle Pineau is a leading light in francophone Caribbean literature. Her diverse oeuvre covering fiction, nonfiction, short stories, and children's literature constitutes one of the most interesting and personal sources of interrogation into the Caribbean past. Pineau's work demonstrates a passionate attention to the emotion of writing and her commitment to relaying individual stories against the backdrop of the francophone Caribbean past. Affectivity infuses her craft as she portrays the dramas of individual characters who are often found at the margins of society. Pineau remains deeply affected by her own familial history as well as the privileged insights into suffering she gains as a result of nursing in psychiatric hospitals in Guadeloupe and France for more than two decades. Pineau does not shy away from depicting scenes of graphic violence, but her literature is always underpinned by a sense of hope. In this way, one can view her contribution to writing as an expression of her fundamental belief in the goodness of humanity and her desire to enact a reconciliation with the past, whether it be at a personal or cultural level: "Je veux aller derrière les masques et les apparences pour toucher ce qui fait la beauté des êtres" (I want to go behind the masks and appearances to touch on what makes the beauty of beings) (Ghinelli, 116).

This chapter will examine how Pineau engages with questions of history, memory, and identity through her three autofictional narratives: *L'Exil selon Julia* (Exile According to Julia) (1996), *Mes quatre femmes* (2007), and *Folie, aller simple: journée ordinaire d'une infirmière* (2010). These books reveal a three-stage process that in some way mirrors the evolution of Glissant's thought—the first part is about claiming a culture, particularly through a connection with nature; the second part is about situating oneself in a genealogical continuum; while the third is concerned with finding the uniting strands between all people—in this case the commonalities between Pineau's patients suffering from mental illness and herself. Carine Mardorossian, in her book *Reclaiming Difference: Caribbean Women Rewrite Postcolonialism*, characterizes this evolving approach privileging multiplicity over binary opposites as a whole new practice of writing that "redefines fragmentation not as the opposite of wholeness and harmony but as their only possible reincarnation" (10). As this chapter will reveal, Pineau's developing style participates in a process of reinterpreting the past that is facilitated through the idea of connecting histories and writing as therapy.

Pineau's work is firmly grounded in the Caribbean context—much more so than Condé's, which has a more cosmopolitan outlook—and yet she also maintains a wider relevance to her themes. Part of Pineau's philosophy derives from the fact that she explicitly writes from her own standpoint as a Guadeloupean woman living and working between the Caribbean and France, but hers is also a story affected by the increasingly influential forces of globalization. However, like Condé, Pineau does not feel the need to theorize and speak in the name of others as she believes some of the *créoliste* writers do: "Je me dis qu'écrire c'est ma liberté de femme sur cette terre: je suis un être humain parmi des milliards d'êtres humains et j'ai ce don d'écrire. Je n'ai pas besoin d'être dans une école ni dans un mouvement. J'écris!" (I tell myself that writing is my freedom as a woman on this earth: I am a human being among millions of humans and I have this gift of writing. I don't need to be in a school or a movement. I write!) (Jurney, 109). Pineau ensures wider links with her works in the way she makes connections between different aspects of her life and her personal and collective histories, which can then be translated into other contexts. For example, her diverse books connect with her country's past, with real and imagined ancestors, and with those suffering varying forms of prejudice. Each book is like an individual story flowing into a network of histories before immersing itself in the vast ocean of History. According to Pineau, "Je n'ai pas besoin de laisser une trace dans la grande Histoire. J'écris des petites histoires et, à mon sens, ce sont des petites histoires qui vont rencontrer les humanités à travers le monde" (I don't need to leave a trace in History with a capital "H." I write small histories and to my sense, these small histories are going to meet humanities throughout the world) (Jurney, 109–10). These lines are reminiscent of some of Édouard Glissant's assertions in *Mémoires des esclavages* and in his joint publication with Patrick Chamoiseau, *Quand les murs tombent*, which emphasize the importance of overcoming barriers and borders of varying kinds. Indeed, her embrace of the concept of *littérature-monde* complements Glissant's vision of a world where differences coexist in an ever-unfolding rhizomatic network.[1] World literature "déverrouille, défait les barrières, abat des murs et élargit les horizons. Elle surprend et étonne" (unlocks, undoes barriers, pulls down walls, and enlarges horizons. It surprises and astonishes) (Jurney, 110). As the last line of this affirmation attests, a distinguishing feature of Pineau's work is her optimism and appreciation of the beauty that exists in the world in spite of an often overwhelming ugliness. For Pineau, it is the very process of writing that allows her to overcome hardship and remain positively engaged in life. "Mes livres sont écrits à l'image de la vie: on se bat, on prend des coups, mais quand même on se redresse" (My books are written in the image of life: we fight, we take beatings, but nonetheless we get up again) (Jurney, 109). Her message, then, is ultimately a positive one in which she highlights the resilient nature of humanity.

Reading and Writing as Therapy

According to an interview with Florence Raymond Jurney, Pineau began writing at the age of seven and has always found solace in the world of literature, as have all the writers in this volume. Against the backdrop of racism and isolation she experienced as a child, reading provided the young Pineau with the possibilities of other worlds while the act of writing became "une bouée de sauvetage" (a life jacket) and "une consolation" (a consolation) (Jurney, 108). Dominique Licops argues that for Pineau, by "identifying a book that mirrors her reality [for example, *The Diary of Anne Frank*, which Pineau explores in *Exile*], Gisèle becomes an agent of and in her own imagination, and imagines a world that includes her in it" (Licops, "Reading and Danger," 259). Licops's analysis explores both Pineau's and Condé's use of different Caribbean and non-Caribbean texts in elucidating their identities, but she demonstrates that in both cases reading and writing are fundamental to their negotiation of complex personal and collective pasts. In "Écrire en tant que Noire," Pineau details some of her literary influences, which span French classics such as those by Zola and, later, writings by black Americans and Africans "qui représentaient des modèles de courage et d'audace dans ce monde de la littérature qui m'apparaissait réservé à une élite" (which represented models of courage and audacity in this world of literature that appeared to me to be reserved for an elite) (291). Ultimately, the writing space is what grants Pineau her freedom while at the same time offering a lifeline to her readers. In Mark Andrews's words, "la littérature est comme un lieu d'accueil pour l'être dépossédé, un espace vital et libérateur capable de créer des réseaux reliant les pays et les cultures, mais apte aussi à explorer les lignes de fracture cachées qui divisent les familles et à souder les générations dans une entreprise solidaire" (literature is like a meeting place for the dispossessed person, a vital and liberating space that is capable of creating networks linking countries and cultures, but also of exploring the hidden lines of fracture that divide families and to weld together the generations in an enterprise of solidarity) (Andrews, 57).

Personal and Collective Pasts

Pineau's personal history marks a fundamental point of departure when considering her writing and her relationship to the Caribbean past. Unlike other distinguished writers of her generation such as Patrick Chamoiseau and Raphaël Confiant, Pineau was born in Paris in 1956 to Guadeloupean parents: "[J]e n'ai pas vécu une enfance antillaise sous les tropiques" (I didn't live a Caribbean childhood in the tropics) (Pineau, "Écrire en tant que Noire," 289). The racism she experienced as a child growing up in a hostile urban environment remains a painful reference point for her and is a period she refers to frequently in her writing. In her essay "Écrire en tant que Noire," she recalls her isolation as the "[s]eule noire à marcher dans les rues sous le regard inqualifiable des Blancs, si nombreux" (the only black girl walking in the streets under the unspeakable gaze of the whites, so numerous) (290). Pineau evocatively portrays her feelings of exclusion through the contrast between the cold, linear lines of Paris and the vibrant colors of the Caribbean that her grandmother, Man Ya (Julia), evokes for her. As we will see in the discussion of *Exile According to Julia*, which features Man Ya, a sense of belonging to her Guadeloupean homeland forms an essential part of Pineau's identity trajectory. Man Ya is the one who endows her with "l'amour d'un pays, son pays, notre pays, loin, de l'autre côté de la mer. Un pays où le Noir marchait parmi d'autres Noirs, fier" (the love of a country, her country, our country, far away, on the other side of the sea. A country where blacks walked among blacks, proud) ("Écrire en tant que Noire," 290).

Part of Pineau's sense of rootlessness as a child arises as a result of her father's career as a soldier, which took him away from his birthplace of Guadeloupe in 1943. Answering Charles de Gaulle's *l'Appel du 18 juin*, Maréchal Pineau enlisted in the Free French to fight against the German invasion in France. Remaining in the army after World War II, Pineau's father undertook a variety of foreign postings in Africa, Asia, and the Pacific. As Pineau later discovered, these experiences also resulted in a series of extramarital affairs, to the point where Maréchal created a whole new family (Loichot, 332–33). Pineau's mother, Daisy, emerged as a long-suffering wife, not only assuming responsibility for the son Maréchal fathered prior to their marriage but also taking care of the "wife" and child he brought to Paris from Asia. In 1961, the family returned to Guadeloupe for a period, before again transferring to Paris, this time with Pineau's paternal grandmother, Man Ya, in tow. Maréchal famously "kidnapped" his mother in order to deliver her from the oppressions of his father, nicknamed le Bourreau (the Torturer). Man Ya's inability to assimilate into Parisian life formed the basis of Pineau's first foray into autofiction in *Exile According to Julia*. Pineau's struggle to forge her own identity caught between the contrasting French and Creole cultures was fundamentally altered by her grandmother's presence as well as by her own firsthand experience of living in France, Africa, and the Caribbean.

In addition to these fundamental negotiations of identity fostered by the continual exchange between France and Guadeloupe, Pineau's writing is also closely linked to her career as a psychiatric nurse. Although Pineau harbored a passion and talent for writing from childhood, she was forced to abandon the literary studies she began in 1975 at the Université de Paris X Nanterre because of a lack of money. She subsequently trained as a psychiatric nurse and began a profession that she has practiced in tandem with her writing since 1979. Her professional placements include over twenty years at the Centre Hospitalier Psychiatrique de Saint-Claude in Guadeloupe and Villejuif in Paris after she moved to the French capital in 2000. She has since established herself in Marie-Galante. Pineau's most recent autofictional narrative, *Folie, aller simple: journée ordinaire d'une infirmière*, reveals the intimate relationship that exists between her writing, her nursing, and her experience of Caribbean history and identity.[2]

Like Condé, Gisèle Pineau situates herself as a writer of the present. However, she has a different relationship to the past than her Guadeloupean compatriot. While for Condé the past is a reference point but not necessarily a dominant force in her work, Pineau situates herself in a chronological continuum. She may write from the present, but her eyes are fixed firmly on the past, and it is as a result of "working through" this past through writing that she is able to look toward the future: "[J]e suis un écrivain d'aujourd'hui, parce que je ne me cantonne pas à écrire sur le passé. Néanmoins, ce passé a toujours des répercussions flagrantes" (I am a writer of today because I don't limit myself to writing about the past. However, this past still has flagrant repercussions) (Ghinelli, 113). Perhaps more than Condé, Pineau's collective and individual heritage forms a fundamental backdrop to her literary project: "Je ne peux pas écrire sans prendre en compte ces histoires, qui pèsent" (I can't write without taking into account these histories, which oppress) (Ghinelli, 113). As we have seen, for Pineau, writing becomes a form of therapy for facing the past, liberating oneself from its negative influence and looking to the future with optimism.

Lucía Suárez argues that Pineau "highlights the role inner vision plays in positioning a Creole identity in, against, and within the rest of the world, most specifically within the interstices of two national cultures" (20). Pineau herself has commented that she does not adopt an intellectual approach to her writing, favoring instead an instinctual, emotional relationship with her subject matter. Clearly placing herself in opposition to writers such as Chamoiseau and Confiant who have a much more cerebral approach to their craft, Pineau argues: "Je suis un écrivain qui écrit avec ses sens. Je mesure le temps et la vie avec mes sens. J'avance d'une manière intuitive, je sens les choses, je les perçois" (I am a writer who writes with her senses. I measure time and life with my senses. I advance in an intuitive manner, I feel things, I perceive them) (Ghinelli, 114). Moreover, the experience of writing is intensely physical for her, mirroring Michael Lambek and Paul Antze's assertion that memory making and grappling with issues of identity draw from our bodies as much as from our minds. As Pineau declares: "[J]'écris réellement avec mon corps, avec mon ventre, avec cette langue créole mêlée à la langue française, avec mon histoire, avec ma vie" (I really write with my body, with my belly, with this Creole language mixed with French, with my history, with my life) (Anglade and Simasotchi-Brones). Critics have also commented on this corporeal and complex aspect of Pineau's writing, with Dominique Licops, for example, declaring: "La poétique de Pineau formule une voie qui va au-delà de l'opposition entre essentialisme et constructivisme puisqu'elle pense l'identité comme un mélange des deux, l'identité et le sens d'une personne étant situés à l'intérieur du corps, mais n'y étant pas réductibles" (Pineau's poetics formulates a path that goes beyond the opposition of essentialism and constructivism since it thinks of identity as a mixture of the two, the identity and sense of a person being situated in the body, but not being reducible to it) (Licops, "Métaphores naturelles," 99). This deep intertwining of the physical and emotional, and the individual and collective, distinguishes Pineau's writing as particularly intimate in its approach. "Writing therapy" becomes an intensely personal medium for engaging with history and claiming an optimistic space defined by relationship and connection with the Self and Other.

While Pineau's work is deeply concerned with "ce qui se passe à l'intérieur des gens" (what happens inside people) (Ghinelli, 118), her writing also has a testimonial element informed by her acute sense of collective responsibility. Her 1998 publication *Femmes des Antilles: traces et voix*, coauthored with Marie Abraham, is indicative of her desire to give voice to those who were denied subjectivity in the past. This book, which came out for the 150th anniversary of the abolition of slavery in Martinique and Guadeloupe, is a historical and imaginative reconstruction of Caribbean women under slavery and beyond. It is both a testimony to the existence of these black women who were "déchirées par les hommes, trompées, violées debout malgré tout" (destroyed, cheated on, raped by men, and standing despite everything) ("Écrire en tant que Noire," 292) and Pineau's attempt to "apporter [une] voix aux autres voix des femmes d'ici et d'ailleurs qui témoignent pour demain" (give [a] voice to these women from here and elsewhere who are the witnesses for tomorrow) ("Écrire en tant que Noire," 295). The idea of speaking for others suggests a relationship that also involves listening, as if Pineau has patiently heard and recorded the tales of her real and imagined forebears. Many critics have emphasized the important role the listener plays in facilitating the healing of victims of trauma. As Jennifer Griffiths asserts, "the listener becomes an integral part of this awareness and the process of creating meaning from the chaos of trauma" (2). Pineau's project thus has significance on many levels, not only as the anchoring point for Pineau's own journey of self-discovery but also as part of a larger quest for the reinscription of history's forgotten individuals into a meaningful narrative.

L'Exil selon Julia

As Maryse Condé demonstrates in the previous chapter, knowing oneself is essential if one is to know and relate to others in a balanced manner. *L'Exil selon Julia* (*Exile According to Julia*) marks a vital first stage in the construction of Pineau's journey of self-discovery and consequently in her quest to reconcile the traumas of her personal and collective past. This book relates the story of Man Ya's "kidnapping" by her son, her move to Paris with the Pineau family (where she struggles painfully with the Metropolitan environment), and her ultimate return to her beloved Guadeloupe. The weaving of Man Ya's individual story into the larger fabric of colonial History is of paramount importance as Pineau portrays her grandmother's many sufferings as a result of her status as an illiterate, black peasant woman from Guadeloupe. Pineau's transformation of her grandmother's story into narrative form serves both to preserve an aspect of history that is in danger of being neglected and to "work through" and understand her own place in the world.

Throughout this personal narrative, Pineau depicts different members of her family struggling with the various challenges to identity that are a result of the colonial experience. The most significant are those encountered by Man Ya, Pineau herself, and her upwardly mobile parents. Each of their struggles demonstrates a different response to the intricacies of carving out an identity in a society dominated culturally and politically by another. The inner journeys Pineau explores through her family relationships underline how the traumatic legacies of history may be passed down families in a pattern of transgenerational trauma, but also how "inner work" and insight can break the cycle and posit a different future. For Pineau, this exploration is possible thanks to the therapeutic attributes of writing, in which her careful observations of her family allow her to develop a more balanced relationship to her personal and social past. In addition, the collective responsibility she assumes as a published writer, particularly in works such as *Femmes des Antilles*, enables her to communicate these views to a wide audience in a gesture of hope for the future and a belief in the ultimate good of humanity.

As we will see in the course of this chapter, it is Man Ya who is most fundamental to Pineau's developing sense of self. The contrast between her grandmother's painful exclusion in France and the sense of peace she feels in Guadeloupe brings into sharp focus the issue of cultural identity in the postcolonial context. During the seven years she spends in Paris, Man Ya's sense of identity is severely challenged. She constantly feels at odds with life in France and commits numerous cultural errors: for example, she arrives at the children's school in her son's army overcoat and kepi to protect herself from the rain, only to be arrested by the gendarmes for displaying a lack of respect toward the French military. "Here the gaping gulf of misunderstanding between people who live on the same soil, yet worlds apart appears derisory on the one hand, but almost impossible to bridge on the other" (Githire, 79). On another occasion, Man Ya sets off on a whim for the Sacré-Coeur with her grandson in tow, with no regard for time or direction.

While those around her are exasperated or pitying in her blatant inability to fit into French society, Man Ya remains unconcerned. In contrast to the educated members of the expatriate francophone Caribbean community who frequent the Pineau family, Man Ya displays no desire to assimilate into Parisian society. She is not interested in speaking French or dressing herself in chic clothes and discussing the latest fashionable topic. Instead, she presents herself as a "vieille négresse marronne dans la campagne" (an old Maroon Negress in the countryside) (Makward, 1209). Unlike those trying to climb the social ladder, Man Ya demonstrates self-assuredness and a singular lack of identity conflict. While the identity she maintains is marginalized in the eyes of others, for Man Ya it is quite simply who she is, and she has no aspirations to be different.

Pineau observes that Man Ya's uncompromising presence invokes a sort of fear in her parents' sophisticated friends, who paradoxically recognize themselves in her. With the benefit of retrospection, Pineau comments that Man Ya symbolizes a former existence defined by slavery and oppression. "Man Ya, in her self alone, represents all the thoughts of slavery that come to them from time to time and that they stifle and repress like the Creole in their mouths" (*Exile*, 59). This fearful attitude demonstrates a central dilemma of francophone Caribbean identity—in order to ascend the social ladder, it is necessary to repress one's Caribbean roots and instead assume a French identity. Pineau's mother, for example, never teaches her children Creole and encourages them to pursue social betterment through a French education. The Pineau family adopts an assimilationist approach to cultural identity that involves obscuring one's cultural origins in the quest to access the advantages of being French. This attitude is reminiscent of Condé's parents, and both Pineau and Condé reject this model themselves. The idea of repressing part of one's self in order to advance socially is not conducive to the idea of relationship and connection, which Pineau's work posits as the way forward. In this scenario, then, Pineau portrays Man Ya as far more secure in her sense of self than her parents and, indeed, elevates her status to one of cultural historian, as Gloria Nne Onyeoziri observes: "[L]a grand-mère...offre à ses petits-enfants un modèle de retour qui, loin de constituer une forme d'évasion, cherche à négocier, à travers la pratique de son oralité, une place dans le monde" (the grandmother...offers to her grandchildren a model of return which, far from constituting a form of evasion, looks to negotiate through her practice of orality, a place in the world) (17).

Pineau depicts another side to her grandmother's character that is not synonymous with autonomy and contentment. Despite the fact that slavery was abolished in Guadeloupe in 1848, Man Ya's relationship with her lighter-skinned husband closely resembles that of master and slave. Asdrubal is a man broken by his experiences fighting for the French in World War I, and he plays out his post-traumatic stress disorder by abusing his wife. Indeed, the attitude of acceptance and resignation that Man Ya adopts reflects Pineau's description of female slaves in *Femmes des Antilles*: "Elles subirent bien des humiliations et des avanies" (They suffered many humiliations and snubs) (Pineau and Abraham, 11). Man Ya's response—or lack of response—to her situation represents one way in which to deal with these and other colonial inheritances. She does not challenge her status but instead turns to the natural environment, her country, and religion for solace. It is almost as if she is trying to find the little gaps in the "system" in order to survive and flourish, just as celebrated Creole figures such as the *djobeurs* do in Chamoiseau's writing (Burton, "*Debrouya Pa Peche*"). This relationship with the Caribbean landscape is of vital importance to the development and preservation of Man Ya's persona, and the image of an Eden-like paradise is a recurrent image in Pineau's literary works. While the land is classically linked to the painful memories of the sugar plantations and slavery in the Caribbean context, Man Ya treats it instead as the very oxygen she breathes. Her deep attachment to the physical environment sustains Man Ya in the difficult years she spends in the Parisian metropolis, far away from her own patch of earth in Guadeloupe.

Pineau's use of the Garden of Eden as a literal and figurative metaphor is a characteristic that has been widely noted by critics (Hellerstein, 49; Casteel, 14). According to Pineau, the garden "expose à lui seul le monde que j'espère" (alone exposes the world that I hope for) (Pineau, "L'Identité, la créolité et la francité," 224). However, an analysis of this imagery reveals that it is not simply a tool for expressing one's affinity with nature. It also serves as a medium for illustrating some of the complexities of the Caribbean relationship to history, memory, and identity. In *Exile According to Julia*, the garden represents a place that embodies the security of home, but it also generates nostalgia and longing. As Sarah Phillips Casteel asserts, the garden "suggests fullness and density, foundations and origins" (14), but it is also "a landscape of labour and of history" (24). Moreover, continual movement and change characterize gardens, where laying claim to a place and therefore an identity "is understood as an ongoing, laborious, and always provisional process" (27). In *Exile According to Julia*, Guadeloupe is embodied above all in the image of Man Ya's garden and the unspoiled natural world. This physical and imaginative space represents an important stage in Pineau's identity trajectory, where her desire to claim her island heritage is expressed in the need to find a Caribbean Genesis untainted by the slave and colonial past. Man Ya's reminiscences of her Creole garden in Guadeloupe fulfills this function for the young Pineau: "She pictures it for us, a wonderful place where all kinds of trees, plants, and flowers grow in abundance in an overwhelming green, an almost miraculous verdure, dappled here and there with a silver light that shines nowhere else but in the heart of Routhiers" (*Exile*, 8; Routhiers is a small town in Guadeloupe). Man Ya's memories of her garden provide an enduring link between her native island and the city of Paris as well as a tangible image with which to sustain her troubled granddaughter. They also illustrate Pineau's writing philosophy in which art reflects nature: "Il y a donc au fond de moi toujours un espoir et comme le dit la nature, quand tout est détruit par des inondations, des coulées de boue, on reconstruit" (There is, therefore, always hope deep inside me and as nature shows, when everything is destroyed by floods, mudslides, we rebuild) (Jurney, 117).

Looking back at her childhood, Pineau attributes her growing appreciation of the multiple strands of her identity to Man Ya. Again and again, it becomes clear that nature is Man Ya's lifeblood, and the natural world is what nourishes her sense of self. Without the capacity to feel the earth in her hands, Man Ya is like a faded flower who cannot thrive. When spring finally bursts forth in Paris, for example, Man Ya immediately gets into the garden, where "[h]andling the earth, turning it over, feeling it between her fingers, delights her" and "[t]illing the soil gives her life, sustains her" (*Exile*, 46). This positive connection to nature is reminiscent of the slave women who were given small plots of land to tend, representing a tiny space for self-expression and autonomy in an otherwise oppressive system. Man Ya succeeds in communicating this love of nature to her granddaughter, and after Man Ya's departure for Guadeloupe, Pineau also draws on the environment to maintain a connection with her grandmother. Looking out of her window in Paris, Pineau hopefully declares that "perhaps, a trade wind will bring me the smells from Man Ya's garden. Vanilla, cinnamon, cocoa, roasted coffee, nutmeg, curry powder" (106). Through the character of Man Ya, Pineau demonstrates that memory and landscape are two intertwined elements of identity, allowing her otherwise marginalized grandmother to locate a sense of personal fulfillment and peace in the world.

While nature emerges as an unequivocally positive influence in her grandmother's life, Pineau reveals that language is another matter. The linguistic battleground between French and Creole is a major point of tension in *Exile According to Julia*, in which Man Ya suffers alienation because she cannot speak French. Like Victoire, Man Ya is excluded from, or excludes herself from, assimilating to the French way of life. In a later echo of this exclusionary power of language, Pineau's inability to speak Creole fluently means that she, too, is alienated when the family first moves to Martinique. More than just a language, Creole governs Man Ya's entire being, providing her with the vocabulary to describe her precious garden and animating her Eden-like memories of her homeland. Creole suffuses her conception of time, which stretches out into infinity, unlike the rigid clock that rules French time. "She can walk in the paths of her youth in the morning and sit in the middle of her garden at noon. If her flesh remembers the Torturer's blows, her mind sets her free; she abandons her body and goes off to bathe her soul in little moments of joy, in her stream, in Routhiers" (*Exile*, 59). Man Ya also uses the Creole language as a way to reject assimilation and maintain her Caribbean identity. However, Man Ya's rigidity means that she finds life in Paris a constant battle, and she becomes profoundly depressed. Her stance represents the other end of the spectrum to the Caribbean people who want to become "more French than the French," such as Pineau's and Condé's parents. While she remains true to her Creole roots, she finds that she can only thrive in her indigenous environment. Indeed, her positing of French as fundamentally opposite to Creole is an example of the limitations of a nonrelational approach to identity. Man Ya is like a tropical plant who wilts and withers when taken away from the sunshine and rain of the tropics. It is only when she is finally reunited with her beloved Guadeloupe that Man Ya begins to grow again. Pineau's observations of her grandmother's suffering in the French environment is one of the factors that drives her to adopt a more flexible approach to identity in her own life, allowing multiple influences to generate her sense of self and not to limit herself to reductive either/or choices.

As a mediator between the Caribbean past and the French present, the character of Man Ya serves above all to satisfy her descendants' needs to know their origins. The cultural history that Man Ya transmits to her grandchildren through her tales, her songs, and especially the memories of her Creole garden fills this gap in such a way that Pineau manages to create her own cultural identity, which continues to nourish her imagination today. Man Ya's memory becomes a place of hope and rebirth that leads to a state of self-realization and belonging for both storyteller and listener. In the closing pages of the book, Pineau passionately acknowledges the precious gift from her grandmother:

> Then we truly understood what Man Ya had done for us.... Cleared the paths of her Creole language. Layered feelings in the rest of us, pale, drooping young forests. Revealed perfumes. She had given us: words, visions, rays of sunlight, and patience in life. She had pointed out to us the three sentinels, past, present, future, that hold the threads of time, had twisted them together to weave for us, day after day, a solid bridge between Over There and Back Home. During all those years of snow and cold, she had kept alight the torch that showed the way. Her hand had never let go of us. (165)

Thanks to Man Ya, Pineau manages to find an alternative to the simple assimilation or rejection of a French identity. Instead, she succeeds in weaving together the strands of multiple identities, highlighting the possibilities of a *métis* existence that understands and respects both worlds. It becomes clear that in the modern-day francophone Caribbean it is inauthentic and unrealistic to discard the diverse elements of one's identity that is the direct result of the region's creolized history. Accepting diversity becomes one way of overcoming exclusion and alienation. For Pineau, such acceptance involves discovering and living "*métissage*, the reality that defines the complex structure of Antillean society" (Sourieau, 179). Like the colorful riot of plants that flourishes in Man Ya's tropical garden, Pineau's identity formation allows for the coexistence of contrasting and often dissonant elements. In this important first phase of her interrogation into her past, Pineau draws extensively on the Caribbean landscape to articulate her personal and cultural dilemmas.

Mes quatre femmes

Pineau's 2007 memoir *Mes quatre femmes* represents another stage of her dramatization of the ways in which the past imprints itself upon the present on both a social and individual level. As Jennifer Griffiths asserts, the "transmission of family stories provides insight into the relationship between collective trauma and individual lives"(70). Pineau's book builds on the explorations into her country's past and her own personal history that she began in *Exile According to Julia*, but this time her focus is on her personal female genealogy. Indeed, Louise Hardwick argues that Pineau's 2007 text "sits in a hypertextual relationship with *L'Exil*" (Hardwick, *Childhood*, 195). Like Condé, Pineau demonstrates the need to connect specifically with her female relatives in order to understand herself more fully. Setting her story in a dark "memory jail," Pineau imaginatively explores how individual and collective experiences inscribe themselves in one's memory and how these memories in turn influence the memories of others. This process of memory making and memory transmission becomes like the ever-expanding rhizome, which constantly reproduces and expands. *Mes quatre femmes* underscores the redemptive possibilities of an outward-looking approach to one's life—in the same vein as Condé's retrospective narratives—and points to its pivotal role in overcoming historical and personal trauma. This book also allows Pineau to assess the redemptive or limiting possibilities of different responses to past traumas.

As in *Exile According to Julia*, *Mes quatre femmes* gives an insight into Pineau's own genealogical history but also into some of the wider concerns of her people's past. The four characters she gives voice to—her aunt Gisèle, her paternal grandmother Julia (Man Ya), her mother Daisy, and her great-grandmother Angélique—allow her to interrogate the ways in which past traumas may either burden or liberate their victim. It becomes clear that those characters who search for connections—whether it be with others, with nature, or with an unadorned vision of their country's past—attain a sense of freedom that is denied those who remain trapped in closed introspection. The narrative also demonstrates the powerful role history has on subsequent generations and the way in which trauma may manifest itself transgenerationally. Through her literary imagination in this book, Pineau is able to explore the histories that make up her own persona, adapting and discarding their lessons while she constructs her own identity. Her varied explorations exemplify Marianne Hirsch's concept of post-memory in which present-day stories may be either silenced or enlivened by the life trajectories that come before them. Pineau's ultimate liberation arrives as a result of "working through" her family's traumas in order to embrace her own truth. Once again, writing acts as her therapeutic tool, with Pineau asserting: "J'écris d'abord pour comprendre" (I write first of all in order to understand) (Ghinelli, 115).

Mes quatre femmes brings together four generations and creates an intergenerational dialog that ultimately frees its youngest descendant—Pineau. The operation of this process is consistent with the idea of a rhizomatic network, for each woman narrates her trauma in a gesture of openness and connectedness to her female family members. The story of each woman is interwoven in the others, and within each woman's story the other women speak—interrupting, reminiscing, redirecting the narrative flow so as to encompass their own past. Historical and personal traumas both emerge as significant factors in the identity construction of these four women as they navigate the micro and macro influences on their lives. Above all, *Mes quatre femmes* provides an imaginative and deeply personal look at how traumatic experience may be overcome through the notion of connecting histories.

The first person Pineau explores in *Mes quatre femmes* is her aunt Gisèle, after whom she is named and whose life is dominated by the unresolved grief caused by her husband's premature death. In the course of Gisèle's story, Pineau reveals that each woman is permitted to take an object into the memory jail that encapsulates her life journey and that offers her solace. For Gisèle, it is a broad-brimmed straw hat, despite the fact that no sunlight pierces the shadows of the jail. Pineau skillfully uses this scene to express connection, or lack of it, in images of the circle. As Gisèle appears more and more oppressed by her sorrowful memories—symbolized by the large hat "qui ombre la moitié de son visage" (that shades half her face) (*Mes quatre femmes*, 32)—Pineau describes the three remaining women attempting to reach out to her in a gesture of physical openness: "Les trois autres font cercle autour d'elle comme si elles entendaient son histoire pour la première fois" (The three others make a circle around her as if they were hearing her story for the first time) (27). Indeed, an early photograph in which her sisters "font cercle autour de Gisèle. Elles constituent une sorte de garde-corps" (make a circle around Gisèle. They constitute a sort of bodyguard) (33), suggests the future vulnerability of this character and her need for protection. However, Gisèle remains resolutely closed to all overtures of help and hope, while the single event of her husband's traumatic death casts a permanent and all-encompassing shadow over her life.

Like a sorrowful incantation, the words "Gisèle se souvient" (Gisèle remembers) reverberate throughout the chapter, drawing the reader into the deep pain that saw her withdraw emotionally from life at the age of twenty-seven after the death of her husband. Defining herself solely in relation to his living presence, Gisèle is unable to cling to life—despite the existence of her three children and despite the revelations that her husband was unfaithful to her—and suffers a premature death herself. Even in the timeless memory jail, Gisèle cannot divorce herself from this sorrow. She refuses to reach out to others and remains frozen in her traumatic experience. The straw hat remains painfully out of place in this gathering of women, reminding Gisèle only of the ephemeral happiness she experienced as an affluent wife. Moreover, it constitutes a symbol of her withdrawal from the liberating possibilities of connection to others: "Elle s'obstine à garder sur la tête ce chapeau de paille qui lui masque la moitié de son visage" (She persists in keeping this straw hat on her head that masks half her face) (13). Far from being the celebrated *femme de combat* characteristic of so many Caribbean women in the face of adversity, Gisèle is carried away by her grief, trapped in the tragedy of her traumatized existence.

As we have seen in *Exile According to Julia*, Pineau, like Glissant and many other Caribbean writers, turns to nature to express her approach to memory. However, unlike the liberating possibilities offered in Glissant's depictions of the Caribbean landscape, Pineau emphasizes the way in which landscape may also oppress. On the day of Gisèle's husband's funeral, for example, the weather reflects the gloomy circumstances of the event. "Ce temps s'embrume. Alentour les visages sont nombreux mais curieusement indistincts. Les figures semblent couvertes de cendre" (The weather is misty. Around the faces are numerous but curiously indistinct. The people seem covered by ash) (16). Pineau also depicts Gisèle's hunger for the red earth. However, it is not, as Pineau's grandmother Julia finds it, a place of refuge, but rather a place to inter herself. Pineau also uses landscape to emphasize the contrast between Gisèle's early life as an ecstatic new bride and her subsequent retreat into depression, highlighting Casteel Phillips's notion of the different connotations of the Caribbean garden: "Y a un temps pour monter et un temps pour descendre" (There is a time for going up and a time for going down) (52). The scene is reminiscent of Toussine's descent into madness in Simone Schwarz-Bart's *Pluie et vent sur Télumée Miracle* (*The Bridge of Beyond*), but, unlike the former's triumphant return to life, Gisèle remains trapped in the shadowy depths of withdrawal and death. Gisèle's refusal to contemplate life outside of her sadness and to allow anyone to reach her shows the oppressive powers of trauma. One could imagine this individual trauma persisting down the family line, as presumably her children would suffer from the lack of an emotionally engaged mother, providing a model that they too may emulate for their children. Gisèle's experience becomes an example of the dangers of not embracing openness and connection to others.

Pineau's portrayal of Julia, the second woman to be explored in *Mes quatre femmes*, builds on the portrait she paints of her grandmother in *Exile According to Julia*. Once again she reveals the close link between landscape, memory, and identity, but in the character of Julia these elements are merged in a positive way. Her relationship with the natural world illustrates Jana Evans Braziel's assertion that history and memory "are interwoven in the Caribbean imagination as it reflects on nature and remembers subterranean and submarine histories" (122), in stark contrast to the tragic Gisèle, who seems to stop history. Pineau establishes early on in the narrative the profound connection between Julia and the land, particularly her beloved garden in Routhiers, Guadeloupe. The relationship is a symbiotic one, in which the boundary between woman and landscape is indistinct. "Julia est une femme de la terre. Elle sait qu'elle est pétrie de cette terre noire, ainsi qu'il est dit dans les Écritures. Julia connaît la terre" (Julia is a woman of the earth. She knows that she is kneaded from this black earth, as it is said in the Scriptures. Julia understands the earth) (*Mes quatre femmes*, 59). In her physical appearance, too, Julia remains indistinguishable from her natural surrounds: "Si elle grimpe dans un arbre pour y cueillir des avocats, des prunes de Cythère, un fruit à pain, elle devient comme invisible, ou plutôt semblable à une branche" (If she climbs a tree to pick avocadoes or plums, a breadfruit, it is as if she is invisible, or rather similar to a branch) (60). There is much to be said about this connection to the landscape, which mirrors Glissant's assertion that "[o]ur landscape is its own monument: its meaning can only be traced on the underside. It is all history" (*Caribbean Discourse*, 11). Although she is excluded from the history that is narrated by colonizers, Julia participates in a different version of the past through her deep connection with the land.

It is through landscape that Julia experiences some of the past's negative effects and through landscape that she is able to achieve a sense of liberty. For example, her husband, Asdrubal, is profoundly altered by his experience as a soldier in the French army in World War I. He returns psychologically damaged by the experience of war and subsequently expresses his post-traumatic stress disorder by abusing his wife. In his eyes, "Julia n'est rien d'autre qu'une méchante terre qu'il laboure, souille et piétine chaque jour de sa vie" (Julia is nothing other than bad earth that he labors, sullies, and tramples on every day of her life) (*Mes quatre femmes*, 84). And yet Julia is not bound by her oppression, finding solace in her garden and the beauty of her surroundings. In a simple yet profound gesture, she exemplifies Glissant's assertion that this "manière d'ouvrir les paysages et d'en faire saisir le sens profond, c'est de la politique; c'est, pour moi, le maximum du politique" (way of opening landscapes and understanding the deep meaning of them is politics, it is, for me, the maximum point of politics) (*Artières*, 80). While Julia cannot be described as a militant political figure, she nonetheless embodies the quiet victory of someone who is at peace with herself.

Pineau reinforces the power of landscape with her depiction of Julia's special object in the memory jail as the branch of a guava tree. With this symbol, Julia embodies the sturdiness of a tree in her ability to resist the trials of life. Despite the traumas she suffers, she adopts an attitude to life that is outward looking and oriented toward the natural world: "La terre est sa seconde mère, celle qui l'a tenue debout, parée à endurer tout ce que le destin dressait sur son chemin" (The earth is her second mother, the one which kept her upright, prepared to endure everything destiny threw her way) (*Mes quatre femmes*, 59). While Julia does not display a particular openness toward other people—remaining above all "une habituée de la solitude" (a creature of solitude) (61) for whom the "jardin est son univers" (garden is her universe) (80)—she nonetheless embraces the idea of relationship. For her, however, relationship comes from and is directed toward the environment. The richness and strength in Julia's character emerges from her simple lived expression of Glissant's complex ideas. She may appear to have an identity more in line with Glissant's conception of a "root identity" that has a single source—a model that he rejects for its denial of difference and diversity. However, while she plants her roots firmly in the Guadeloupean landscape—"Ses racines sont plantées solides dans la terre de l'île Guadeloupe" (Her roots are planted firmly in the soil of the island Guadeloupe) (*Mes quatre femmes*, 98)—she proves more open to the liberating possibilities of the future than many of her compatriots. Indeed, Julia is a luminous figure in Pineau's story, conveying considerable strength in the face of the traumas of her personal and national history. She is not only able to transcend the painful legacies of the past in her own life, but she also transmits a positive model to her descendants, giving a model of transgenerational reconciliation.

Pineau's mother, Daisy, comes next in the book and—in contrast with the exalted terms by which Pineau describes Julia—is depicted as a woman limited by the legacies of Guadeloupe's colonial history, in a similar manner to the way in which Condé views her parents. In Pineau's eyes, this unhealthy attitude is expressed in Daisy's passionate desire to emulate the French—in language, costume, and habit. Her chosen object for the memory jail is a book that not only symbolizes her affinity for French culture but also creates an escapist outlet from the challenges of her everyday existence: "Daisy connaît la vie grâce aux romans" (Daisy knows life thanks to novels) (*Mes quatre femmes*, 73). While Daisy is outwardly more open than her sister Gisèle, she nonetheless displays a certain closure from the true nature of her being. Her connections with others are limited to the people she perceives as upwardly mobile like herself. However, Daisy's reality never quite reflects the dreamy existence she envisions for herself. For example, she imagines a photo of her family that she would send back to relatives in Guadeloupe, in which her materially prosperous life in Paris would be on full display: "Elle aurait été cette femme rayonnante face à l'objectif. Épouse et mère comblée. Plénitude et perfection" (She would have been this dazzling woman facing the lens. A wife and mother who couldn't wish for anything more. Fullness and perfection) (109). Sadly, though, her real life does not reflect this utopian vision, and reading becomes the only activity that allows her to live out her imagined happiness.

This image of Daisy's unreasonable attachment to the cultural riches of France demonstrates the psychological alienation that occurred so frequently as a result of the Caribbean's slave and colonial experiences. Pineau highlights the material advantages that may arise from adopting a path of assimilation with the French, but that equally reveals the dark underside of denying one's true self. In Glissant's model of cultural identity, it is vital for Caribbean people to reject this one-way, idolatrous relationship with France and instead embrace Relation in a deep and lasting connection with other people, other cultures, other languages. Moreover, we can see in Daisy's story many of the ongoing social consequences of Guadeloupe's painful history. While outwardly Daisy's husband manages to carve out a prosperous career in the army and comfortably settles his family in Paris, he nonetheless displays the unstable family structures characteristic of slavery. For example, he returns from one of his postings in Indochina with another "wife" and two young children, whom he proceeds to temporarily house in the Pineau family home. For Daisy, "[i]l n'y pas à discuter. . . . C'est ainsi qu'on bâtit une descendance" (There was no discussion. . . . That's how we built our descendants) (*Mes quatre femmes*, 106). It is almost as if Maréchal were compelled to create as many family lines as possible in order to counteract the possibility of another shattering of the Caribbean family. Furthermore, Daisy suffers from a deep sense of alienation when the family temporarily relocates to Africa, evocatively mirroring the experiences Maryse Condé describes in her first novel, *Hérémakhonon*, and later in *La Vie sans fards*. The end result of these diverse experiences is that Daisy is weighed down by some of the legacies of her country's past. She valiantly attempts to create a better life for herself through assimilation with the French, but this redirection of her history arises at the cost of her true self.

To some extent, Daisy demonstrates some of the same tendencies as her sister Gisèle. She is steadfastly devoted to a man who betrays her, and she searches for a sense of identity outside herself. For Gisèle, selfhood is located in her husband; for Daisy, it is embodied in the blue, white, and red that symbolize France. While her sister gives up, Daisy resists, staying strong for her children. At the end of her story, she reflects with some pride that it was her children and her books that gave her the strength to survive. From Pineau's point of view, though, this survival meant suppressing part of her true identity. In some sense, Daisy represents a more successful example of someone who is able to reach out to others and achieve a sense of liberation from the shackles of her past. However, Pineau reveals that her mother is alienated from herself and therefore has not embraced this gesture of openness within. She survives and has traveled up the social ladder, but her daughter ultimately chooses not to emulate the identity path of her mother.

The final woman explored in the book is Gisèle's great-grandmother Angélique, a former slave who was liberated with the abolition of slavery but who continues to suffer the psychological legacies of slavery throughout her life: "Toute ma vie, j'ai dû me battre" (All my life I had to fight) (*Mes quatre femmes*, 143). In the first page of her story, she lists a series of activities that she asserts she could have done if she had not been bound by the shackles of slavery: "[J]'aurais pu m'asseoir dans une berceuse ... j'aurais pu mourir du mal d'amour ... j'aurais pu voyager à travers le monde ... j'aurais pu avoir un jardin" (I could have sat in a cradle ... I could have died of a broken heart ... I could have traveled around the world ... I could have had a garden) (143). With her story forming the final chapter of *Mes quatre femmes*, Pineau emphasizes the ongoing presence of slavery in the contemporary Caribbean imagination. History with a capital "H" infuses Angélique's story, and, as she affirms in a conversation with Daisy, this History of master narratives has irrevocable consequences for the myriad "small" histories that exist. Despite Angélique's liberation from slavery—symbolized in the page from the *Gazette Officielle de la Guadeloupe* that announces her legal liberation and the object she carries with her into the memory jail—the psychological repercussions of slavery continue. Angélique constantly reminds the reader that freedom "c'est pas pour nous dans le pays Guadeloupe ... c'est pas pour les nègres de notre espèce" (isn't for us in Guadeloupe ... it's not for the black people of our kind) (150). By placing Angélique's story at the end of the book with its firm grounding in the history of slavery, Pineau emphasizes the continuing influence of the past on contemporary life.

However, in many ways Angélique displays a resilience similar to Julia's. They are the two who are most directly affected by History, and yet they are also the two who remain most open to the possibilities of freedom within the confines of their social position. Angélique may regret her limited opportunities, yet she succeeds in achieving legal liberation from slavery and demonstrates a strength of character that proves exemplary for her descendants. For Pineau, this direct link with her slave ancestry means that the oppressive past will never be forgotten. Pineau's inclusion of extracts from "real" social documents such as Le Code Noir in *Mes quatre femmes* establishes the presence of History very firmly, but she relates it in a way that is deeply personal. Angélique's openness to the small gaps of autonomy that exist within her situation allows her to positively subvert a state of historical determinism and give a sense of hope to her descendants.

At end of the book, Pineau emphasizes the constructed nature of memory and in a light-hearted manner asserts that "il ne faut pas croire toutes les histoires" (you mustn't believe all my stories) (*Mes quatre femmes*, 185). However, her message is a powerful one. Through the careful and self-conscious crafting of her ancestors' stories, she reveals that memory is essential to the construction of identity. Her work shows that by reconciling with one's past and the past of one's ancestors and country, it is possible to achieve a sense of liberation and insight into one's own present and future. Such connections lead to a sense of sovereignty over one's own life in which previously external circumstances may have proved overwhelming. Importantly, though, the book shows people's different responses to memory—Gisèle's withdrawal from life, Julia's openness to nature, Daisy's embrace of material opportunities but oppression by self-alienation, and Angélique's ability to profit from the small gaps offered within the dominant system as we have seen with Man Ya in *Exile According to Julia* and Chamoiseau's *djobeurs*. Pineau structures the book a bit like a physical enactment of relationship, with the sharing of each of her ancestors' stories allowing her to positively construct her own subjectivity.

Folie, aller simple: journée ordinaire d'une infirmière

The third stage of Pineau's identity trajectory is her exploration of the complex relationship that exists between past and present in her 2010 narrative *Folie, aller simple: journée ordinaire d'une infirmière*. This book is an intimate portrayal of her role as a psychiatric nurse and the way in which her story becomes intertwined with those in her care. Psychiatric nursing is an activity that has always existed alongside Pineau's writing, and, fittingly, this narrative draws together both aspects of her professional craft. Framed and intertwined with the suicide of one of Pineau's patients, Sophie R., who ends her life by jumping in the path of a metro train in Paris, Pineau explores different strands of her own life and those for whom she cares. Her narrative reveals the often fragile separation that exists between madness and "normality," connection and disconnection, and points to the deeply binding similarities that unite us all.

Early in the narrative, Pineau situates herself in relation to the island of Guadeloupe, remembering her childhood gathering shells on the beach. Pineau draws on the literal and figurative image of the shell as a way to place her story in a Caribbean context, but one that is sufficiently open to embrace both Caribbean and non-Caribbean identities. Pineau's likening of the shells' weathering by the waves to the trials all people experience in life establishes her outward-looking perspective from the outset: "Déjà, à l'époque, j'imaginais qu'ils avaient tous souffert de quelque chose, d'une mauvaise rencontre au fond des mers, d'une existence miséreuse" (Already, at the time, I imagined they had all suffered from something, from a bad meeting at the bottom of the seas, from a miserable existence) (*Folie*, 11). Pineau's evocative description leads to the repeated phrase: "*On n'arrive jamais à l'hôpital psychiatrique par hasard*" (*One never arrives at a psychiatric hospital by chance*) (12; italics in original), which echoes the lament of "Gisèle se souvient" (Gisèle remembers) in *Mes quatre femmes*. Pineau subjects the former sentence to a word-by-word dissection, eventually arriving at the conclusion that "[t]els les coquillages jonchant les plages de la Guadeloupe, les personnes qui se trouvent à l'hôpital psychiatrique arrivent d'un long voyage" (like shells strewn on the beaches of Guadeloupe, people who find themselves in a psychiatric hospital arrive after a long journey) (*Folie*, 14). These opening paragraphs are important in establishing the evolution of Pineau's thought in relation to identity, suffering, and the burdens of the past. Although she announces her affinity to Guadeloupe at the start, characteristically drawing on natural imagery to convey her vision, she nonetheless seeks to illuminate the bonds that unite rather than divide us in a context that is wider than that of the Caribbean.

While Glissant's explorations of the unifying properties of Relation are on the scale of culture, for Pineau they are found on a more intimate scale. We may like to consider that people suffering from mental illness are far removed from us, but Pineau repeatedly underlines the connections that exist between the mentally unwell and those who are more emotionally robust. Relating her personal example of the fragile border that exists between "normality" and madness, Pineau demonstrates that we all experience the same challenges; it is just a question of degree. Much of Pineau's narrative is composed of lists of words or adjectives, running like fault lines through her work, echoing the ruptures that historians like Michel de

Certeau and Paula Hamilton describe in their work on history and memory. Images of disconnection and breakage abound in Pineau's text, emphasizing the urgent need for reconnection on a variety of levels: "Il y a des déchirures, des nécroses, des entailles si profondes qu'on pourrait croire des canyons. Il y a des fractures irréductibles, des lésions sans nom qui ulcèrent et démangent" (There are tears, necroses, cuts that are so deep they feel like canyons. There are irreducible fractures, lesions without names that ulcerate and itch) (15). *Folie, aller simple* paints a graphic and evocative picture of the internal wounds that afflict human beings. Like Carine Mardorossian's assertion that fragmentation can become a positive attribute in a reimagining of identity, Pineau attempts to draw these seemingly negative elements into some sort of narrative that allows them to exist without threatening one's very source of identity. For Pineau, this end is achieved above all by the therapeutic properties of writing and the accompanying processes of speaking and listening that characterize her work as a nurse.

As we have seen, a major theme of Pineau's philosophy is the closely intertwined poles of writing and psychiatry. She illustrates that in her life the two are symbiotic, each one necessary to sustain her sense of self. Pineau has written extensively of her early passion for reading and writing and the fact that literature was always going to be a part of her professional life. However, it is only as a result of her qualification and the practice of nursing that she is able to live out her calling of helping and understanding herself and others. Writing provides a uniting path between self and other, allowing her to navigate the torments of her own life, understand those of her patients, and somehow keep her from crossing the line into madness: "Je dis que ce métier d'infirmière équilibre ma vie, me permet de ne pas m'échapper dans un monde virtuel, de garder le contact avec le réel" (I say that this profession of nursing balances my life, stops me from escaping into a virtual world, to stay in touch with the real) (*Folie*, 170). At the same time, however, Pineau wonders if writing is in fact "une manière élégante et transversale de délirer?" (an elegant and transversal way of being delirious?) (173). Pineau's narrative shows that madness forms part of the make-up of us all: "[O]n se ressemble tous, parce qu'on est tous fragiles comme de la porcelaine ou des coquillages, tous si vulnérables, tous plus ou moins brisés de l'intérieur" (We all resemble each other, because we are all fragile like porcelain or shells, all so vulnerable, all more or less broken from inside) (113). Toward the end of the book, Pineau recalls the wisdom of an old nurse in a psychiatric hospital in Guadeloupe who tells her that madness is a completely natural state for the hostile world in which we live. Indeed, sometimes escaping into the irrational is the only way in which we can endure our suffering and remain in life.

For Pineau, though, writing provides a way out: "Je crois qu'on peut briser le cycle de cette violence en utilisant l'écriture pour parler de l'universel" (I think we can break the cycle of this violence by using writing to talk about the universal) (Jurney, 116).

In *Folie, aller simple*, Pineau exemplifies the fluctuating line between universal and particular by intertwining her personal reflections with the stories of some of her patients. Employing images of brokenness, muteness, and the absence of memory, Pineau attempts to rehabilitate her charges, giving them a voice and a purpose in a society that does not value those who do not conform to "normality." For example, Sophie R. "a comme perdu la parole" (has lost her words), and for her, everything "est flou. La mémoire incertaine" (is hazy. Memory is uncertain) (*Folie*, 23). For Gabrielle S., who has three days of madness, "elle n'a gardé aucun souvenir. 'Le trou noir. Tout oublié'" (she has no memory. "A black hole. All forgotten") (45). When the mother of a seventeen-year-old schizophrenic comes to visit him, "elle n'avait pas de mots. Elle se contentait de regarder son fils comme s'il était devenu une bête curieuse" (she didn't have any words. She was happy to look at her son as if he had become a curious beast) (210). Against these images of muteness and lack of power, Pineau repeatedly stresses that these negative judgments arise as a result of people's fear and ignorance. Indeed, people "voient des morceaux d'eux-mêmes dans la folie des autres" (see pieces of themselves in the madness of others) (67), while the mad "représentent toutes les couches de la société. Ici, les barrières sociales s'effondrent face à la maladie" (represent all layers of society. Here, social barriers collapse in the face of sickness) (68).

In Pineau's typical style, though, she reveals that beauty may appear in the most wretched of scenarios. She contrasts the heart-wrenching suffering of many of her patients with the profound lessons of humanity that they have taught her: "J'ai appris la patience et l'humilité, la rigueur et l'observation, la compassion et l'écoute silencieuse" (I've learned patience and humility, rigor and observation, compassion and silent listening) (146). Pineau's patients also reveal a profound openness to others, giving a physical expression to their desire for connection. When the nurses join their patients at quiet moments in the day, the others "ouvrent le cercle d'une manière conviviale" (open the circle in a convivial manner) (153). This gesture of openness allows the patients to place themselves in a meaningful social network while also allowing the nurses to relate to their charges in a different way: "Ici, on tente de soigner, de soulager, d'accompagner. . . . On n'a pas de grande prétention. On ne se fait guère d'illusions. Mais on se bat pour l'humanité et ce combat n'est jamais vain" (Here, we attempt to look after, to soothe, to accompany.... We don't have any pretension. We don't have any illusions. But we fight for humanity and this fight is never in vain) (158). In Pineau's hands, the profession of psychiatry reveals itself as particularly open to the idea of interrelationship and inclusion, where people are accepted regardless of their "couleurs, compositions, complexions, confessions, continents" (colors, composition, complexion, confession, continents) (197).

As in *Exile According to Julia* and *Mes quatre femmes*, Pineau draws on nature to express some of her key ideas. In these and other works by Pineau, such as *La Grande Drive des esprits*, we have seen that the garden is a dynamic entity that can offer solace and beauty on the one hand and reflect the harshness of life on the other. In *Folie, aller simple*, Pineau likens her patients' experience to the changing fortunes of the garden, observing that "chacun cultive son délire comme un jardin clos planté d'arbres extraordinaires qui donnent des fruits en toutes saisons" (each one cultivates his or her delirium like a closed garden planted with extraordinary trees that produce fruit in all seasons) (166). However, this place of fecundity and beauty has the power to change rapidly: "Un jour, le gentil jardin se transforme en forêt et vous prenez peur. Les tiges volubiles prolifèrent et menacent de vous étrangler" (One day the gentle garden changes into a forest and you become scared. The voluble stems proliferate and threaten to strangle you) (175). This delicate balance between the garden as a place of refuge and a place of fear is crucial to Pineau's elucidation of identity. While peace does not necessarily have to be found in a carefully manicured garden, as Julia's garden in Routhiers attests, the threat of a garden growing out of control is ever present. The chaotic merging of roots and flowers, overpowering its inhabitants and bequeathing a sense of instability, shows that the path to reconciliation must be negotiated carefully. For this reason, gardens in both a figurative and literal sense must be attended to, respectfully treated, and ultimately allowed to grow in their own unique manner if they are truly to blossom. *Folie, aller simple* demonstrates through the potentially uniting properties of the garden that a sense of liberation is possible for every person, regardless of their individual challenges. The book is a firm statement of Pineau's belief that just like nature, people can be reborn after hardship.

As the above discussion illustrates, Pineau's literary project is driven by her desire to expose the bonds that exist between individuals even in the most unlikely of situations, to bridge the gaps between past and present with creativity and imagination, and to open up a space where the potential for human resilience may thrive. While Condé's tone is ironic and self-assured, Pineau's is more serious, deeply passionate, and underpinned by a sense of hope, despite the heart-wrenching scenes she often describes. In an interview with Chantal Anglade and Françoise Simasotchi-Brones, Pineau asserts that, for her, "le livre est le seul espace de liberté" (the book is the only space of freedom) (Anglade and Simasotchi-Brones, 7), a medium that allows her "to share with others" (Loichot, 329). Writing in Pineau's hands becomes a powerful therapeutic tool, one that is firmly grounded in her personal circumstances but that is sufficiently flexible to reach out to others in their difference:

> Écrire en tant que femme noire créole, c'est vivre l'espérance d'un monde vraiment nouveau, peuples, langues, races, religions, cultures mêlés, imbriqués, s'enrichissant, se découvrant sans cesse, se respectant et s'acceptant dans la belle différence.
>
> (To write as a black Creole woman is to live the hope of a world that is really new, peoples, languages, races, religions, cultures that are mixed together, linked, constantly enriching each other, respecting each other, and accepting each other in beautiful difference.) (Pineau, "Écrire en tant que Noire," 295)

CHAPTER 3

PATRICK CHAMOISEAU
Memory, Relation, and the Creolized Imaginary

Patrick Chamoiseau is one of the most innovative writers in the francophone Caribbean, known both for his attention to the craft of writing and his commitment to expressing Creole culture through his literature. Like Maryse Condé and Gisèle Pineau, he has practiced a dual occupation for decades—in his case, social work alongside his distinguished writing career. His literary oeuvre is wide and varied, encompassing fiction, theoretical reflection (in recent years these publications were frequently coauthored with Édouard Glissant), stories for children, and collaborations with photographers. His writing has been recognized by a plethora of literary awards, most notably the 1992 Prix Goncourt for his historical novel *Texaco*. Chamoiseau is also one of the key theoreticians of Créolité, or Creoleness, and with Jean Bernabé and Raphaël Confiant penned the 1989 manifesto *Éloge de la Créolité* (*In Praise of Creoleness*). Considered a key intellectual development that follows on from Aimé Césaire's Négritude and Glissant's Antillanité, Créolité emphasizes the need to embrace all that is Creole—language, history, and cultural traditions—and this belief underpins all of Chamoiseau's writing. In contrast to Condé's and Pineau's self-proclaimed intuitive and anti-intellectual approach to the past, Chamoiseau reveals himself to be a more cerebral writer, although he remains deeply attuned to the music of language and how it expresses emotions. His later thought is marked by an increasing adherence to the notion that creolization—of which the Caribbean is a prime example—constitutes a living model of Glissant's Relation. Chamoiseau uses the notion of the creolized imaginary as a way to unlock new ways of relating to past, present, and future and as a powerful means to draw together people from diverse communities.

This chapter will examine how Chamoiseau extends Glissant's notion of Relation and dramatizes a creolized imaginary through his childhood narratives, plotting a path that moves from a more sensuous recalling of 1950s Martinique to a world that is increasingly marked by globalization. Chamoiseau's autofictional narratives *Antan d'enfance* (*Childhood*) (1990), *Chemin d'école* (*School Days*) (1994), and *À Bout d'enfance* (2005), which are grouped together under the banner *Une enfance créole*, form the basis of the discussion. Chamoiseau's explorations of the personal and collective effects of Martinique's history, revealed dramatically through these three volumes, highlight various facets of engaging with the past. *Childhood* introduces the topic of memory, colorful Caribbean figures such as the *conteur*, the *femme matador*, and the Syrian merchant, as well as the social stratification of the French and Creole languages; and *School Days* paints a portrait of the colonial school as a microcosm of Creole society, through its three main characters—the *négrillon*, the *maître* and Gros-Lombric (Big Bellybutton)—illustrating three ways of responding to French cultural dominance. Finally, *À Bout d'enfance* returns to some of the themes of *Childhood* with further musings on the unreliability of memory, Creole traditions, and a certain nostalgia as Chamoiseau realizes that his childhood is coming to an end and he must face a world beyond his Caribbean island. Each volume is guided by Chamoiseau's portrayal of the creolized imaginary as the key to understanding the historical process, which is characterized by continuous movement and a direct link to the future. Embedded in the history of Martinique itself, it is "la Créolisation américaine [qui] va produire du *nouveau culturel valable pour tous*" (American Creolization [that] is going to produce a new cultural model that is applicable for everyone) (Chamoiseau, *Césaire, Perse, Glissant*, 20; italics in original). This intellectual framework allows for Chamoiseau's notion of unity in diversity—or *diversalité*—to become a possibility.

Before proceeding to an analysis of *Une enfance créole*, it is important first to understand how Chamoiseau's personal history inflects his writings. Patrick Chamoiseau was born in Fort-de-France, Martinique, in 1953, the youngest of five children. His mother, Man Ninotte, who is a key character in his childhood memoirs, is an embodiment of the celebrated Caribbean *femme matador*, while his father is a quieter individual who changes professions from shoemaker to postal worker and luxuriates in the beauty of the French language. Unlike his *créoliste* counterpart Raphaël Confiant, Chamoiseau grew up in the urban environment of Martinique's capital city, and this experience had a profound influence on his conception of

Creole identity. In an interview with Paola Ghinelli, he asserted that his city background was problematic for him (Ghinelli, 20). As Creole traditions are more manifest in the countryside, Chamoiseau had to forge his own approach to the past, revealing different aspects of the repressed Creole culture and language that are central to the *créoliste* philosophy. His portrayal of disappearing cultural practices in towns such as the Creole *conteur* (storyteller), the Caribbean market, and resourceful characters such as the *djobeurs* (odd-jobbers) forms an essential part of his conception of Créolité. After completing his secondary studies in Martinique, Chamoiseau undertook a law and social economics degree in France. He worked as a social worker in the Metropole before returning to Martinique as a counselor at the Juvenile Justice Tribunal in Fort-de-France. He remains a politically engaged writer and is outspoken on a variety of issues such as the importance of preserving the natural environment.

Language, Culture, and Identity

While both Condé and Pineau openly declare the imaginative elements that form part of their memoirs, Chamoiseau's self-conscious stance toward his autofictional writings is even more overt. As in his wider oeuvre, there is no question that his texts are highly constructed entities with their frequent authorial intrusions, footnotes, explanations, and meandering between fact and fiction. In her authoritative study *Patrick Chamoiseau: A Critical Introduction*, Wendy Knepper argues that the Martinican writer dons various masks for the purpose of exploring different facets of his personal and collective life. According to Knepper, "the invention of identities, such as Word Scratcher or Warrior of the Imaginary, serves as an authorial strategy for exploring the interactions among the world, the self, and the word through the activity of 'la dérive' or imaginative wandering" (4). Like his Caribbean counterparts, Chamoiseau uses writing to conjure up new worlds and new ways of being, but his "shifting narrative ground defies certain knowledge and the formation of fixed identities in favor of a poetics where the negotiation and rerouting of identities, genres of narrative, languages, histories, and places enter into new imaginative fields of interactive, transformative relations" (Knepper, *Patrick Chamoiseau*, 4–5). As Chamoiseau himself asserts: "Le berceau de l'Écrire est dans *la relation de tout à tout*, comme l'aurait dit Glissant" (The cradle of Writing is in *the relation of everything to everything*, as Glissant would have said) (*Césaire, Perse, Glissant*, 23). At the heart of

Chamoiseau's conception of identity is his belief in the profoundly transformative process of creolization and its potential in liberating intellectual thought. According to Chamoiseau, such creolization can be characterized as "the accelerated, massive coming together of several peoples, several languages" (Thomas, 165), leading to the melding of Amerindian, African, and European influences but also contributing to an overwhelming ambiguity attached to the notion of identity. As a result of their political, economic, and cultural domination by France, the Martinican people have suffered from deep alienation regarding their cultural identity, a situation worsened by the fact that France operates both as the "Other" (the island was first a colony and since 1946 has been an overseas department of France) and the "Same" (Martinicans have interiorized the values and language of France). Chamoiseau has reflected on the Caribbean's creolized status in many different forums, but he repeatedly stresses its result in the creation of a hybridized people, a history that cannot be referred back to a genesis story and the primacy of the oral tale: "[T]here is no absolute—not linguistically, not racially, not culturally, not historically; we are in an extreme relativization of traditions, a chaos of diversity" (Morgan, 447). However, Chamoiseau does not view this as a negative attribute but as a deep positive in which it is the *imaginaire* (imaginary) that gives rise to connections between people. Chamoiseau coins the term *diversalité* (diversality) as a way to structure this imaginary, where "[u]nity opens to diversity; diversity opens to unity, and the two maintain each other; and that's why rather than to say 'universality' in language, let's say 'diversality' since universality has the tendency to line us all up along Western values under the pretext of looking for unity" (Morgan, 451). Embodied in the notion of the creolized imaginary, diversality is a way in which to look toward the future.

An important stage in Chamoiseau's theoretical trajectory is his role in the development of Créolité. Along with Bernabé and Confiant, Chamoiseau is one of the key thinkers behind this theoretical movement, which contrasts with Césaire's Négritude and Glissant's Antillanité. While Césaire's approach to literature and identity advocates the reclaiming and revalorization of the Caribbean's African roots, and Glissant's early theorizations liken the Caribbean to a rhizome where islands burst forth like new buds from a network of roots that are interconnected, Créolité is grounded firmly in the Creole nature of the islands: "Neither Europeans, nor Africans, nor Asians, we proclaim ourselves Creoles" (Bernabé, Chamoiseau, and Confiant, 75). Above all, this intellectual current underscores the importance of the Creole language and culture in Martinican society;

this emphasis is evident in Chamoiseau's diverse publications, particularly his earlier ones such as *Chronique des sept misères* (*Chronicle of the Seven Sorrows*) and *Solibo magnifique* (*Solibo Magnificent*). Créolité attributes a fundamental role to the writer, who is charged with the responsibility of rewriting into existence the forgotten players of the colonial chronicle. According to *Éloge de la Créolité*, "[m]ore than anyone else, the writer's vocation is to identify what, in our daily lives, determines the patterns and structure of the imaginary. To perceive our existence is to perceive us in the context of our history, of our daily lives, of our reality" (Bernabé, Chamoiseau, and Confiant, 100). This belief in the power of literature is reinforced in Chamoiseau and Confiant's later publication, *Lettres créoles*, in which they assert that literature "est mêlée à l'oxygène des vies. Elle a connu les pays, les peuples, les hommes.... Elle sait les sentiments, connaît les émotions, s'articule dans les langues de la tour de Babel et se love dans chacune des conceptions du monde" (is mixed with the oxygen of lives. It has known countries, people, men, and women.... It knows feelings, emotions, articulates itself in the languages from the Tower of Babel, and coils itself up in each of the conceptions of the world) (Chamoiseau and Confiant, 12). In the three volumes of *Une enfance créole*, the Creole characters, language, and traditions of Martinique's unwritten history form an indispensable backdrop to Chamoiseau's meditations on his personal and his country's past and his battle with the unreliability of memory that refuses to fix any moment in time.

In 1997, Chamoiseau published *Écrire en pays dominé*, a part-theoretical, part-autobiographical text in which he reflects on the fundamental question: "Comment écrire, dominé?" (How to write, dominated?) (17). According to Luciano Picanço, the double-edged style of this text allows Chamoiseau to "démythifier la vérité autobiographique et ainsi à prêter au fictionnel la solidité nécessaire à l'explication non pas, tout simplement, de sa biographie personnelle, mais surtout de la réalité culturelle de son peuple" (demythify autobiographical truth and therefore to lend to the fictional the necessary solidity not only to explain his personal biography but, especially the cultural reality of his people) (194). This commitment to portraying the collective through the personal is one of the defining characteristics of Chamoiseau's work. In *Écrire*, he characterizes his role as a "guerrier de l'imaginaire" (warrior of the imaginary) (274), a position that Lorna Milne believes is fundamental to his aesthetic and political project (*Patrick Chamoiseau*, 181), for it is through writing that he advocates change. Chamoiseau underlines, furthermore, that "écrire n'est pas certitude, mais découverte" (writing is not certitude, but discovery) (*Écrire*, 279), which clearly illuminates the notion of openness that is fundamental to Chamoiseau's approach toward the contemporary world. In relation to language, which is a philosophical battleground in colonial Martinique, Chamoiseau gives a suggestive example of how this can be viewed differently through his concept of diversality. In a letter he wrote to the translators of *Childhood*, which they reproduce in the preface to the English edition, he emphasizes the idea of diverse interconnections that can occur without domination:

> In the use of French, I try not to forget my Creole language, my Creole imagination, my Creole perception of the world.... I want to feel [language] trembling, to feel its availability to all other languages of the world. I want it to stop behaving as if it were the only one capable of expressing the world but rather for it to be relativised, informed of the splendid possibilities of other languages, which are placed on the same plane. I want the language to be "open." (vii–viii)

Chamoiseau's thought is closely related to Glissant's, as the above statement attests, and the two frequently collaborated on literary projects. Indeed, Chamoiseau thanks Glissant "dont l'oeuvre et les paroles nourrissent cet Écrire et m'anime" (whose work and words nourish this Writing and animate me] (*Écrire*, 321) and in a 2009 interview with Maeve McCusker credits Glissant with liberating his whole imagination (McCusker, "On Slavery," 79). The Glissantian terms that Chamoiseau most often invokes are Relation and *tout-monde* (whole-world). Both of these models emphasize plurality, openness, and connection; it is no longer a question of the Same versus the Other but a situation where "the 'other' is already there—everywhere. So, what you have are emanations, networks, and presences ... the complexity of places, of multiple belongings, and of diverse cultural presences in a country" (Morgan, 449).

Chamoiseau and Glissant argue that creolization is not unique to the Caribbean and in fact has occurred in many different settings. Naturally constituting a model of Relation, creolization opens the space for Chamoiseau's understanding of the term *mondialité* (globalism), which is a fundamental influence in the contemporary world. "To speak of mondialité is to say, hold on: these elements of contact and relation have always been part of the progression of cultures and humanities, they have become more pronounced, and we are now destined to envisage our individual and collective fulfillment through an imaginary that inhabits the wider world" (McCusker, "On

Slavery," 77). In Chamoiseau's investigations of his childhood, he reveals that a first step in this process of global understanding is to articulate where you come from. Building on Glissant's idea of *la trace*, developed in *Le Discours antillais* and other works, Chamoiseau introduces the concept of *traces-mémoires*. According to Chamoiseau, "memory-traces"—objects of memory that may include things as diverse as old cabins and tools—"nous ouvre à une mémoire bien plus complète que celle qui serait tout simplement liée à une trace écrite ou à la parole verbalisée" (opens us to a memory that is much more complete than one which would simply be linked to a written trace or a verbalized word) (Ghinelli, 18). In his 1994 collaboration with photographer Rodolphe Hammadi, *Guyane: traces-mémoires du bagne*, a literary and photographic investigation of a ruined prison in French Guiana, Chamoiseau provides a graphic example of a history informed by "memory-traces" "dont la portée symbolique, affective, fonctionnelle, dont les significations ouvertes, évolutives, vivantes, dépassent de bien loin l'équation immobile des traditionnels monuments que l'on répertorie dans la Mémoire occidentale" (whose symbolic, affective, functional impact, whose open, evolutionary, living significances surpass by far the immobile equation of traditional monuments that are recorded in western Memory) (Chamoiseau and Hammadi, 16). With this nontraditional approach to history, then, it is appropriate to proceed to an analysis of Chamoiseau's autofictional narratives, which are guided by the subjective nature of memory and encompass the diverse elements of his Creole childhood.

Une enfance créole I: Antan d'enfance

Wendy Knepper argues that the three volumes of *Une enfance créole* show that the "child's life is a site of tension whose narrative repeats in a compressed time scale and *en miniature* the collective history of instabilities that have contributed to the cultural psyche of Martinique" (Knepper, *Patrick Chamoiseau*, 131). While numerous critics have commented on the intermingling of personal and collective in his work, Chamoiseau also asserts that "il n'y a pas un seul pays où je suis passé et que les gens ne m'ont pas dit que j'avais décrit leur enfance" (there is not a single country that I went to where people didn't tell me I had described their childhood) (Ghinelli, 29). *Une enfance créole* is thus both a very Caribbean portrayal of growing up in Fort-de-France in the 1950s and 1960s and a chronicle that has more wide-ranging insights. Thematically and stylistically, there are uniting elements in all three volumes, but each contributes a different aspect to Chamoiseau's portrayal of the past. The first book, *Childhood*, is divided into two parts—"Sentir" (Feeling) and "Partir" (Leaving)—and describes the narrator's early years during which he progresses from a life entirely defined within the home to one in which he gradually ventures outward. As Suzanne Crosta observes, place is of primary importance in this book, and the "déplacement du 'qui suis-je?' à 'où suis-je?' met en valeur les lieux d'identification dans la formation identitaire" (displacement of "who am I?" to "where am I?" emphasizes the places of identification in one's identity formation) (4). Edgard Sankara argues that "Chamoiseau's autobiography constantly refers to a particular audience, and this is likely a narrative strategy that Chamoiseau borrows from the folktale, especially in its performance or delivery" (99). These two assertions underscore the heart of Chamoiseau's project: the Caribbean context, which is vital to the book's meaning, and a narrative strategy taken from an oral Creole tradition that supports his literary aim.

In writing the trilogy of his childhood and adolescence, Chamoiseau "is making a theory about autobiography that establishes as its premise the unreliability of memory when writing autobiographies" (Sankara, 101). Crosta also emphasizes this constructed nature of the autobiographical project, arguing that there "existe cette zone floue entre la mémoire et l'imagination, que le narrateur essaie de réconcilier avec lui-même et de communiquer au lecteur" (exists this gray area between memory and imagination, that the narrator tries to reconcile with himself and to communicate to the reader) (5). As previously stated, Paula Hamilton identifies a recent trend in historiography that celebrates "a return to the storytelling function in history" (25), and Chamoiseau's historical strategy, which combines the factual and imaginative, corresponds to this view. Like Condé and Pineau, Chamoiseau specifically refers to the selective nature of memory and gives no impression of relating his "true" life story to his readers: "[I]s it I who remember, memory, or you who remember me?" (*Childhood*, 4). Memory emerges as an autonomous character as much as the narrator himself, and there is a constant process of negotiation between the two. As Maeve McCusker observes more negatively, the character of memory is "presented throughout all three texts as a locus of struggle, due to the dialectical relationship between experience and narrative, between narrated and narrating self" (McCusker, *Patrick Chamoiseau*, 52). Chamoiseau's manner of treating memory allows him to portray a kaleidoscope of recollections and observations in which the trivial and significant intermingle and are presented as equally important in his construction of self. By the same token, his own story and those of his culture coexist to provide a portrait of Caribbean society that is both particular and universal. Moreover, memory appears as a kind of rhizomatic network defined by the constant shifting of interpretation and significance. There is never a sense of fixity or completeness, which reflects the notion of Relation and the creolized imaginary.

Chamoiseau's approach to memory also allows him to portray the past in a more impressionistic way than that of an "objective" historian sifting through the "facts." Like the conjurer in a magic show, Chamoiseau depicts himself as the creator of memory, not the passive recipient of his childhood reflections: "O selective memory . . . Memory, that is my decision" (*Childhood*, 29). According to Knepper, "the idea of memory as a creative activity becomes a powerful tool for reorienting oneself toward a new understanding of history and narrative" (*Patrick Chamoiseau*, 151). This self-conscious nature of Chamoiseau's memory writing highlights the storytelling aspect of his autobiographical project as well as demonstrating that any act of writing contains within it the personal bias of its author. Thus, while History purports to be an accurate representation of the past, it emerges as both selective and creative, as critics such as Mireille Rosello and Nicola King have pointed out. Chamoiseau's interrogation of "Truth" and the impossibility of creating a totalizing, unbiased version of the past is echoed in the narrative strategies he employs. His splintering of his narrator into three "voices"—"il" (le négrillon), "tu" (his young self), and "je" (the adult autobiographer)—"reinforces the idea of modern autobiography as the fracturing of the Self into many entities" (Sankara, 104). Chamoiseau's employment of intrusions and commentaries in his text only serves to reinforce the notion of autobiographical writing as a highly constructed activity. Although Chamoiseau does not portray himself as a historian, his engagement with the past nonetheless mirrors some of the tasks of the contemporary practitioner of history and memory. In particular, his hard-won synthesis of archival and emotional sources into a meaningful narrative reflects how memory making is physical as well as intellectual, a ceaseless process of "remembering and forgetting, assimilating and discarding" (Lambek and Antze, xxiv). Knepper likens the process to that of "[a]utoethnographic performance [that] not only situates the exiled adult in relation to childhood and the mysteries of the child as other, but opens up a space of resistance between the individual (*auto-*) and the collective (*-ethno*) where writing (*-graphy*) becomes a process for rewriting given affiliations and relations" (*Patrick Chamoiseau*, 153).

Despite Condé's and Pineau's portrayal of male Caribbean writers as overly cerebral and theoretical, Chamoiseau asserts that he, like them, writes with his senses: "[L]orsque j'écris, je ne suis plus en réflexion, je suis en émotion, je suis dans mon rire, dans mon inquiétude, dans mon envie de partage, dans mes amusements, dans mes effets de style" (When I write, I am no longer in reflection, I am in emotion, I am in my laugh, in my anxiety, in my desire to share, in my amusements, in my effects of style) (Ghinelli, 29). In this way, then, it is not surprising to read of a landscape of emotion in the reminiscence of Chamoiseau's past: "What predominates is the memory of impatience" (*Childhood*, 21). McCusker characterizes this approach as the exploratory privileging over the explanatory, thereby opening up the possibility of multiple understandings (*Patrick Chamoiseau*, 53). Chamoiseau's portrayal of his childhood in sensuous terms, emphasizing color, feeling, and fragmentary memories, appeals to a different aspect of the historical project. It connects more deeply to the imagination, to perception rather than definite memories, and in this way allows the recollections of his childhood to form its own narrative structure. Moreover, this fluidity allows readers to make their own connections with Chamoiseau's story and to find parallels with their lives, putting into action the notion of a creolized imaginary. Knepper adds another layer to this more sensual way of recalling the past, arguing that Chamoiseau deliberately alludes to the Proustian madeleine in a scene describing the Creole sweets his mother makes, but reworks it in a subversive manner: "Rather than a delicate Proustian bite into the past, releasing the flow of memories, Chamoiseau evokes the past-present dynamics of French-Martinican relations through the rewriting of the Proustian in a local context" (*Patrick Chamoiseau*, 135). There are thus multiple layers that can be read into different scenes from Chamoiseau's childhood, ranging from a simple and sensuous recollection of a childhood treat, to a commentary on relations between the Caribbean and the Metropole, to a dialog between Chamoiseau and his literary forebears. This approach could be considered an example of the imaginary creating meaningful links between people that draw on one's physical, emotional, and intellectual experiences of the past.

On a different level, *Childhood* brings to life a number of memorable figures who address Chamoiseau's wider aim of recording both Creole history and his own family background. The book demonstrates a particular period in time that stands in contrast to the later *À Bout d'enfance*, which displays the hallmarks of increasing globalization. We meet his mother, Man Ninotte, a *femme matador* who keeps her family on a firm path toward social success. This revered figure in francophone Caribbean society has attained almost mythic-like status in her ability to courageously resist life's trials. In a 2000 interview with Maeve McCusker, Chamoiseau argues that "la réalité sociologique de la Martinique, c'est que les femmes sont très présentes, et ce sont de fortes femmes" (the sociological reality in Martinique is that women are very present and they are strong women) (McCusker, "De la problématique du territoire," 730). Indeed, in reading other works by Chamoiseau such as *Texaco*, it is clear that his mother's steely strength infuses his conception and even idealization of the strong Caribbean woman. In *Childhood*, Chamoiseau depicts his eldest sister Anastasia, nicknamed La Baronne (the Baronness), in the same vein, a woman who "had inherited from Ma Ninotte an aptitude for conquering life, for foreseeing everything, for knowing everything, for organizing everything" (14). We learn more generally in *Childhood* that "mamas never rested" (43) and that Man Ninotte, like many women, had a deep understanding of the Caribbean market. "Better than anyone, she knew its laws" (81). This close association between women and Creole traditions such as the marketplace is important as it underlines the fundamental role women play in preserving the Creole past. Chamoiseau also depicts his mother as closely in tune with nature, demonstrating her deep implantation within the Caribbean landscape: "Her body was plugged into the seasons of the moon" (107). Chamoiseau's portrayal of his mother and sisters as *femme matador*–like figures aligns him with a tradition in Caribbean writing in which women are frequently the ones who preserve and transmit cultural memory. The most striking example of this trend is Simone Schwarz-Bart's *Pluie et vent sur Télumée Miracle* (*The Bridge of Beyond*) in which Reine Sans Nom (Queen without a Name) imbues her granddaughter Télumée with the strength and spirit of her forebears. In depicting his own female relatives in this way, Chamoiseau serves both to cement his own personal history and to paint a larger portrait of Caribbean society in 1950s Martinique. He also contributes to the further mythification of this Caribbean cultural figure.

Chamoiseau's recollections in *Childhood* lie against the backdrop of the Creole society that existed in Fort-de-France in the 1950s. He depicts, for example, the complex networks of the Creole grocery store, which "was a world unto itself" (87), and the way in which the plethora of Syrian merchants "spoke several languages, Creole for familiarity, French to strike deals, their native tongue to simulate idiocy when the client had spunk" (78). The differences used to describe the hair of Chamoiseau and his siblings gives an indication of the racial distinctions that form the basis of Caribbean society after slavery (64–65). Time appears both measureless—the "house was as old as eternity, it seems: the little boy never met anyone with a memory long enough to recall a time of splendor" (16)—or structured according to the seasons: "From his window the little boy could detect two seasons, times that were rainy and times that weren't" (107). We learn the challenges that face the Creole culture in which "Creole medicine was losing its paths of transmission.... A people becomes feeble and dies when its traditions are invalidated even to itself" (57). Such reflections detail the growing intervention of the adult narrator who can set these childish observations against the larger narrative of a society faced with erasure by French cultural dominance and increasing globalization. The importance of retaining the Creole culture and language are of paramount importance to Chamoiseau's literary project, even when it is focused on the seemingly individualist subject of his life story.

The universe Chamoiseau paints in *Childhood* as well as the subsequent volumes of *Une enfance créole* underline the continuous and value-laden struggles that exist between French and Creole in Martinican society. Linguists such as Ellen Schnepel have detailed the state of diglossia characteristic of Martinique and how French is linked to promotion and privilege in society while Creole is associated with backwardness and dying traditions. The work of the *créolistes* has done much to refute this simple binarization, and indeed, Chamoiseau's own contribution to revalorizing the Creole language has been considerable. In *Childhood*, he depicts some of the linguistic battles seen from the vantage point of both the child and the adult narrator. We learn, for example, of the richness of the Creole language: "It fascinated us, as it did all the children, by its ability to contest ... the French order that governed speech.... There was mutiny in the language" (33). A young girl from the countryside, Jeanne-Yvette, brings evocative Creole tales to the town, where storytellers are rare: "She taught the little boy the astonishing richness of Creole orality. A universe of canny resistance, of salvational cruelty, rich with several genies" (70). Like the *femme matador*, the *conteur créole* is valorized in *Childhood* through the character of Jean-Yvette and is a figure whom Chamoiseau returns to at numerous intervals in his fictional and nonfictional works. Both form part of his long-standing project of safeguarding Creole history through the production of a written narrative. McCusker attributes an almost archaeological role to Chamoiseau, asserting how he "attempts to recover (bring back) the memory of the past [and has] contributed to a collective and individual coming to terms with, and, potentially, a recovery from, its effects" (*Patrick Chamoiseau*, 19–20). Knepper also comments on this aspect of Chamoiseau's writing, arguing: "What is experienced as a split consciousness, a Creole private self and a French public self, is pulled apart and knit together through the fictions of memory and the art of storytelling" (*Patrick Chamoiseau*, 142).

As already stated, Chamoiseau's commentary about childhood underlines both the universal and the particular aspects of his experience growing up in 1950s Martinique. "You never leave childhood, you hold it tight inside. You never detach from it, you repress it. It's not a process of improvement that leads to adulthood, but the slow sedimentation of a crust around a sensitive state that will be the core of what you are" (49). These primal transformations that occur in the transition from childhood to adulthood could be considered akin to the way in which the past plays a fundamental role in the development of a society. While many writers from the Caribbean place slavery and colonization at the heart of their narratives, Chamoiseau's approach defuses the power of any one "event" and situates past experiences into a network of Relation. With memories reduced to unattached entities that jostle in relation to others, societies, like individuals, can make choices about how much power they attribute to different experiences. One of Chamoiseau's final observations in *Childhood* stresses the autonomy that exists in memory if we allow it to: "Memory, who remembers for you? Who fixed your laws and procedures? Who keeps inventory in your thieving caves?" (106). History and memory thus remain in the power of their creators, and Chamoiseau shows that anyone can become the *Marqueur de parole* (Scribe) of their own story.

Une enfance créole II: Chemin d'école

In *School Days*, Chamoiseau extends the preoccupations he develops in *Childhood*, centering particularly on his growing awareness of the gaps between the dominant French culture of the public sphere and the Creole values and language that reign in the domestic realm. The struggle of the young narrator to develop his own identity amid these competing influences forms a striking contrast to some of the other characters in the book, who demonstrate a variety of reactions to these differentially valued cultures and languages. While the protagonist eventually manages to strike a balance between the French and Creole cultures and take the best of both worlds, his schoolmaster gains prominence in society only by rejecting his Creole roots.

Divided into two parts, entitled "Envie" (Longing) and "Survie" (Survival), the book explores the life of the young Martinican boy confronted with the French education system that was imposed on and continues to reign in the Caribbean islands of Martinique and Guadeloupe. These two sections summarize the central conflict of French Caribbean identity: before going to school, the young narrator is fascinated by the mysterious place that his brothers and sisters visit each day, and he is brimming with desire to be a part of such an adventure. However, he soon realizes that there is a huge difference between the French universe that dominates at school and the Creole one that characterizes his home life. From the point of view of the author, the major problem of the French national education system that operated in Martinique as he was growing up is that it did not recognize the specificities of the island and tried to transform Caribbean children into subjects of Metropolitan France. While at school, for example, the narrator discovers maps of a mysterious hexagonal country and pictures of wintry landscapes on the wall. Moreover, he observes his teachers wearing pants, jackets, waistcoats, and ties despite the tropical climate. The world with which the narrator is confronted clearly reflects the *mission civilisatrice* philosophy of the French educators: to create and maintain a "little France" in the Caribbean. Chamoiseau's narrative dramatizes numerous examples of the conflict between the dull world of the French teachers and the vibrant colors of the Creole children as well as the damaging psychological effects of the education system on these young students.

Although the teachers described in the book are black Martinicans, they firmly model themselves on their Metropolitan counterparts. For this reason, Chamoiseau's teacher only speaks French, and he constantly sings the praises of what he perceives are superior French values. He is a classic example of Fanon's *Peau noire, masques blancs*. The use of Creole at school is punished to such an extent that the narrator declares that the teacher had rendered him mute. At first glance, the teacher appears to embody real cruelty in his civilizing mission toward the children, but Chamoiseau partly explains these attitudes through references to the past in the book. For example, when the teacher calls the roll and the children reply timidly, he reminds them that it was not so long ago that slaves did not have the right to their own names and therefore that they should be proud of theirs. For the teacher, as for the French colonizers, pride and self-esteem can only be found in the wholehearted adoption of a French identity, which they consider the emblem of civilization against the "savagery" of the Creole world. His intentions are thus complex, fluctuating from frustrated outrage at the children's ineptitude in speaking French and a genuine belief that his educational methods will give them the best possible start in life.

Chamoiseau underlines the difficulty of living the duality of French Caribbean identity in the way he shows the teacher's recourse to his native Creole in times of stress: "He would also, in the occasional moment of fatigue, skimp on his *r*s or lose his *u*s. But he'd catch himself in a flash" (*School Days*, 63). Despite his vigilance toward these moments of weakness, the teacher finds himself completely undone in a dramatic scene symbolizing the clash of French and Creole cultures and the rare victory of the latter. When the young schoolboy Gros-Lombric (Big Bellybutton), depicted as a Creole person who cannot assimilate himself to the French model, arrives at school with a snake's head in his pocket, all hell breaks loose. Associated with the negative effects of black magic, the snake is an animal that stimulates fear in many Caribbean people, even those who think themselves above such superstitions. The teachers are paralyzed with fear and find themselves returning to their native Creole—the same language that they try to erase from the vocabulary of their students. Chamoiseau highlights the constant tension that forms an integral part of French Caribbean identity in the contrast between the teachers unraveled by the appearance of the snake's head and their efforts to regain their dignity by cursing the Creole culture: "Without even giving the order to sit down, the Teacher started haranguing us about Negro-Creole customs and the hopeless perdition of that barbarous people" (83). Obviously, if the teachers were secure in their French identity, there would be no need to affirm themselves by diminishing the importance of another culture.

As this scene amply demonstrates, language in fact constitutes a key battleground for the elucidation of francophone Caribbean identity. For the teachers in *School Days*, speaking Creole ties Caribbean people to the injustices of the slave past and prevents them from advancing toward the future, which is, in their opinion, a French future. The fact that Martinique is heavily subsidized by France (despite the efforts of a number of intellectuals who remain committed to the island's independence), and that the majority of the population is happy to remain "French," seem to reinforce this idea of a prosperous future equaling a French one. However, certain sociologists have demonstrated that the inequality between the French and Creole languages serves to fortify French dominance and, consequently, to denigrate the Creole influence. According to Ellen Schnepel, these two languages "are differentially evaluated. French is held in high prestige: its power equated with that of its speakers.... Until quite recently, Creole was considered to be a deformed variety of French, a stigmatized *patois* associated with slave culture and lack of education, and the index of an inferior social status. At one and the same time, the two languages reflect and reinforce local systems of stratification and inequality" (249). Language is thus transformed into a powerful tool for social acceptance or rejection in the French Caribbean: speaking French offers the opportunity for social promotion, as in the case for the schoolteachers in Chamoiseau's book. However, if an individual is content to speak only Creole, he or she risks remaining imprisoned in the lowest social categories.

Gros-Lombric emerges as a character who does not have the possibility of exceeding the limits of his social milieu, in large part because of his inability to master the French language. Unlike the narrator, Gros-Lombric does not manage to assimilate the French values learned at school because they remain too far removed from his daily experience. Described as the possessor of an "arcane expertise in the plant kingdom" (69), a gift reserved for rural Caribbean people who remain closely attached to the land, he nevertheless succeeds in carrying off small victories over the French education system. For example, the day he brings in the snake's head he causes uncontrollable panic among staff and students at school. On another occasion he arrives with a stick that he had found deep in the forest after the teacher encourages the students to bring in canes that he can later use on them in class. The teacher is delighted that Gros-Lombric has found such a terrifying-looking cane, but he soon realizes that it causes no harm to the children—a moment of intense satisfaction for Gros-Lombric.

Despite these brief moments of victory, the character of Gros-Lombric serves to establish a poignant comparison between the ideals of French culture and the realities of everyday life in the French Caribbean. In class, for example, the teacher insists on telling stories about Petit-Pierre from the children's reader as if they were the norm in the Caribbean: "Our reading material talked about farms, geese, harvest moons, wooden shoes, hares, chimneypieces, squirrels" (116). As a child in a family of ten brothers and sisters, Gros-Lombric shares a single dry straw mattress with them in their one-room cabin, a situation that has little in common with Petit-Pierre. Every day, he gets up before dawn to tend to the animals and domestic tasks, runs two or three kilometers to go to school, and then carries out the same routine in the evening. This reality is evidently far removed from the snowy forests and violins that the teacher presents to his students through the stories of Petit-Pierre. As for the teacher, he is so convinced by the truth of his teachings that he is shocked to learn of the difficulties of his student's life.

He expresses this shock in his decision to no longer harass this young boy, who cannot assimilate himself to the French model. The narrator makes a revealing comment about the divergence between the French and Creole worlds and its effect on the schoolchildren when he writes: "To Big Bellybutton, the Petit-Pierre we read about seemed like an alien from outer space, but as we read further along in these sacred texts, it was Petit-Pierre who began to seem normal to Big Bellybutton and most of his classmates" (118). Chamoiseau's statement is a poignant example of the French education system's attempt to force the young schoolchildren to forget their origins and to impose those of France as the norm. His comment also demonstrates how French Caribbean people interiorize French values, and, consequently, how the Other (France) becomes the Same (the Caribbean) and vice versa.

While the narrator succeeds in negotiating a path between these two vastly different ways of life, Gros-Lombric does not achieve the same success. After having learned of the hardships of his family life, the teacher decides that Gros-Lombric is a lost cause, and he forgets him completely—despite his gift for math and his profound knowledge of nature. According to Chamoiseau, the French colonial education system does not have a place for those who do not conform, and Gros-Lombric is let down by the inability of his educators to adapt to his needs. From the point of view of Gros-Lombric, the content of the school's lessons has no connection to his own experiences, and he arrives at a point where he feels it is no longer worth pursuing an education. Gros-Lombric represents a failure for the teacher's civilizing mission, but more poignantly he demonstrates the difficulty of adapting to an identity that is not one's own.

The rejection of geography is further evidence of the refusal of the educators to take account of the French Caribbean landscape, which is so completely different from that of France. For example, in the eyes of the teacher, Gros-Lombric's knowledge of nature is useless and a sign of his savagery. Apart from mathematics, Gros-Lombric is not a gifted student, but his understanding of the natural world is profound—evident in his capacity to trick the teacher with his threatening but ultimately useless cane found deep in the woods. The schoolchildren are obliged to wear French-style clothes, which are completely inappropriate in a tropical climate. The main objective of the French education system is to transplant the Metropolitan world into the Caribbean without regard for the psychological consequences for the Martinicans. By alienating the French Caribbean people from the natural environment that surrounds them, the French colonizers reinforce the alterity of French Caribbean identity.

Raphaël Confiant offers a novel and more contemporary reflection on the dissonance that exists between the French and Creole identities from the point of view of geography. While Gros-Lombric feels the cultural differences between the two worlds in his daily existence, Confiant highlights the geographical aspect that complicates the question of French Caribbean identity. In a 2001 interview (Thomas, 179–80), Confiant explains why he has a map of the Americas pinned up on his wall, affirming that it is to remind himself that the Caribbean is a part of America, at least geographically, rather than of Europe. He declares, furthermore, that despite the geographical proximity of the United States, he madly prepares for a week for a trip that lasts only one or two hours. However, when he travels to France, which is a plane journey of eight hours, he packs his bags on the same morning as his departure. Confiant's personal experiences demonstrate another way in which French Caribbean people have absorbed the values of their colonizers as if they were their own—an interesting admission from an intellectual who fights passionately for the Creole cause. France becomes an extension of the Caribbean landscape and represents the mother country for the Martinican people—despite the fact that there is no geographical link between the two countries. Up until recently, French Caribbean identity has been based on the wholehearted adoption of French cultural values coupled with the denial of any geographical links with neighboring islands. In a recent article, Lorna Milne demonstrates further complications of identity for Martinican intellectuals such as Confiant and Chamoiseau with her assertion that Chamoiseau's 2007 novel *Un dimanche au cachot* "might also be read as the troubled autofictional projection of an individual struggling with the accumulated bonds of his real-life work and art: after all, while Chamoiseau is a creative writer and pro-independence activist, as his own ironic references remind us he nevertheless works for the French *fonction publique* in an intrinsically conservative and culturally metropolitan institution" ("Working, Writing and the Antillean Postcolony," 211). How to negotiate these contrasting and often opposed identities remains an issue of consequence today.

In *School Days*, however, Chamoiseau strikes an optimistic tone despite the pain the narrator experiences in his initiation into school life. All the breathless hopes he had before starting primary school, beautifully captured in the chapter title "Longing," soon give way to the disappointing demands of the French education system. However, in contrast to Gros-Lombric, the narrator succeeds in making the transition between the Creole and French worlds. Unlike the teachers who are perfectly assimilated to the French style, the narrator manages to weave a thread between the two cultures and to integrate the best aspects of both in his attitude toward life. After the linguistic battles that left him dumb at the beginning of the book, he arrives at a point where he can appreciate and profit from both French and Creole. It is certain that the narrator of the book has all the benefits of retrospection, yet nonetheless the narrative is peppered with childish observations that trace the intellectual trajectory of the author. It is remarkable that at the end of the book, for example, the protagonist writes: "Bit by bit, the homey little Creole in his head was joined by scraps of French, words, phrases.... There was no looking back" (143). At this tender age, and under the oppressive influence of the colonial education system, the narrator is more interested in mastering the French language than his mother tongue. However, later in life it is Creole that revitalizes his role as a writer of French, and Chamoiseau has become one of the most creative and beautiful writers of a literary *français créolisé* (creolized French).

Perhaps the most revealing line in the book is the last one: "He would have needed the ancient gift of second sight to divine that—in this sacking of their native world, in this crippling inner ruination—the little black boy bent over his notebook was tracing, without fully realizing it, an inky lifeline of survival" (144). Like the secret paths of the runaway slaves from the past, the narrator demonstrates his capacity to survive and exceed the limits of the system imposed on him by the French. His use of the third person to speak of his childhood character and the word *négrillon* (little black boy) reinforces the idea that his *chemin d'école* is inspired by history and reflects the experiences of many francophone Caribbean people of the era. This book represents not only the author's autobiography but also the collective expression of a culture.

School Days is therefore an important book for demonstrating the different responses to the complexities of French Caribbean identity. In an environment where two cultures and two languages exist, the different characters attest to the range of possible reactions—while the teachers choose total assimilation to French values, Gros-Lombric takes the other direction and remains firmly Creole. But it is the narrator who is the most interesting character, for he represents a victory for French Caribbean subjectivity. In the complex world of the French Caribbean, his capacity to allow the multiple influences to exist in his character make him an exemplary figure: a sort of modern French Caribbean hero. As H. Adlai Murdoch asserts, Chamoiseau engages in "a form of discursive excavation and reconstitution, but one predicated on intersection and interconnection rather than exclusion and exclusivity" (21). In this way, he contributes to an illustration of the connected and multiple possibilities of Glissant's model of Relation.

The intertextual elements to Chamoiseau's books are also important and reveal a desire to place himself in a cultural continuum as he finds himself at home—or not—among the different literary influences to which he is subject under the French education system. Like Condé and Pineau, reading and writing provide the nurturing medium with which to explore his identity. For the narrator, as for Chamoiseau himself, multiple influences constitute his literary self and empower him to engage with the oppressive past of slavery and colonialism. As Louise Hardwick points out, Chamoiseau's childhood trilogy exposes the cohabitation of different cultural influences that range from Caribbean authors such as Saint-John Perse, Aimé Césaire, and Joseph Zobel to classic French writers such as Jean de La Fontaine, George Sand, Alphonse Daudet, Antoine de Saint-Exupéry, François-René de Chateaubriand, and Victor Hugo (Hardwick, *Childhood*, 78). In 2013, Chamoiseau published *Césaire, Perse, Glissant: les liaisons magnétiques*, in which he pays explicit homage to three of his greatest influences while alluding to Glissant's 2007 publication *La terre magnétique*. Hardwick also notes that "Chamoiseau's récits d'enfance have established another important feature of the post-1990 tradition: the trilogy, with its own interlocking dynamics of intertextuality, sits in a porous relationship with his wider oeuvre ... creat[ing] a backdrop, or literary key, against which other works may be more readily explored; a reader familiar with *Antan* will be all the better prepared for *Texaco*" (Hardwick 2013, 62). Just as for the other writers in this volume, Chamoiseau's works have multiple, connected strands that stage a dialog with the literary past.

Une enfance créole III: À Bout d'enfance

In the third part of his childhood autobiography, Chamoiseau returns to some of the concerns outlined in *Childhood*. The magnifying glass, which he used to illuminate the striking characters of his entry into the school system in *School Days*, now shifts back to paint a more general portrait of life as he enters into puberty and a changing world. As in all three parts of his autobiographical reflections, *À Bout d'enfance* underscores both the universal and typically Caribbean experiences of the different stages of his childhood. In a departure from the previous two volumes, the present one is not divided into two sections but has eight chapters. However, two significant events mark the book, so the idea of an ordering dualism again comes into play. À *Bout d'enfance* is driven by the time before and after "la fatale découverte de l'existence des petites-filles" (the fatal discovery of the existence of girls) and "le mabouya" (the mabouya lizard) (31), which Knepper likens to the quest narrative (*Patrick Chamoiseau*, 136–37). These two experiences intertwine the particularities and generalizations that make this book so powerful. In the lives of many boys, the discovery of girls is significant—the narrator thus explicates a stage that is common to many, yet at the same time grounds it in the specific context of his island, which influences, for example, his description of the physical attributes of the girls (277–78). So, too, the discovery of the *mabou*, a stage of initiation that is particularly Caribbean, with this lizard species native to the region acting as a sort of universal reference point for the process of transitioning from boyhood to manhood. As in the previous volumes of *Une enfance créole*, À *Bout d'enfance* enacts a model of interconnected histories as the strands of the *je*, *tu*, and *il* narrative voices weave themselves into a braid of *diversalité*.

One of Chamoiseau's great gifts in this book is his ability to creolize the universal aspects of childhood while safeguarding their general appeal. In his early discovery of girls, for example, Chamoiseau describes in heart-wrenching detail how the young boys planned their verbal approaches in the tiniest detail, only to be delivered the Creole *Tchip*, which would instantly reduce them to a gibbering mess (160). Chamoiseau reveals the nuances of language as the boys attempt to stammer out the phrase "What time is it?" in a variety of elegant French expressions, which they think might better impress the girls: "Le français conférait le léger avantage de vous ouvrir l'audience, encore fallait-il le manier avec le bon accent et une claire justesse" (French conferred a small advantage of opening the audience to you, but you still had to manage it with the right accent and exactness) (161). The linguistic subtleties of French and Creole that are explored so painfully in *School Days* are given a different angle in À *Bout d'enfance*. While French is clearly given the higher authority in *School Days*, Chamoiseau shows that it is Creole that contains more power in À *Bout d'enfance*. Significantly, Creole is the language that the young girls employ to put the boys in their place, and Creole is the language that dominates Chamoiseau's home life. As we have seen in each volume of *Une enfance créole*, Man Ninotte is the determining force in his family, and her language of choice is Creole. By contrast, Chamoiseau's father may express himself in lyrical French, but he is shown as largely ineffectual. Ultimately, though, all three of Chamoiseau's memoirs highlight that knowledge of both languages and an appreciation of their contrasting riches is the most valuable lesson to learn in life. In Chamoiseau's model, the Creole imaginary allows for the existence of all influences, not just those that dominate.

In *À Bout d'enfance*, Chamoiseau reinforces the idea of memory as a continual process of construction and reconstruction through his narrative structure, as memories flow from his mind in varying degrees of completion. Memory emerges as a proliferation of images (32), an omnipresence of colors (97), and a place where there are "que de mensonges dans ces fragments de souvenirs, ce clignotement de la mémoire soumis à des odeurs, des associations, des sensations, et des reconstructions que l'on sait fausses mais dessinent du vrai!" (so many lies in these fragments of memories, this twinkling of memory subject to smells, associations, sensations, and the reconstructions that we know are false but that are drawn true!) (101). In her book *Patrick Chamoiseau: Recovering Memory*, Maeve McCusker draws a distinction between the French terms *mémoire* and *souvenir*, which are both translated into English as "memory," arguing that Chamoiseau disrupts the interchangeability of the former as "raw material, and as active, critical process" (56), and the latter as its end product. In this way, Chamoiseau, according to McCusker, resists the "temptation of transcendence and closure, of soft focus or mawkish nostalgia" (57), and instead sets the three elements of *mémoire, souvenir*, and forgetting in a constantly changing network configuration. Indeed, Chamoiseau employs a distinctly Glissantian vocabulary when describing how individual memories intersect with collective memories and fictions move alongside "truths":

> Mais les souvenirs s'entrelacent. . . . Les mémoires s'interpellent . . . elles se croisent aux mêmes endroits sans trop se rencontrer, ou alors se contredisent pour mieux se compléter. . . . Il faut tant de mémoires pour fonder une mémoire, et tant de fiction pour en affirmer une.

> (But the memories intertwine. . . . The memories call each other . . . they cross each other at the same places without meeting each other too much, or contradicting each other in order to better complement each other. . . . You need so many memories to found a memory, and so much fiction to affirm one) (56; italics in original)

In a broader context, Chamoiseau uses the concept of memory in Relation to explore the creeping "bétonisation" (concretization) of contemporary Martinique, which is burying its lush vegetation beneath ugly and dehumanizing concrete: "*Du béton sans visage a remplacé de vieilles façades au bois*" (*faceless concrete has replaced the old wooden façades*) (177; italics in original). Writing in the preface to a volume by Martinican ecologist and politician Garcin Malsa, Chamoiseau asserts that ecosystems embody a positive system of interrelation in which "[t]out est lié" (everything is linked) (Preface to *L'Écologie ou la passion du vivant*, 10). According to Chamoiseau, ecosystems not only are an example of Relation in nature but can also exemplify the complex interactions of the mind. Like the "petits miracles inexplicables, non maîtrisables, dont il nous faut tenir compte et que nous devons apprendre à connaître, comprendre et respecter" (small miracles that we cannot master, that we need to take account of, and that we must learn to know, understand, and respect) (Preface to *L'Écologie ou la passion du vivant*, 9) that occur in nature, one should also allow for the possibility of positive interaction among humans. In a sad reflection of contemporary life, Chamoiseau asserts that it is our poor treatment of the environment that unites us: it is "le combat commun de tous les peuples, de toutes les nations, de toutes les identités de la terre" (the battle common to all peoples, all nations, all identities of the earth) (10).

Chamoiseau's lyrical writing in *Une enfance créole* bears the indelible influence of his collaborator and mentor Édouard Glissant. However, he also delineates his own path to a life lived in a connected manner through his celebration of the urban Creole environment, his depiction of the benefits of appropriating and individualizing one's cultural and personal influences in the ultimate goal of *diversalité*. Thus, while his setting is distinctly Caribbean, his lessons could be adapted to any setting. In *À Bout d'enfance*, Chamoiseau draws on his beloved city of Fort-de-France to encapsulate his concept of a creolized imaginary that is Relation itself, a place characterized by movement and transformation. "*Cette ville créole n'a de rigidité qu'en nervures, traces subtiles, fidèle à son principe elle ira au mouvement qui ne se fixe pour encore bouger . . . moi-même ainsi, mon négrillon*" (*This Creole town only has rigidity in its veins, subtle traces, faithful to its principle it will go toward a movement that only settles in order to move again . . . therefore me too, my little black boy*) (178; italics in original). Chamoiseau's narrator becomes part of his environment, intimately intertwined with the literal and figurative traces of his history. Together, the three books provide a heartwarming and illuminating example of the creolized imagination and how embracing its multiple connections allows one to live in an increasingly complex world. As Chamoiseau states in *Césaire, Perse, Glissant*: "Il ne s'agit plus d'"universaliser," mais de mettre en relation le foisonnement des diversités.... Il s'agit de diversaliser" (It is no longer about universalizing, but putting into relation the profusion of diversities.... It's about diversalizing) (36).

CHAPTER 4

EDWIDGE DANTICAT
Connecting the Political and Personal

Edwidge Danticat arrived on the literary scene with the publication of her first novel, *Breath, Eyes, Memory*, in 1994 and quickly garnered the admiration and acclaim of writers and readers alike. In the foreword to the first monograph dedicated to her work, *Edwidge Danticat: A Reader's Guide*, Dany Laferrière describes her as "nothing less than a contemporary classic" ("A Heart of Serenity in the Storm," viii), while Maryse Condé in the same volume asserts that her writing is as "beautiful as nascent oxygen" ("Finally Edwidge Arrived," 167). In November 1994, the *New York Times* declared her among "thirty artists, thirty and under ... likely to change the culture for the next thirty years," and in 1996 she was included in *Granta* magazine's list of the twenty best young American novelists. She has been described by the *New Yorker* as one of "twenty writers for the twenty-first century," and, as a testament to her global impact, Oprah Winfrey selected *Breath, Eyes, Memory* for her televised book club. Danticat's stylistically beautiful writing is distinguished above all by her attention to the relationship between the personal and political realms. As Martin Munro affirms, "Danticat's work explores *both* the personal and the political, so that she personalizes politics and, conversely, politicizes the personal" (*Exile*, 220). Through three quite different autobiographical texts—*After the Dance: A Walk through Carnival in Haiti* (2002); *Brother, I'm Dying* (2007); and *Create Dangerously: The Immigrant Artist at Work* (2011)—this chapter will underline how Danticat's works intertwine the historical and local, the collective and individual, demanding that each be read in relation to the other. In a very concrete and personal way, Danticat demonstrates that an individual story also tells the story of the collective.

Edwidge Danticat was born in Haiti in 1969, where she spent the first twelve years of her life before immigrating to New York to join her mother and father. Danticat was separated from her parents for much of her early life, as her father moved to New York when his daughter was two and Danticat's mother joined him two years later. Like so many others, Danticat's parents left their homeland in search of a better life, and it was only when Danticat was twelve that they were finally able to support their children in the United States. In the meantime, Danticat and her younger brother, Bob, were left in the care of their paternal uncle, Joseph—one of the subjects of *Brother, I'm Dying*—and his wife, Denise. The bond that grew between Danticat and her uncle was so intense that when the time came for her to emigrate, it felt as if she were leaving a second father.

Danticat's key educational experiences took place in the United States, where she first studied French literature at Barnard College in New York and later completed a master's in fine arts (creative writing) from Brown University. Her thesis at Brown became her first published novel, *Breath, Eyes, Memory*. This book immediately launched her into the public eye, and her writing has not lessened in impact since then. In addition to her literary career, Danticat has taught creative writing at New York University and the University of Miami and she has collaborated with filmmakers Patricia Benoît and Jonathan Demme on a number of Haitian-related projects. She is also an active member of the National Coalition for Haitian Rights, and her role as an advocate for minority groups, particularly Haitians, forms an integral part of her professional life. She currently resides in Miami with her husband and two daughters.

History and Identity

In her laudatory examination of the importance of Danticat's place in literature, Maryse Condé affirms the singular way in which Danticat has sparked a rethinking of history through her writing. According to Condé, Danticat's unique position as a Haitian who writes in English, depicting a time of globalization that does not involve the chains of slavery but that nonetheless forces her to live in an unknown country where the people speak a different language, has resulted in a distinct literature: "Her novels restarted the stopped clock of time. They transformed the referent" ("Finally Edwidge Arrived," 166). Most significantly, Condé asserts that Danticat's literary perspective challenges notions of identity and belonging in a postcolonial world. In contrast to theorists such as the *créolistes* who insist on the intrinsic importance of slavery and colonization and who reify Creole language and culture, Danticat's work expresses a different point of view that constantly infuses the personal with the political and vice versa. Condé summarizes the challenges Danticat poses for the contemporary postcolonial writer in her evolving conception of identity:

> Identity has wrongly been considered a garment that is sewn once and for all.... Neither European, nor African, nor Asian in the terms of the *Éloge*, can [Danticat] still be proclaimed Creole? If so, what is the nature of her Creoleness? Is it the one defined by a now obsolete discourse? Or rather, isn't it the outcome of a History that has been restarted and that has taken into account the trials of our present? If so, isn't this a new phenomenon? And shouldn't we try to grasp it in its new form and study it? ("Finally Edwidge Arrived," 166)

Without pushing a particular political platform, Danticat proposes a novel way of viewing identity. First of all, she writes in a language that is not her mother tongue; second, she refuses to separate the personal and political; and finally, she writes from a perspective that could be considered compatible with Dany Laferrière's idea of the New World, a place that is distinguished by its openness toward both the universal and the local and that stretches across the Americas. Condé's questions constitute important food for thought when considering Danticat's place in Caribbean literature, and indeed in the relevance of her contribution to the notion of connecting histories. To some extent, her writing reinforces many of the concepts that have already been explored in this volume—the interrelationship between History and histories, the way in which the "I" of autofictional reflection serves to capture the collective stories that have been erased as a result of slavery and colonization, dictatorships, and natural disasters, and the importance of connection and interrelation in order to move forward positively. Danticat herself has affirmed how past, present, and future are linked for her: "Though my life is going forward here [in Brooklyn], I look to the past—to Haiti" (Anglesey, 36). In a manner akin to Laferrière's belief in the importance of the single and intimate voice in contemporary writing, Danticat argues: "I've always been fascinated by these individual voices in history and the fact that one person's voice adds to another and that creates a chorus" (Anglesey, 36). Danticat's assertion relates to Antonio Benítez-Rojo's idea of a polyphonic composition in which each voice is necessary, despite the fact that individual elements may conflict. Danticat does not claim to speak for everyone, but she does highlight that each individual story links together to create a whole. In this way, her work also serves as an example of Chamoiseau's belief that unity can be found in diversity, or *diversalité*. Furthermore, as Jo Collins asserts, "Danticat's writing 'I' is mobile and contingent, taking up different positions in relation to the family, nation, and region, with differing levels of identification" (8).

Danticat explores questions of history and memory through her contrasting depictions of the storyteller and historian in her writing. For Danticat, who believes that individual voices participate in the creation of history, the overlapping of the two can sometimes come into conflict or be conflated into an undistinguishable whole. Particularly in relation to her first novel, she discovered the perils of such an approach to literature, in which people associated Danticat's presentation of different aspects of her personal and her country's history as a definitive statement of sociological "truth.""When you belong to a minority group, even when you write fiction, people think it's sociology or anthropology" (Pulitano, "An Immigrant Artist at Work," 49; see also Lyons, 190). In *Breath, Eyes, Memory*, many fell prey to the temptation to link the narrator Sophie's experiences to those of all Haitian women. While Danticat undoubtedly borrows from her individual and collective past, she considers her role as an artist rather than a historian. "What I am trying to do is tell the history through one voice" (Shea, "Travelling Words," 50). Danticat uses the image of the collage to characterize this approach, in which she pastes together elements from her own life along with elements from the lives of those she knows as well as those who are more distant: "[I] merge my own narratives with the oral and written narratives of others" (*Create Dangerously*, 62). In the epilogue to her book of short stories, *Krik Krak*, she draws on a different image, concluding that writing is "like braiding hair. / Taking a handful of coarse unruly strands and / attempting to bring them unity," while Collins argues that "her particular *bricolage* produces decentred and relational authorial stances" (11). All these images emphasize the interconnectedness of every facet of life, joining other memorable metaphors of postcolonial identity such as the polyphonic composition, the rhizome, the mosaic, and the mangrove. They also suggest that there is no such thing as a life, a culture, or a history lived in isolation from others.

In several interviews (Anglesey, 38; Pulitano, "An Immigrant Artist at Work," 48), Danticat comments on the resonance she finds in Julia Alvarez's book *Something to Declare*. According to Alvarez, a Dominican American, there is great autonomy writing from "the hyphen" of two cultures and two languages: "Being in and out of both worlds, looking at one side from the other side.... These unusual perspectives are often what I write about. A duality that I hope in the writing transcends itself and becomes a new consciousness, a new place on the map, a synthesizing way of looking at the world" (173). Reminiscent of Homi Bhabha's concept of the "third space" in *The Location of Culture*, Alvarez's position emphasizes the impossibility of living identity in a binary way in which acceptance and rejection are the only options. Carine Mardorossian argues that writers like Danticat and Alvarez "refuse to be either assimilated or marginalized, and insist on redefining Americanness itself rather than on integrating discrete versions of otherness into its misconceived dominant incarnations" (23). In the Haitian context, Danticat's experience of hyphenation lies in her position as a member of the "*dyaspora*"—an insider who is living outside the country. According to Munro, the *dyaspora* "is neither one place nor the other; it is 'floating,' indeterminate, and evolving; its connection to Haiti is 'ideological,' that is, through an ongoing commitment to the country's political and social fate" (*Exile*, 207–8). Danticat displays an unwavering determination to portray the collective and personal aspects of Haitian history, a perspective that is enhanced by her experience of living both within and outside of her country of birth. Indeed, as Munro asserts, "she styles herself an immigrant rather than an exile or even a Haitian American. In doing so, she stresses that the process of immigrating remains unfinished and that her own status has not significantly changed since arriving in the United States at the age of twelve" (*Writing on the Fault Line*, 29).

In her introduction to the anthology *Haiti noir*, Danticat argues that migration "is such an integral part of the Haitian experience that those living outside of the country were once designated as part of a 'tenth department,' an ideological auxiliary to Haiti's first geographical nine" (14). She demonstrates, furthermore, that this diasporic status has both advantages and disadvantages. On the one hand, it lends itself to ambiguity and a lack of affiliation: "When I say 'my country' to some Haitians, they think I mean the United States. When I say 'my country' to some Americans, they think of Haiti" (*Create Dangerously*, 49). On the other hand, it allows a depth of understanding that is not possible if you belong to a single country and a single history. Danticat's insights into the two cultures she moves between are compelling in the way they continually underscore the notion of interconnection and relatedness, but also in the fact that the process of migration is never complete, as Munro suggests. Indeed, as we will see in the next chapter on Dany Laferrière, questions about home and belonging remain deep in the recesses of one's body and mind, even in those who adapt "successfully" to new contexts.

Alongside her "hyphenated" approach to experience, Danticat distinguishes herself from her Haitian counterparts by her choice of language. Munro remarks that her use of English "marks a rupture with a long tradition of Haitian writing in French" (*Exile*, 208). On the website *Île en Île*, which is devoted to the study of francophone literatures, it is noted that Danticat is the first writer to be listed on their database who does not write in French.[1] Elvira Pulitano has noted that this linguistic difference has also served to isolate Danticat, as she does not fall simply into the category of a "francophone" writer. Pulitano tells the story of trying to submit a paper for a panel on "islands and ocean representation in the new Francophone writing" only to be told that "Danticat cannot be considered a Francophone Caribbean writer" ("Landscape, Memory and Survival," 2). This anecdote highlights another way in which language can be exclusionary—in contrast to the French Creole dichotomy of previous chapters in this book—and that Danticat's uniqueness in writing in English reinforces her innovative engagement with colonialism's legacies. Danticat's position could be considered a living example of Patrick Chamoiseau's assertion that it is not a common language that unites people, but, rather, it is the structure of the imaginary (see Gauvin, 37).

Condé asserts that Danticat's choice of English as her literary language not only widens the accepted mode of self-expression among Caribbean writers but in fact results in a revolution for Guadeloupean and Martinican writers who have long struggled between the "choice" of French or Creole as their written and spoken language. According to Condé, "Edwidge Danticat proves to us that identity, the tributary of historical vicissitudes, can express itself in any idiom" ("Finally Edwidge Arrived," 166). Danticat gives a different slant to the linguistic question, arguing that English acts as her "stepmother tongue." "I never thought of those images of the bad stepmother. I thought of a stepmother tongue in the sense that you have a mother tongue and then an adopted language that you take on because your family circumstances have changed, sometimes not by your own choice" (Shea, "The Dangerous Job," 387). Danticat also notes that English provided a forum where, for the first time, she was able to speak and write in the same language. On arriving in New York at the age of twelve, she frequently had to do translations in her head between French, Creole, and English and between the vastly different physical and cultural landscapes that exist in Haiti and the United States. "I wrote in a language I didn't speak regularly

[French] and spoke a language I couldn't write [Creole]. When I came here and learned English, it was the first time I could speak and write the same language" (Lyons 189). Her use of English, then, constitutes an important tool that allows her to create meaningful connections between her differing lived experiences.

Danticat's literary project is driven above all by "the [individual and collective] need to be remembered" (Shea, "Travelling Words," 49). However, bearing witness to the legacies of history through personal and individual stories raises important questions about who has the authority to testify. "I have this mental split because I wonder, am I the one to write this story? Maybe someone who went through it should write it. In some ways, I feel presumptuous, as though I were taking their place, but in some ways to be able to write it, you have to feel as though someone is lending you their voice, their story, as you're the mediator" (Shea, "Travelling Words," 50). Munro acknowledges the burdens that such a role may entail, arguing: "For all the talent she possesses and the success she has enjoyed, Edwidge Danticat is in some senses in an unenviable situation as a writer ... conferr[ing] on her the status of unofficial spokesperson for her country of birth" (Munro, *Writing on the Fault Line*, 25). However, despite these expectations, Danticat has taken on the responsibility to record her country's histories in a number of different settings in her work. In *Create Dangerously*, for example, she relates the story of a Jamaican sculptor who perished at the World Trade Center in New York on September 11, 2011. The physical artworks that survived in different parts of the world allowed him to leave "something behind that speaks not only for himself but also for them too" (125). Again in *Create Dangerously*, she recounts the life of Daniel Morel, a photographer who witnessed executions as a child and immediately decided to become a photographer in order to document Haiti's history. According to Morel, the graphic violence that appears in some of his images is not because he wants to portray Haiti in a negative light, but to show "people the way things are because maybe if they see it with their own eyes, they'll do something to change the situation" (141). To some extent, Morel's aim in his photography is similar to Danticat's in her literature. It is about bearing witness, "provok[ing] debate, ... shak[ing] readers' consciousness, ... incit[ing] action" (Pulitano, "An Immigrant Artist at Work," 42). Danticat's distinct style of relating a larger history through the telling of an individual tale "fights complete erasure. It forces others to remember that we were—are—here" (*Create Dangerously*, 147). As the proceeding discussion will illustrate, Danticat's creative use of autobiographical witness in three different literary genres constitutes an imaginative way of engaging with history that emphasizes connection and belonging. It also demonstrates that Danticat's technique of "*bricolage* is a self-conscious strategy to incompletely and provisionally broach the (historical) 'gaps' by overlaying available resources from oral and written histories and other cultural sources" (Collins, 18).

After the Dance: A Walk through Carnival in Haiti

In 2002 Danticat published *After the Dance: A Walk through Carnival in Haiti* as part of the Crown Journeys travel series. The title comes from the Haitian proverb "After the dance, the drum is heavy," which emphasizes the cyclical nature of life and how bad times may follow the good. This book explores carnival as one of the foremost cultural traditions in the Caribbean. While the focus of the book is the meaning and context of this important festival, Danticat presents it in such a way that her personal history forms an integral part of the story. Indeed, she notes that before her research into the tradition, she had never actually experienced a carnival due to her religious uncle Joseph's dislike of the tradition. This intermingling of the personal and political is, as we have seen, typical of Danticat's style, and in her travelogue she consistently underlines the links that exist between individuals and the larger society that she describes. Charles Forsdick asserts that the book "nuances the author's own explorations of the complex itineraries and entangled memories—her own and those of others—that connect Haiti with North America and elsewhere ... a work that is in dialogue with her own fictional [and nonfictional] writing" (99). Forsdick asserts, furthermore, that the "walk" suggested by the title allows Danticat's narrator to slow down and "pay attention to the entangled detail—both historical and contemporary, lived and fictional—that characterizes the city of Jacmel and its surrounding area" (109). Danticat's explorations in this work of autobiographical travel writing give an innovative spin on the way in which the personal embeds itself in the political and vice versa.

Danticat opens the book by situating the Haitian carnival in a specific time and place: the town of Jacmel in 2001. This town, as Danticat reveals through her conversation with carnival expert Michelet Divers, has hosted two carnivals on consecutive weekends since 1992: a national one attended by Haitians from around the country and the diaspora and a Jacmelian one drawing together Jacmel's residents. Throughout her narrative, Danticat describes the lead-up to 2001's national carnival, all the while interspersing her observations with reflections on the carnival's history, the country's history, and her own experience of carnival past and present. Early in the narrative, Danticat establishes some of the principles of the Haitian carnival: it is a festival that allows long-suffering Haitians to "release themselves temporarily from personal and global concerns" (15), while at the same time it dramatizes Haitian history: "Every costume, every mask portrays a part of our story and concerns" (17). Collins observes, too, that in the book "Danticat dons different masks, altering her position in relation to Haiti" (Collins, 13), again underscoring the merging of the individual and collective. As Divers explains to Danticat, carnival weekends are a way for Jacmelians to establish both their singularity with and difference from broader Haitian society. Danticat inserts herself into the story here, noting her appreciation of an image from Greek theater that depicts a half-laughing, half-sorrowing mask and that she believes embodies the spirit of Haiti: "This mask has always seemed to me a representation of the country where I was born, especially during carnival" (16). As *After the Dance* progressively reveals, carnival comes to symbolize Haiti and its people, displaying both a collective experience through the overall gathering of the crowd and the differences among its individual players as all persons have their own costume and interpretation of what Haiti means to them.

Danticat travels throughout Jacmel in the company of poet and publisher Rodney Saint-Éloi, making commentaries about contemporary Haitian reality that are projected through the prism of the carnival. At one point they visit a cemetery, which Danticat affirms is one of "the best places to become acquainted with the tastes of the inhabitants, both present and gone" (25). She notes in particular the employment of the Haitian cross in the cemetery, which is spherical in shape and emphasizes "the circular motion of human souls" (31), an observation recorded by art historian Robert Farris Thompson in his book *Flash of the Spirit*. This image of circularity and continuity can be harnessed to encapsulate the spirit of carnival itself. It is a tradition that stretches back to the past, as far back as the original inhabitants of the island, the Arawaks, who are often represented through masks in the present-day carnival. It provides Haitians with a "break from life" (*After the Dance*, 118), and it forms a rhizomatic continuity so that "a child who cannot even walk yet can say he saw the same thing at the carnival as his grandmother and grandfather did" (136). The carnival provides a forum in which Haitians can reflect on their past and project themselves into the future, while taking a much-needed pause from the present. As the narrative progresses, Danticat reveals both the crippling problems that plague Haiti and its inhabitants' unyielding belief in the future of their country.

Danticat identifies a conflicted relationship between Haitians and their history. On the one hand, they have the distinction of being the first independent black republic in the world, a fact that makes them immensely proud and that distinguishes them from their Martinican and Guadeloupean counterparts, who remain in an ongoing relationship of dependency with France. On the other hand, they have experienced a level of poverty that is unrivaled in the Caribbean and that continues to besiege the country today. In a concrete embodiment of this dissonance, Danticat and a friend search for a small cluster of cannons that were used in the battle for independence when a man informs them that they are to be moved to a different location. "'Won't they lose their context?' my friend asked. 'No,' the priest replied. 'They will still be the same cannons. That will never change'" (49). These remains of a glorious past, uprooted from their historical resting place, join a number of other important "memory-traces" that are relegated to an ambiguous physical and historical space: "Simón Bolívar's house is a dress shop. Ogé's fort is a soccer field. Anacaona is living in Providence, Rhode Island. History is moving on" (49). These material traces of the past that are not housed in the sanctuary of a museum but are left to deteriorate or are moved from place to place underline Haiti's problematic relationship with history. Through these images, past and present relate to each other in a disconnected way, underscoring the great rupture between the achievement of independence and the hardships of contemporary reality. Moreover, the succession of challenges that Haiti has faced since 1804 only serves to strengthen a narrative of breakage. What Danticat's work repeatedly underlines is that these elements can be pasted into a collage of meaningful connections, shaped above all by the coexistence of the personal and political.

Like Glissant, who asserts that the natural world may act as a monument to the past, Danticat views the degradations of the Haitian environment as a physical embodiment of Haiti's history and a constant reminder of its contemporary marginal status. Haiti's bald landscape as a result of deforestation is the most striking example of this. As a result of her discussions with a peasant called Ovid, Danticat finds that rural people, who form the majority in Haiti, "are like Maroons in their own country, excluded from any national decision-making process, remaining symbols more than anything else of the bread basket of a country that increasingly looks for its bread abroad, valuing imported goods above those produced at home" (58).

Danticat's reference to the Maroon past, however, contrasts with Glissant's reification of this historical figure because of their rejection of slavery. In his 1964 novel *Le Quatrième siècle* (*The Fourth Century*), for example, Glissant depicts two possible responses to the experience of slavery through the characters of Longoué and Béluse: the former escapes into the hills within minutes of setting foot on the island, while Béluse opts for tolerance and resignation by accepting his slave status. Richard Burton draws attention to the value judgment Glissant attributes to these varying approaches, noting that "la partie supérieure—moralement comme topographiquement—appartient aux Longoué et la partie inférieure aux Béluse" (the superior part—morally as topographically—belongs to the Longoués and the inferior part to the Béluses) (*Le Roman marron*, 70). In the context of *After the Dance*, the Maroons are considered as outcasts, symbolic of the way Haiti's peasants are left unsupported in their country's pursuit of foreign markets.

Danticat reveals that it is not just the land and the peasants that are being abused but also the traditional artisans, who are being increasingly overlooked in Haiti's bid to augment its global presence. Danticat meets, for example, Marlène, a dressmaker whose "craft, once essential to Haitian life, is slowly being rendered obsolete by the flood of used ready-made clothes from abroad" (*After the Dance*, 102). Reminiscent of the situation of the peasants, whose crops are being overlooked in favor of foreign imports, Haiti's artisans are slowly losing the distinctiveness of their craft through this similar obsession with markets abroad. The result, according to Danticat, is zombification, "a state of deterioration based on the loss of one's *ti bonanj*, one's good angel, which turns one into a vacuous shell of one's former self" (69). Glissant has written extensively on such a state in his theoretical writings as well as in novels such as *La Case du commandeur* (*The Overseer's Cabin*) through the character of Pythagore. The degradation of the land and the drain of its talented citizens to migration and exile mean that Haiti's present-day situation runs the risk of a similar zombification of society.

Despite these threats, however, Danticat depicts a situation in which Haitians overwhelmingly maintain their faith in their country. We see, for example, Paula Hyppolite, a jewelry maker who lives in the mountains of Cap Rouge and who says: "My body was in New York ... but my soul was here. I had to come back to connect the two" (85). A bumper sticker announces: "NO ROADS, NO ELECTRICITY, NO RUNNING WATER. NO TELEPHONES ... BUT I STILL LOVE HAITI" (113), while a man who owns a rope that leads down to a trio of pools near the waterfall in the Bassin Bleu asserts: "A love for a place like Haiti is a love that cannot be explained. It has its good and bad side, but at times the bad part can make you love the good part even more. You love her. You hate her. You pity her. You want to protect her. That's how it is with Haiti" (114). Danticat explores her own optimism through her search for the wheels of a Watt steam engine: "I had thought of them as symbols of Haiti— ... weathered and depreciated, but still robust and stalwart at the core" (61). All of these commentaries attest to a remarkable country that has suffered deeply and yet continues to survive. Danticat's weaving together of her own reflections, insights from those she meets, and an engagement with certain material remains creates a historical narrative in which everything has a place and is connected.

Against the backdrop of these musings on Haiti's relationship to past and present, Danticat emphasizes the carnival's pivotal role as a dramatization of the living past, drawing together individuals in a harmonious collective. For a short period of time during carnival, Haitians are able to forget the very real miseries of their daily struggle to survive. The carnival allows Haitians to reconnect with the more positive elements of their past, situates them in a historical continuum, and bands them together in a colorful wave of hope for the future. Finally, the Haitian carnival is a profound statement of Haitians' capability of surviving no matter what, and their incredible capacity for creative expression. As Danticat asserts in her introduction to *Haiti noir*, "Haitian creativity has always been one of the country's most identifiable survival traits" (10). Her final reflections underscore the way in which carnival is itself a demonstration of positive relationship, an experience that is both individual and collective: "In that brief space and time, the carnival offers all the paradoxical elements I value in life: anonymity, jubilant community, and belonging" (*After the Dance*, 147).

Brother, I'm Dying

Danticat intertwined the personal and political in a vastly different way with the publication of her autobiographical narrative *Brother, I'm Dying* in 2007. As Wendy Knepper observes, this book blends "memoir and Creole storytelling traditions together with investigative reporting about injustice and criminality" ("In/justice and Necro-Natality," 192). The principal characters of the story are her father and her paternal uncle Joseph, both of whom are beloved to Danticat and who eke out vastly different lives within the challenges of Haiti's past and present. Danticat's father, affectionately nicknamed Mira, had migrated to New York when Danticat was just two, in search of a better life. After separations of two years from his wife and twelve years from Danticat and her brother Bob, the family finally reunites in the United States. Joseph, by contrast, elects to stay in his beloved Caribbean homeland, working as a minister and attempting to help his fellow Haitians "on site." The brothers experience most of their lives apart in a physical sense but are deeply connected emotionally, particularly as Mira's two children are left in Joseph's care until they are able to join their parents in New York. Alongside the intertwined stories of Joseph and Mira is that of Danticat herself, who discovers that she is pregnant with her first child on the same day she learns that her father has been diagnosed with terminal pulmonary fibrosis. Indeed, the book opens with the powerful lines: "I found out I was pregnant the same day that my father's rapid weight loss and chronic shortness of breath were positively diagnosed as end-stage pulmonary fibrosis" (3). Danticat's own story becomes linked with that of her father and uncle in the telling of this personal tale. Equally important is the political backdrop to the story, which illuminates Haiti's plight and exposes the far-reaching injustices experienced by Haitian and other migrants in the United States. *Brother, I'm Dying* is a compelling and disturbing account of Danticat's direct experience of the way the personal embeds itself in the political and vice versa.

In a number of interviews, Danticat reveals that a major motivation for writing *Brother, I'm Dying* is political, in contrast to what she had first imagined: "I thought I was going to write it for therapeutic reasons" (Pulitano, "An Immigrant Artist at Work," 43), as a way "to pay tribute to my father's and uncle's lives" (Shea, "A Family Story," 188). However, it became much more than that, serving as a "testimonial narrative" and "bear[ing] witness" (Knepper, "In/justice and Necro-Natality," 200) to the brutality of life under a dictatorship and to immigration-detainee mistreatment. *Brother, I'm Dying* becomes a searing examination of the injustices to which many potential migrants are subject, seen through the eyes of her uncle Joseph, who ends up losing his life while in custody in the United States. At every point in the book personal and political collide, particularly in relation to Joseph's life under the Duvalier dictatorships and Mira's struggles as an exile in the United States. Their diverse experiences show that exile and immigration do not simply constitute a flight-or-fight response but are complex and constant negotiations between two countries in which movement is both physical and psychological. For Mira, exile is the only option with which to safeguard his family's future, but he never loses his attachment to Haiti and to his family that remains there. For Joseph, the reasoning is the same, but his tactic is different: "Someone has to stay behind, to receive the letters and greet family members when they come back" (140). Viewing the different layers of Mira's and Joseph's experiences unravels a complex network of new, old, and modified allegiances. Both men and their families must negotiate a place for themselves in an external environment that is often hostile but that is underpinned by a deep commitment to family and personal betterment.

Against the backdrop of exile, immigration, and the negotiations of identity, the place of papers, history, and the transmission of culture through storytelling becomes even more crucial. Another of Danticat's aims in *Brother, I'm Dying* is to record a single history, *her* history, which was in danger of fading into invisibility. However, in writing for her family she is also writing as part of a wider group. We see, for example, the familiar position occupied by a Caribbean grandmother in the character of *tante* Denise's mother Granmè Melina, who, like many rural Haitians of her generation, "didn't have a birth certificate and could only vaguely recall, as she'd been told by her parents, that she was born when a man named Canal Boisrond was president of Haiti" (68). However, this same person, who at first glance appears a marginal character, is the centerpiece of her family's memory, recounting lively stories as soon as the sun goes down. Like Dany Laferrière's grandmother Da, Granmè Melina favors the gallery, literally and symbolically open to the street and wider world, as the setting for her colorful riddles and tales. Danticat, too, sees herself as the preserver of family memories, and in writing her father's and uncle's story she begs them: "*Please tell me more. Both of you, together, tell me more. About you. About me. About all of us*" (161; italics in original). The notion that the individual contributes to an understanding of connecting histories is evident in Danticat's explicit intermingling of her family stories from the very first page of the book.

In a similar way to his niece, Joseph reveals himself to be concerned with preserving history, obsessively recording observations of his town and his people with the intention of one day writing a book. Sadly, however, his notes are destroyed in a raid, re-creating the colonial situation of having few physical traces of the past. Joseph and his son Maxo are left to seek refuge with the antigang unit of the Haitian national police and record all the tangible losses of their existence: "birth certificates, old report cards, family photos, school diplomas, the kind of things one might need to restore even the smallest fragments of a life" (204). Danticat demonstrates that the threat of invisibility from history carries over into the new world, where she discovers that her dead cousin Marius had "left no trace of his more-than-five-year undocumented stay in Miami" (194). In the face of these obliterations of family memory, photos take on a role of particular importance for Danticat, falling into the realm of Chamoiseau's *traces-mémoires*. As signposts of important moments in her personal history, several photos are among her most treasured possessions: a photo of Mira and Joseph taken at *tante* Denise's funeral, a photo of her parents that she takes with her into the delivery room for the birth of her first daughter Mira, and a photo of the two Miras before her father dies. These visual images become vital anchor points in Danticat's personal history and give an important insight into her past. Charles Forsdick asserts that objects such as photographs provide both connection and distance; "they are the props whereby connections are maintained and the mobility of a diasporized culture signaled" (104). Viewed from this angle, history becomes more a collective expression of diverse voices, supported by different historical sources rather than an individual chronicle penned by a master historian.

Brother, I'm Dying contains a strong testimonial element, attesting to the way in which "l'écriture du moi dépasse le niveau interpersonnel pour s'intéresser aux rapports du sujet avec le monde" (the writing of the self exceeds the interpersonal level to interest itself in the relationships between the subject and the world) (Gasparini, 12). This aspect of the book raises it out of the purely personal realm and fixes it as an important document of social history. Danticat's role as advocate for her people is an integral part of her literary motivation, and her uncle's story represents but one example of many. The lack of concrete materials forms a barrier to Danticat's task, and she is forced to draw from diverse resources to create her powerful narrative, as we have already seen in the work of Condé and Pineau, who use the imaginative alongside the concrete materials they find. "I write these things now, some as I witnessed them and today remember them, others from official documents, as well as the borrowed recollections of family members" (*Brother, I'm Dying*, 25). In her acknowledgments, Danticat focuses attention on the access to different materials she gained as a result of the US Freedom of Information Act. Elizabeth Walcott-Hackshaw observes that the section about Joseph's detention and death in the United States signals a contrasting tone to the rest of the book: "There are few editorial comments from Danticat; instead, she positions herself as an observer and maintains a measured, restrained tone, relying primarily on recorded facts and the recollections of those who actually witnessed what happened to Joseph Dantica[t]" (76). Danticat's relating of her uncle's death in custody is delivered through the objective and dispassionate tone of official documents in which Joseph is reduced to the status of "alien 27041999" (*Brother, I'm Dying*, 214). The magnification of this personal incident, which delivers an accusing message to immigration authorities in the United States, ensures that the book occupies a place wider than that of simple autobiographical reflection. The story stresses Danticat's belief in the importance of voice and having that voice heard, an issue that also arose in a literal sense when Joseph lost his voice box at the age of fifty-five. As a child, Danticat became her uncle's interpreter when he lost his voice, and, although he benefited from the use of an artificial voice box later in life, she remained his spokesperson by writing this book.

In the closing pages of *Brother, I'm Dying*, Danticat draws together the different strands of her internal and external worlds through the deaths of her father and uncle and the birth of her daughter Mira. She recognizes her unique position as a literal embodiment and transmitter of family history, her body forming a space in which "the dead and the new life were already linked, through my blood, through me" (249). Sadly, Joseph never gets to meet his great-niece, but her father manages to hold on long enough to cradle his granddaughter in his arms. However, he is careful to free his daughter from the burden of seeing him die, driven by a desire not to impose his physical death on her when he believes that life must be directed toward the living. Complicated questions of relationship arise in these last pages of the book, where Danticat is caught between life and death, her uncle having passed away in the brutal confines of immigration's custody and her father's tortured thoughts about his brother being exiled from Haiti in death. "He would become part of the soil of a country that had not wanted him. This haunted my father more than anything else.... 'If our country were ever given a chance and allowed to be a country like any other, none of us would live or die here'" (251). The story, however, ends on a positive note with the two brothers "sharing a gravesite and a tombstone in Queens, New York, after living apart for more than thirty years" (269). The overwhelming feeling of the book is that of reconciliation—between past and present, between countries, between life and death—and in this way Danticat opens up a space in which she can project herself and her family into a more positive future. "This is an attempt at cohesiveness, and at re-creating a few wondrous and terrible months when their lives and mine intersected in startling ways, forcing me to look forward and back at the same time. I am writing this only because they can't" (26). *Brother, I'm Dying* is a poignant account of how the individual voices of Danticat and her family contribute to a larger collage of the Haitian experience of exile and immigration and how all combine to create connecting histories.

Create Dangerously: The Immigrant Artist at Work

The final book under discussion in this chapter, *Create Dangerously*, moves between the genres of memoir and essay, exploring the themes of artistry, exile, and "the responsibility of the immigrant artist to bear witness when her country of origin is living tragic times" (Pulitano, "An Immigrant Artist at Work," 41). Danticat announces the wider importance of the work from the outset, dedicating it to the "two hundred thousand and more" who were the victims of the 2010 earthquake in Haiti. The book is in fact framed by two tragedies—the execution of two young men, Marcel Numa and Louis Drouin, on November 12, 1964, by Papa Doc Duvalier's firing squad, and the catastrophic earthquake of January 12, 2010. Danticat explains that all writers have creation myths that haunt and obsess them, and the double execution "is one of mine" (*Create Dangerously*, 5). Her personalization of this political event emphasizes her belief in the need not only to bear witness to one's own life but also to preserve a wider collective history. By explicitly placing herself in a historical continuum, Danticat attempts to create links between past, present, and future. Martin Munro notes, furthermore, that Danticat's writing in *Create Dangerously*, with its "reworking of the notion of the engaged, self-sacrificing writer and the idea of dangerous creation[,] mark to some extent a return to a previous set of concerns that largely tied Haitian writers' fate to that of the nation" (*Writing on the Fault Line*, 30). In contrast to an author like Laferrière, who had heralded in a new tradition of Haitian writing with his focus on style rather than politically committed content in his books, Danticat appears to signal a return to more pressing social concerns.

The consequences of the Haitian earthquake of 2010 cast a long shadow over the book and cause Danticat to reflect on her role as a writer. Like many other well-known Haitians, she was asked to write her reaction to the event in various articles, usually in 1,500 words or less: "They were therapeutic for me, these media outings, and helpful, I hoped, in adding one more voice to a chorus of bereavement and helping to explain what so many of us were feeling, which was a deep and paralyzing sense of loss" (*Create

Dangerously, 158). Moreover, this situation forced her to reflect on her position as an immigrant: "Maybe that was my purpose, then, as an immigrant and a writer—to be an echo chamber, gathering and then replaying voices from both the distant and the local devastation" (159). Danticat's assertions underline her belief that it is important to combine the individual voice with others in order to make a collective impact. At the same time, however, her position as an expert commentator and echo chamber does not always sit comfortably with her. In contrast to Laferrière, a direct observer of the event whose "role was to bear witness and he did it beautifully, going on the radio and television and writing his essays of fifteen hundred words or less to add one more voice to our chorus of bereavement and paralyzing loss" (161), Danticat felt uneasy: "You were not there. You did not live it. You have no right even to speak—for you, for them, for anyone" (159). Danticat subsequently turned to books—both as a reader and a writer—in order to confront these complex questions, signaling once again the way in which literature proves to be a sheltering site.

Like Laferrière, in the early aftermath Danticat locates the earthquake as a definitive moment in Haitian history. "From now on, there will always be the Haiti of before the earthquake and the Haiti of after the earthquake. And after the earthquake, the way we read and the way we write, both inside and outside of Haiti, will never be the same" (162). Far from simply devastating the physical landscape and affecting its people in a material way, Danticat argues that the psychological fractures of the earthquake are perhaps the most powerful. In the way it flattened out all distinctions between social classes—such a palpable characteristic of life under a dictatorship—the earthquake threw all its inhabitants into a collective hole in the ground and forced them to start from the beginning. As Laferrière suggests in *Tout bouge autour de moi (The World is Moving Around Me)*, the "year zero" may not be the most appropriate way to characterize the event, but this natural disaster permanently changed the way in which Haiti relates to the past and the future. Indeed, as Munro states in his definitive study following the earthquake, *Writing on the Fault Line*, in "its own way, the earthquake seemed likely to become as significant a historical landmark as the revolution itself, though the memories it would transmit to future generations would carry none of the comforting national myths of the former event" (31–32). Somehow this "new" present needed to be integrated into the national and individual psyche, and for Danticat this task lies in unearthing points of connection. As Danticat has already made plain in her other literary works, Haiti and its people demonstrate a remarkable survival instinct, and this trait is what emerges alongside the devastation.

Danticat's personal contribution is to write this optimism, drawing on individual stories to convey the resilient spirit of Haitians. As she writes in a short article published in the aftermath of the earthquake, "Living and Loving through Tragedy": "They are each living Job. Yet they still manage to love their neighbours. I think that's an extraordinary example for everyone who is willing to open their eyes and hearts to witness it" (11). While the earthquake is not the only focus of *Create Dangerously*, it does bring into focus a number of important concerns about the way Danticat participates in the recording of momentous historical events.

Create Dangerously also allows Danticat to return to the familiar theme of the transmission of cultural memory through her strategy of literary collage. As in her earlier works, Danticat inserts herself into the narrative, and her personal experiences form an important part of the story. In one incident, she walks with Nick, her cousin Maxo's son, up the mountains to see her oldest living relative, *tante* Ilyana. Along the way, they "retell each other fragmented stories ... the furthest that memory and history go back in our family, vague tales that we've gathered from older family members" (22). The fragmentation Danticat finds in her family background resonates with the ideas of many historians who write of questions of history and memory. However, Danticat does not see such discontinuity as a negative—rather, each memory, each experience, becomes part of a greater patchwork in which all elements are necessary. Equally important is the presence of a custodian of cultural memory, in this case *tante* Ilyana, whose "vocation is nothing less than to maintain our family's physical legacy, to guard a very small house in the ancestral village, to sustain a faraway world to which we could return, if we wanted to, and find traces, however remote and faint, of who we are" (38). *Tante* Ilyana's careful guarding of her family's story helps her descendants to construct their own narrative of their past and to engage with history on both an individual and a collective level, creating connections between the two.

Returning to a less personal angle, Danticat draws on the stories of immigrants who have successfully negotiated the difficulties of identity formation in a new environment. They reveal that the most common challenge is how to assimilate the conflicting traditions of old and new, so aptly described by Laferrière as nostalgia for the past and the long hoped-for future. For Jean Dominique, the Haitian journalist and agronomist, those from the diaspora should be viewed positively, as "people with their feet planted in both worlds" (*Create Dangerously*, 51). Rather than not fitting in anywhere, they have privileged insights into more than one country and are therefore able to relate in a more integrated way to the world around them. The famous painter Jean-Michel Basquiat, whose mother was fourth-generation Puerto Rican and whose father was Haitian, demonstrates a different way of relating to one's cultural and historical background: "I've never been to Africa. I'm an artist who has been influenced by his New York environment. But I have a cultural memory. I don't need to look for it, it exists. It's over there, in Africa. That doesn't mean that I have to go live there. Our cultural memory follows us everywhere, wherever you live" (*Create Dangerously*, 132). Basquiat's concept of carrying cultural memory within allows for a multiplicity of connections between different cultures and time periods, embodying a flexible approach to identity that is reminiscent of postmodernity. "Basquiat did not belong to any fixed collective. He freely borrowed from and floated among many cultural and geographic traditions" (*Create Dangerously*, 133). Dominique's and Basquiat's personal identity quests constitute two contrasting but equally valid examples of how to function as an immigrant. The former favors a firm rooting in one's past and present; the latter floats between different contexts, taking on those elements that are most useful to him. Together, they contribute to the intricate mosaic of immigrant life, in which each person assimilates and discards in an individual way those elements that are personally most significant.

Martin Munro asserts that "Edwidge Danticat's story is that of modern Haiti" ("Inside Out," 25), and her works continually attest to the intricate layering of past, present, and future in this complex Caribbean nation. Danticat's engaged and passionate love of her island homeland ensures that she acts as an advocate for Haiti while preserving her own preoccupations in narrative form. She records Haiti's history by dramatizing individual stories and speaks out against the injustices she observes in a beautifully crafted style that is appreciated by readers and literary critics alike. The defining philosophy of her work is the weaving of the personal and political, a manner that underlines the impossibility of one element existing without the other. This strategy of collage allows her to place the notions of memory and belonging in a continuously evolving relationship in which the art of writing itself is what forges a path toward the future. As she states in *Create Dangerously*: "to create dangerously is also to create fearlessly, boldly embracing the public and private terrors that would silence us, then bravely moving forward even when it feels as though we are chasing or being chased by ghosts" (148).

CHAPTER 5

DANY LAFERRIÈRE
"I Write as I Live"

Dany Laferrière is an exciting, irreverent, and original writer who has been described as "a one-man literary movement" (Munro, "Master of the New," 176) and "the voice of a new generation of Haitian writers" (Dash, *Culture and Customs*, 113). Laferrière has produced one of the most prolific and provocative bodies of work in contemporary Haitian literature. The composition of his writing belies categorization into any one genre, intertwining fiction, autobiography, commentary, truth, lies, humor, provocation, and poignancy. This chapter will focus on three aspects of Laferriere's work—first of all, his self-proclaimed *Une autobiographie américaine* (*An American Autobiography*) (1985–2001), which is composed of ten works of fiction and nonfiction; second, his 2009 autobiographical novel *L'Énigme du retour* (*The Return*), a poignant meditation on exile and return following the death of his father; and finally, *Tout bouge autour de moi* (*The World Is Moving Around Me*) (2011), an emotional exploration of being a witness to the devastating earthquake that hit Haiti in 2010. The theme of connecting histories manifests itself in different forms in Laferrière's life and work and is heavily conditioned by his family's experiences of the Duvaliers' dictatorships and his consequent exile to North America. The first two works mentioned above shed light on the tools Laferrière developed as an exile in which he forged a path that avoided a nostalgic longing for the past or a utopian future by firmly situating himself in the present. The later *The World Is Moving Around Me*[1] has a different focus, with the dramatic and traumatic event of the earthquake challenging many of Laferrière's perceptions about his birthplace and the way it is viewed on the international stage. Like Maryse Condé, Laferrière frequently adopts a self-conscious role as a provocateur, but he also makes profound observations about his native and adopted homelands and life's universal challenges. Like Condé, too, Laferrière values his individualism and declares that the ultimate compliment would be "de me voir comme un écrivain libre de toute catégorisation" (to see me as a writer free of any categorization) (Sroka, 163). Ultimately, his philosophy mirrors the title of one of his books: *J'écris comme je vis* (*I Write as I Live*), in which the intertwining of writing and life are characterized by a conscious grounding in the present, the successful inhabitation of multiple cultural spaces, and a style that is both humorous and compassionate.

Dany Laferrière was born in Port-au-Prince in 1953 to Marie Nelson and Windsor Klebert Laferrière. His life was marked by exile at a young age, after his father was forced to flee the country when his son was just four years old. In fact, father and son shared the name Windsor Klebert Laferrière, but Laferrière junior was given the name Dany to protect him from being associated with his father's radical political activities. Laferrière's father was a journalist and politician who was firmly opposed to François Duvalier's dictatorial regime. In a 2000 interview, Laferrière stated that he only learned the reason for the discrepancy between "Dany" and his official name much later in life, affirming that this situation also influenced his career as a writer: "Dans mes livres, le narrateur n'a jamais une identité propre: soit il n'a pas de nom, soit il porte un nom qui ressemble visiblement à un pseudonyme" (In my books, the narrator never has his own identity: either he doesn't have a name or he has a name that is obviously a pseudonym) (*J'écris comme je vis*, 16). After his father went into exile, Marie sent her young son to live with his grandmother, Da, in Petit-Goâve, a pretty provincial town near the Caribbean Sea. As Laferrière recalls in *J'écris comme je vis*, Petit-Goâve was a tranquil and economically autonomous place until the arrival of Duvalier. Laferrière had an idyllic childhood in Petit-Goâve with his beloved grandmother until he reached high school age, at which time he returned to Port-au-Prince to be with his mother.

Like his father, Dany was to experience exile firsthand as a young man. In the 1970s, Laferrière worked in Port-au-Prince at *Petit Samedi Soir*, a weekly politico-cultural paper, and on the radio with Haïti-Inter. Along with many others, Laferrière was closely watched by the dictatorship, and on June 1, 1976, one of his closest friends and colleagues, Gasner Raymond, was murdered at the age of twenty-three. Raymond's death led Laferrière into immediate exile, a story he recounts in *Le Cri des oiseaux fous*. As he recalls: "Deux issues possibles: la mort ou l'exil. Gasner Raymond meurt, et je quitte Haïti" (Two possible outcomes: death or exile. Gasner Raymond dies, and

I leave Haiti) (*Les Années 80*, 11). Laferrière arrived in Montreal during the 1976 Summer Olympics, encountering a vastly different world where he experienced both crippling loneliness and heady freedom. After nine years working in various factory jobs in Montreal, Laferrière published his first novel in 1985—the provocatively titled *Comment faire l'amour avec un Nègre sans se fatiguer* (*How to Make Love to a Negro without Getting Tired*)—to great acclaim. For Laferrière, this book represented his only escape from a life of poverty and menial employment. The narrator of the book, like Laferrière, declares the book "a handsome hunk of hope. My only chance" (*How to Make Love*, 117). In 1989, the filmmaker Jacques Benoît adapted this outrageous and much talked about novel to film, heralding a new direction in Laferrière's varied career. Since the transformation of his first published novel into film, Laferrière has collaborated on other cinematic productions of his work, and cinema remains a major interest for him.

Integral to Laferrière's literary project is his loathing of labeling in which he is reduced, for example, to the category of "Haitian writer," "Caribbean writer," "Canadian writer," or "immigrant writer" (see, for example, *Je suis fatigué*, 29; and *J'écris comme je vis*, 85). By contrast, he sees himself as "Dany Laferrière, le fils de Marie et de Windsor Laferrière, point!" (Dany Laferrière, the son of Marie and Windsor Laferrière, that's all!) (Sroka, 177). The concept of an "American" identity that he elaborates in his literature allows him to adopt a certain flexibility in relation to national, linguistic, and cultural borders. His refusal to be reduced to a single-rooted identity like Glissant's *identité racine unique* gives him the possibility of moving between different contexts and finding a meaningful place for himself in all of them. As he declares in *Je suis fatigué*: "[E]n acceptant d'être du continent américain, je me sens partout chez moi dans cette partie du monde . . . je ne me considère plus comme un immigré, ni un exilé. Je suis devenu tout simplement un homme du Nouveau Monde" (By accepting myself as being part of the American continent, I feel at home everywhere in this part of the world. . . . I no longer consider myself an immigrant or an exile. I have simply become a man of the New World) (74). He argues, moreover, that his "Americanness" allows him to retain both his specificity and his universality: "Pour moi, l'espace américain n'est pas du tout un espace vaste et vague. C'est un espace très large, celui du continent, et aussi très local, celui de chaque endroit où l'on se trouve" (For me, the American space is not at all a vast and vague space. It is a very wide space, in the continent, and it is also very local, in each place one finds oneself) (Ghinelli, 100). Like Glissant before him, Laferrière draws parallels between all the Americas, claiming a whole spectrum of identities for himself. This strategy is reinforced in his writing style, which has been variously described as "une écriture métisse" (a metisse writing) (Vitiello, 349); a "métissage culturel" (cultural mixing) (Berrouët-Oriol, 63); and creating "un effet d'hybridité esthétique" (an effect of hybrid aesthetics) (Mathis-Moser, 275).

Writing and Identity

In December 2013, Laferrière was elected to Seat Number 2 of the Académie Française, the most prestigious institution of French letters. He joined only a few non-French citizens to take on the role of an *immortel* (immortal) and occupies the seat previously presided over by Argentinean writer Hector Bianciotti and other such luminaries as Montesquieu and Alexandre Dumas, fils. With his ascension to this influential post, it is not surprising that everyone wants to claim Laferrière as their own—the Haitians,[2] the Canadians, the Québécois ... but as Laferrière explained in a 2014 interview about his election: "[J]e ne crois pas que ce soit une bonne chose d'identifier les écrivains par leur nationalité. On est écrivain, tout simplement, comme on est médecin" (I don't think that it is a good thing to identify writers by their nationality. One is quite simply a writer, like one is a doctor) (Dainese, 393). On May 28, 2015, Laferrière was inaugurated into the Académie, and in a speech imaginatively directed at his predecessor Bianciotti, he reflected further on his role as a writer unfettered by restrictive bonds. He credited the Haitian voodoo god Legba as the one who had enabled him to meet Bianciotti, in a statement that acknowledges his Caribbean past but that also extends beyond his own personal context: "Ce Legba permet à un mortel de passer du monde visible au monde invisible, puis de revenir au monde visible. C'est donc le dieu des écrivains" (This Legba allows mortals to pass from the "visible" world to the "invisible" and then to come back again. It is thus the god of writers) ("Discours de réception," 1). During his speech, Laferrière drew out a number of encounters with the Americas that link him, Bianciotti, and even Dumas fils and Montesquieu to the point where he declared, tongue in cheek, that "ce fauteuil est le siège de tant d'aventures reliées à l'Amérique que je ne serai pas étonné qu'il devienne un jour le fauteuil américain de l'Académie" (this seat is the site of so many adventures linked to America that I will not be surprised if it becomes one day the American seat of the Academy) ("Discours de réception," 1). Finally, Laferrière credited the three founders of Négritude, Aimé Césaire,

Léon-Gontran Damas, and Léopold Sédar Senghor (the latter was the first black writer elected to the Académie), with forging a path of dignity for black writers, but also acknowledged the uniting and enriching features of authors the world over: "Chaque fois qu'un écrivain, né ailleurs, entre sous cette Coupole, un simple effort d'imagination pourra nous faire voir le cortège d'ombres protectrices qui l'accompagnent" (Each time a writer, born elsewhere, enters this Dome, a simple effort of imagination will enable us to see that procession of protective shadows that accompany him or her) ("Discours de réception," 7). As Laferrière declared in an earlier interview, in his opinion it is a writer's library more than nationality that is revealing of that person's identity: "J'aime surtout lire des auteurs éloignés de moi.... Comme je dis toujours, il n'y a aucune distinction de race ou d'origine dans ma bibliothèque. Elle est pluriethnique" (I especially like to read authors distant from me.... As I always say, there is no distinction of race or origin in my library. It is pluri-ethnic) (Dainese, 394). The writing space, encompassing writer, text, and reading, becomes, in Laferrière's hands, a powerful force for articulating and negotiating the complexities of the modern world.

In a 2005 interview, Laferrière reflected on the notion of place, asserting that, like Glissant in *Philosophie de la Relation*, "le lieu est incontournable. On vient d'un lieu" (place is imperative. We come from a place) (Ghinelli, 100; Glissant, *Philosophie de la Relation*, 46). However, Laferrière went on to express his rejection of theory and his desire to see "s'il était possible d'écrire sans avoir d'assise théorique derrière soi, en se fondant sur l'intuition, sur l'instinct" (if it was possible to write without having a theory sitting behind you, by basing yourself on intuition, on instinct) (Ghinelli 100). In his 2008 novel *Je suis un écrivain japonais* (*I Am a Japanese Writer*), Laferrière explores such concerns in a comical, yet serious, way. Early in the book, he poses the question: "[W]hat is a Japanese writer? Someone who lives and writes in Japan? Or someone who was born in Japan and writes in spite of it? ... Or someone who was not born in Japan, who doesn't know the language, but who decided one fine day to become a Japanese writer?" (8). According to Laferrière: "We're born in one spot, and afterwards we choose our place of origin ... [w]hich means that when a Japanese person reads me, I immediately become a Japanese writer" (10, 14). While Laferrière's assertions may appear flippant, they underline how notions of identity are continually changing in a globalized world and also contain the possibility of multiple connections. With large-scale migration, the influence of the Internet, and the desire by so many to form part of the capitalized marketplace, the world's citizens are being increasingly homogenized. The provocative statements Laferrière makes in *I Am a Japanese Writer* encapsulate the impossibility of fixing one's identity in a particular time and place. As his *autobiographie américaine* amply demonstrates, identity is always in flux and inseparable from the diverse historical, cultural, geographic, and linguistic elements that continually influence our subjective journeys.

Being open to the dynamic nature of life gives one the chance to adapt to life's changes in a manner that avoids nostalgia and idealism; for Laferrière, this approach is contained in his attachment to the present. Central to his literary style and his continually metamorphosing notion of identity is his use of the present tense when writing, allowing him to create a sense of immediacy and drama: "[J]e ne connais qu'un seul temps. Pour moi, le présent est une densification du passé et de l'avenir" (I only know one tense. For me, the present is a densification of the past and the future) (Ghinelli, 102). The use of the present tense enables Laferrière to enact his philosophy of life, which acknowledges the role of past and future but which is focused on what is unfolding around him. By contrast, he argues that those who come from the Third World, or who are exiles or migrants, are often caught between a nostalgia for the known, often painful past and a dreamed-of future (Ghinelli, 103). Laferrière's literary approach is like that of a photographer, taking snapshots that capture the moment with precision but that also allow for multiple possibilities of interpretation. Perhaps this way of relating to his craft is a result of his increasing interest in cinema, a trend evident in books such as *I Am a Japanese Writer* and *The Return*. In the former, for example, he asserts: "I film ... from my point of view. No editing. And no hesitation about using my imagination to fill in the conversations I'm too far away to hear, or the hidden emotions" (35); while in the latter he writes: "Let us carefully observe the scene. / Close-up on ..." (58). This cinematic style that is constructed around powerful images allows Laferrière to draw the reader in with concrete and accessible imagery, building a story that is projected through the prism of the present.

Laferrière's use of the French language is equally pivotal to his writing project. Like Condé, he has been routinely criticized for his use of the "colonizer's" language, but also like Condé he argues that he has made French his own. In his contribution to the collection *Pour une littérature-monde*, he asserts:

> J'ai perdu trop de temps à commenter le fait que j'écris en français. Et à debattre du fait que ce ne soit pas ma langue maternelle. Finalement, tout cela me paraît aujourd'hui assez théorique, et même un brin ridicule. Cette

langue française s'est infiltrée dans mes neurones, et son chant rhythme mon sang.... J'écris et je lis en français partout dans le monde. C'est cette langue qui m'accompagne en voyage.

(I've lost too much time commenting on the fact that I write in French. And on debating the fact that it is not my mother tongue. In the end, all that seems quite theoretical today, and even a bit ridiculous. This French language has infiltrated my neurones and its song makes a rhythm in my blood.... I write and I read in French everywhere in the world. It is this language that accompanies me on my travels.) ("Je voyage en français," 87)

Laferrière demonstrates that language is as important as place in influencing one's identity trajectory. However, he sees it as part of one's literary tool kit, taken up as needed and used with the aim of expressing one's inner reality. In an interview with Ghila Sroka, Laferrière discussed this notion in reference to Aimé Césaire's *Cahier d'un retour au pays natal* (*Notebook of a Return to my Native Land*) and its influence on his book, *The Return*. Rather than treating his own work as a homage to Césaire, Laferrière sees his discussion of Césaire as a response and continuation of the celebrated Martinican's work. Where Césaire speaks passionately for those without a voice, Laferrière sees himself as someone who encourages the expression of one's own, individual voice: "Je reproche à ceux qui s'adressent à la metropole le fait qu'on n'entende pas leur voix intime, leur voix personnelle.... J'ai donc pensé qu'il était possible de faire entendre cette voix-là, de faire entendre quelque chose qui va au plus profond de soi, qui peut être traversé par l'histoire, par les questions sociales, mais à soi" (I reproach those who address the Metropole the fact that they don't let their intimate voice be heard, their personal voice.... I thought therefore that it would be possible to make this voice heard, to make something heard that goes to the deepest part of the self, that can be traversed by history, by social questions, but which is yours) (Sroka, 154). Although Césaire wrote in French against colonialism, just as Laferrière does, the manner in which they approach this topic differs considerably. Césaire speaks on behalf of the collectivity, forcing a rethinking of history through evocative, graphic, and surreal poetry. On the other hand, Laferrière employs a single point of view in the present and uses the colonial past as a backdrop to his explorations of the past, present, and future. Césaire helps to lay the groundwork for a renewed vision of the colonial subject; Laferrière benefits from this foundation and continues the interrogation of the same subject in a more contemporary setting. The following analysis of Laferrière's works will reveal his unique way of engaging with history.

Une autobiographie américaine

Une autobiographie américaine, one of Laferrière's most extensive achievements, comprises ten books written in nonchronological order, which, as Dennis Essar argues, "reflect[s] the order in which the narrator recollects past events" (932). This nonconventional approach to autobiography is but one example of Laferrière's many challenges to received ideas. In chronological order of Laferrière's life, the books unfold as follows: *L'Odeur du café* (*An Aroma of Coffee*) (1991), *Le Charme des après-midi sans fin* (1997), *Le Goût des jeunes filles* (*Dining with the Dictator*) (1992), *La Chair du maître* (1997), *Le Cri des oiseaux fous* (2000), *Chronique de la dérive douce* (*A Drifting Year*) (1994), *Comment faire l'amour avec un Nègre sans se fatiguer* (*How to Make Love to a Negro without Getting Tired*) (1985), *Éroshima* [*Eroshima*] (1987), *Cette grenade dans la main du jeune nègre est-elle une arme ou un fruit?* (*Why Must a Black Writer Write about Sex?*) (1993), and *Pays sans chapeau* (*Down among the Dead Men*) (1997). These books span his childhood in Petit-Goâve, his adolescence in Port-au-Prince, his exile to Montreal in 1976, and his physical and literary migrations in North America, and they terminate in 1997 with his return to Haiti after a twenty-year absence. As Laferrière states: "Mes livres sont parus d'une manière dispersée mais ils sont liés" (My books appeared in a dispersed manner but they are linked) (Tervonen, 103; see also Sroka, 153). These varied works expose the challenges of constructing one's identity, as Laferrière inhabits different parts of the Americas and reflects on his status as an exile and a writer.[3] Each place marks him in a different way; as he memorably states in *J'écris comme je vis* while residing in Miami: "[J]e suis un homme en trois morceaux: mon coeur est à Port-au-Prince, mon esprit à Montréal, et mon corps à Miami" (I am a man in three pieces: my heart is in Port-au-Prince, my mind/spirit in Montreal, and my body in Miami) (49). In an interview with Sroka, Laferrière declared that with his "American autobiography," "j'avais le sentiment d'avoir témoigné. Tout me semblait sphérique, un cercle parfait" (I had the impression of bearing witness. Everything seemed spherical to me, a perfect circle) (Sroka, 155). However, with the passage of time, he began to feel dissatisfied with his work and undertook a process of rewriting some of these texts, in what he terms "un travail de broderie" (a work of embroidery) (Sroka, 155). This process of writing and rewriting demonstrates one aspect of the flexible approach he takes to his identity and the way he views the world. While many writers would prefer to see their works fixed in time, an enduring testament to the emotions and ideas of the period of writing, Laferrière views his as a work in progress, testifying to the changing interpretations of time.

One of the most important contributions of *Une autobiographie américaine* and the first phase of this anthology is the decisive role played by Laferrière's early childhood in Haiti. Bénédicte Boisseron argues that *An Aroma of Coffee*, chronologically the first book in the series, can be seen as "le livre genèse de son écriture" (the genesis book of his writing) ("La Galerie de Dany Laferrière," 21). Laferrière himself affirmed in a 2009 lecture: "Je suis obsédé par l'idée de faire savoir au monde que j'ai eu une enfance heureuse. Et cela malgré la dictature.... Aujourd'hui, du moins en tant qu'écrivain, elle me permet d'exister. C'est le moment fondamental de ma vie" (I'm obsessed by the idea of showing the world I had a happy childhood. And that in spite of the dictatorship.... Today, at least as a writer, it allows me to exist. It is the fundamental moment of my life) (*Un art de vivre*, 3). It is interesting that Laferrière places such emphasis on beginnings in the development of his vocation, particularly as many writers try to avoid locating their identity formation at any one point in time. At first glance it appears to be against the notion of an identity in flux, seeming more like Césaire's concept of a single-rooted identity. However, it becomes apparent on reading any of Laferrière's works that childhood serves not so much as a fixed origin but as a secure starting point that permits him to negotiate the varied challenges that come his way. In fact he asserts that his move to Petit-Goâve to join his grandmother as a young child constitutes his first exile, a realization he comes to forty years after the event (*Un art de vivre*, 11). Significantly, though, this exile is an overwhelmingly positive experience, opening up the notion of exile to new possibilities that do not equate only with fear, loneliness, and duress.

Laferrière's *autobiographie américaine* enters a dramatic new phase with his arrival in Montreal after the death of his friend and colleague Gasner Raymond in Haiti, which he details in *Le Cri des oiseaux fous*. In the books set in North America, Laferrière critically reassesses his place in the world—a view that metamorphoses from a nostalgic longing for his homeland, to constant comparisons between Haiti and his adopted continent, and finally to an appreciation for the contrasting attributes of both places. Daniel Delas argues that "tout écrivain exilé a dans un premier temps une vie double, une vie emplie du rêve du pays natal et une vie réelle consacrée à intégrer de nouvelles données culturelles" (all exiled writers have a double life for the first period, one life filled with the dream of the native land and a "real" life devoted to integrating the new cultural norms) (90). In *A Drifting Year*, Laferrière explores this double consciousness through a series of snapshots of his first year in Montreal. Early in his stay, it is clear that he is still attached to the country of his birth, fantasizing about the Haitian colors and scenes he evokes so beautifully in *An Aroma of Coffee* and *Le Charme des après-midi sans fin*. He also becomes aware of his skin color for the first time, an issue that he analyzes in many of his subsequent books. In addition to the shock of realizing that the majority of Québécois do not resemble him physically, he also becomes aware of the vastly different standards of living between the two countries when he observes a young woman putting out her cigarette in a salad she has barely touched. Laferrière, by contrast, "can choose between having one good meal with wine and fasting the rest of the week, or eating pigeon and rice for seven days" (*A Drifting Year*, 27). This book pivots on a binary ordering of his existence in which the familiar and new are constantly presented in contrast to each other, an approach that proves unsatisfactory until Laferrière is finally able to reach a point where he is able to reject the either/or, self/other option and instead embrace a model where different influences coexist. "I can't tell you exactly when this city ceased being a foreign city for me. Perhaps when I stopped looking at it" (*A Drifting Year*, 117). The definitive rejection of a dualistic way of viewing exile, identity, and migration occurs in his first novel, *How to Make Love to a Negro without Getting Tired*, which unsettled a whole host of subject positions with its provocative portrayal of Haitians, Africans, feminists, and African Americans (see Tervonen, 101).

In *Why Must a Black Writer Write about Sex?*, Laferrière pursues his reflections on the multiple roots of identity and the complexities of migration. One of the foremost points Laferrière establishes is his dislike of North Americans' obsession with his Haitian origins. When he is commissioned by an influential east coast magazine to write an extended piece on America, the narrator is disgusted at their assumption that his Caribbean past will form an inevitable part of his article. "The same old garbage! People are supposed to write about where they came from! I write about what's going on around me, here and now, where I live" (*Why Must a Black Writer*, 13). He asserts that he has worked hard to overcome his past and to forge a new existence for himself in North America, thereby bypassing the need to continually muse on his Haitianness. Another way Laferrière subverts the expectation that he will focus on his Haitian past is by offering controversial insights into American culture. He argues that the United States functions on false myths that trick immigrants into thinking they have a chance to achieve the American dream. There are many layers to this provocative book, but the common thread lies in Laferrière's dislike of pigeonholing and his continued assertions of his hard-won and valid place in North America.

Why Must a Black Writer highlights Laferrière's personal observations of life as an immigrant as well as shedding light on more general challenges for those who do not form part of the white American majority. This North American phase of his writing demonstrates Laferrière's commitment to his life as a "man of the New World"—that is, a product of a particular history, but one who is able to successfully integrate all aspects of his experience rather than remaining in a restrictive category.

The final phase of Laferrière's *autobiographie américaine* occurs with his return to Haiti after a twenty-year absence. *Down among the Dead Men* brings together the multiple strands of Laferrière's "New World," American identity, revealing not only his deep attachment to his homeland but also the insights he gains as a result of his insider/outsider status in both countries. Martin Munro asserts that the book "forms an extended textual allusion" to Jacques Roumain's classic Haitian novel *Gouverneurs de la rosée* (*Masters of the Dew*) (Munro, "Master of the New," 178), and Laferrière also evokes Glissant's *Pays rêvé, pays réel* with his alternating chapters "Real Country" and "Imagined Country." In reference to the latter, Laferrière asserted in a 2014 interview: "Je suis planté dans le rêve et le réel, toute la littérature pour moi est une sorte de rêve" (I am planted in the dream world and the real, all literature for me is a kind of dream) (Dainese, 397). This dream-like element haunts the book as he moves between its interlocking chapters and explores the changes in his home country since his move to North America, as well as the changes in himself, through the character of Vieux Os (Old Bones). Upon arriving in Haiti, the narrator is instantly struck by the sensuality of his country, recording his feelings in a prelude to the book entitled "A Primitive Writer." In a Proustian moment, Old Bones raises a steaming cup of coffee "and breathed in deeply. My whole childhood rose to the surface" (*Down among the Dead Men*, 18). Installing himself under a heaving mango tree and typing feverishly on his typewriter, Old Bones tries to recapture and concretize a past that has been lost to him for twenty years. His mother anxiously questions a neighbor about the possible madness of her son, only to be told: "No. He just has to learn to breathe again, and feel, see and touch things differently" (10). This early scene establishes one of the main themes of the book, which is how returning exiles can find a place for themselves in the country they left and in the place they now inhabit. As Old Bones works through some of these questions in his detailed observations of his return to Haiti, he arrives at the conclusion that only a firm grounding in the present can release one from nostalgia for the past and an idealistic future. He also proves that connecting the histories of different places, times, languages, and characters carries great enriching potential.

A short vignette entitled "The Green Lizard" from "Real Country" brings into sharp focus some of the dilemmas of exile and return, as Old Bones describes his paralyzing fear when a green lizard jumps onto his shirt. Despite such creatures being commonplace in Haiti, Old Bones reveals his distance from his birth culture when his reaction to the lizard causes him livid fear, and he asks himself: "What did it see when it looked at me? Did it know I'd just returned this very day? Did it know how long I'd lived up north? Did it know there are no lizards where I'd been? So many emotions, sensations, and impressions in so short a time (ten or twelve seconds)" (50). While there is much anthropomorphosis in this scene, the narrator's reflections reveal his self-conscious unease at being absent for so long and his anxiety that he has forgotten how to be "Haitian." The theme of needing to relearn one's culture is picked up at a number of points in the text—for example, when Old Bones is reminded of the Haitian tradition of serving the dead before the living when he receives a cup of coffee (30), and his friend Philippe commenting: "We're going to have to teach you how to dance the merengue all over again" (136). In a poignant affirmation of his own situation, the narrator is struck by the topic of debate at a local radio station, which asks: "Should people who have lived overseas too long be considered Haitians?" (166). The question of what constitutes Haitianness is in fact a recurrent theme in Laferrière's work and one that he explores in different settings, including *The Return* and *The World Is Moving Around Me*. *Down among the Dead Men* dramatizes some of the different forums in which the narrator explores and experiments with his shifting identity, and how he manages to enunciate a new place for himself that is inclusive of all his experiences.

As a writer, Laferrière attempts to articulate the complexities of this status as a returning exile using language as a key arena. In the chapter "Language" in "Dream Country," Old Bones records the fetal-like bliss he feels when immersing himself in his mother tongue of Creole. "I dive headfirst into this sea of familiar sounds. An old tune that comes easily to the lips, even if you haven't heard it for ages. A chaos of words and rhythms in my head. I swim effortlessly. The word is liquid" (70). In *The Return*, Laferrière describes himself as "an aquatic animal—that's what I am" (10), and many of his books feature Laferrian characters sinking into a comforting bath. The deep sense of contentment he attains in water clearly has overtones of the peace and security of the womb and the importance of a deep connection with the maternal. Later reflections in *Down among the Dead Men* underscore the naturalness that comes only when plunging oneself in one's first culture and language. As Old Bones remarks to Philippe: "You're only at home in your mother tongue, and in your own accent. There are things that I can only say in Creole. Sometimes the meaning doesn't even matter. I just want to say the words for their music and the heat that rises off them. There are words I haven't used in twenty years, and I can feel how much my mouth misses them. I want to roll them on my tongue and chew them with my teeth and swallow them" (160). This very sensuous relationship to language forms a stark contrast to Laferrière's more cerebral commentary on his use of French in his contribution to the *littérature-monde* manifesto. While French becomes his language of daily life, travel, and literature, it will nonetheless never occupy the status of his mother tongue. As he states in *Down among the Dead Men*: "Sometimes, up there, I feel so completely alone I just want to scream. There's no one who knew me from before. It's like I never had a 'before.' Like I only have a present. The present is fine. I like living in the present, but there's no present without the past" (160). In some way, Creole represents his past, his "before," and displays all the effortless of one's early childhood; French is his present, a deep source of culture and insight, but one that can never replace his mother tongue. Language, then, becomes one measure of how Laferrière understands his experience of exile and migration.

Down among the Dead Men also brings to light some of the profound differences that exist between Haiti and North America. After the initial joy of reuniting with his family and city, Old Bones becomes aware of the terrible realities of life in Haiti. "It's as if two countries were living side by side, without ever meeting. . . . The real country: the struggle for survival. And the dream country: every fantasy of the most megalomaniac people on earth" (40). Further incompatibilities emerge in relation to space with the overpopulation of Port-au-Prince compared to the relative sparseness of North American cities. In one memorable scene, in Bombardopolis (a commune in northwestern Haiti), the Americans are conducting a secret census and ask a woman how many children she has. When she answers that she has sixteen, only seven of whom are alive, the man refuses to record sixteen while she insists that he count all of them. As the narrator asserts: "Two different visions. Americans subtract their dead, while we continue adding ours up. Our characters are incompatible" (77). A similar lack of comprehension between the two cultures occurs in the vignette "A Primitive Painter" in the final chapter, entitled "Real Country/Dream Country." When a New York journalist questions an illiterate Haitian painter about why he always paints pictures of abundance rather than the poverty that surrounds him, he answers: "'I paint the country I dream.' 'What about the real country?' 'The real country, sir? I don't need to dream it'" (212). While these scenes illustrate the seemingly unbridgeable differences that exist between North America and Haiti, Laferrière emphasizes that it is possible to transcend such incompatibilities. Using the example of his own life, he learns to move between contrasting spaces in a complex process that involves both mind and body, distance and proximity:

> Je n'écris pas uniquement avec des idées, j'écris avec mon corps. Ce corps a beaucoup voyagé et il est resté très longtemps dans un autre pays. Donc cette sorte d'expérience m'habite. Je n'arrive pas à rêver d'une ville quand je suis dans la ville; il faut que j'en sorte pour qu'elle puisse m'habiter. Quand je suis dans une ville, je l'habite. Quand je suis ailleurs, c'est elle qui m'habite.
>
> (I don't write only with ideas, I write with my body. This body has traveled a lot, and it has spent a long time in another country. Therefore this sort of experience inhabits me. I can't dream about a city when I am in that city; I have to leave in order for it to inhabit me. When I am in a city, I live it. When I am elsewhere, it inhabits me.) (Sroka, 157)

Down among the Dead Men, and indeed the entire collection that makes up *Une autobiographie américaine*, constitutes an extended, original, and provocative manner of relating to the past. The contrasting volumes allow Laferrière to try on different masks as a way to make sense of his experiences and to find a place in the present in which he is happy to be himself. His articulation of an "American" identity that is inclusive and outward looking provides the framework for these reflections and forms an important stage in his negotiations of identity.

L'Énigme du retour

Laferrière's maturing approach to questions of exile and the intersecting paths of past, present, and future becomes increasingly evident in his later works. In 2009, Laferrière published *L'Énigme du retour* (*The Return*), which is a poetic meditation on his father's life and death as well as the exile experienced by both father and son. While officially categorized as a novel, this work is heavily influenced by Laferrière's personal experiences and pivots on the phone call he receives about his father's death in New York, followed by his journeys to Brooklyn and then Haiti. The majority of *The Return* is expressed in the form of an extended poem, a technique that allows Laferrière to adopt his familiar "snapshot" style of writing but that also expresses a softer side to him. The book is divided into two uneven parts: "Slow Preparations for Departure" and "A Return." These two subtitles underline the narrator's attempts to come to terms with his father's death and to probe the different layers of the idea of return. As Laferrière stated in his inauguration speech at the Académie Française: "L'un des apports les plus significatifs de l'exil dans la littérature, c'est la notion du retour. D'autant plus intéressant qu'il s'avère impossible dans la réalité. On ne retourne pas au point de départ car le mouvement est incessant" (One of the most significant contributions of exile to literature is the notion of return. What is even more interesting is that it turns out to be impossible in reality. We cannot return to the point of departure because movement is constant) ("Discours de réception," 6). Moreover, *The Return* highlights the transgenerational effects of exile by placing three male characters in the spotlight: Windsor the father, Windsor/Dany the son, and Dany the nephew. Each is marked by exile in a different way, and in some sense they symbolize the past, present, and future of Haiti. Laferrière's dedication of the book to "Dany Charles, my nephew, who lives in Port-au-Prince" suggests his faith in the ultimately redemptive nature of life. For a man who has lived exile so deeply, this book gives him the opportunity to reflect on different aspects of this enforced lifestyle choice: the way exile is experienced both individually and collectively, the fragmentary and sensory nature of memory, the transgenerational processes of trauma and healing, and finally a sense of completion as the narrator ends one phase of his journey.

Early in the book, the narrator expresses the rupture that his father's death introduces into his life, even though the two had not spoken for many years: "I've lost track of myself. / Memories run together in my mind. / My life is just a small damp package / of washed-out colors and old smells" (23). Laferrière's meditations on the loss of his father underline a series of profound emotions in relation to exile, revealing it to be a complex process of identity construction, deconstruction, and reconstruction that penetrates into the tiniest recesses of one's existence. Traveling to Haiti in the wake of his father's death forces the narrator to reconnect with a part of himself that he has had to repress in order to carve out a new life in exile. "Returning South after all these years / I am like someone / who has to relearn what he already knows / but had to forget along the way" (94). Moreover, the experience is a bodily one: "Everything I banished from my mind back there in order to live without the bonds of nostalgia has a concrete presence here. Those things sought refuge in my body where the cold froze them in place.

Now my body is slowly warming. My memory is thawing: that little puddle of water in the bed" (113). This sensuous image demonstrates the profundity of the experience of exile. Far from being a linear process that involves leaving one's homeland behind in order to embrace the opportunities of the new, exile also requires the reappraisal of one's past life and how it is going to fit into the present. Indeed, Laferrière demonstrates that the continuing presence of the past lies dormant in one's body, ready to erupt at any moment to remind the exiled person where he or she came from.

The Return picks up many of the themes previously explored in *Down among the Dead Men*, and the two books complement each other in Laferrière's exploration of exile and return. With more than ten years between the two publications, there are both continuities and discontinuities in the way the narrators perceive their past. When the narrator travels to Haiti in *The Return*, he grapples once again with the notion of how to relate to one's place of birth after such a long period of absence. Haiti proves to be both familiar and foreign. In surveying Port-au-Prince, the scene of his adolescence, the narrator declares: "I promised myself not to look at the city / with yesterday's eyes. / Images from the past constantly try / to superimpose themselves on the present. / I am navigating through two worlds" (137). The centrality of women in concretizing his sense of identity also comes to the fore as Laferrière reminisces that he has lived thirty-three years "far from my mother's eyes" (15). In a similar manner to *Down among the Dead Man*, the narrator comments that he has "lived too long without witnesses" (15), and the fact that he has spent most of his life away from his roots is an experience that only those who have left, voluntarily or by force, can understand. Indeed, the narrator argues that "the real opposition is not / between countries, no matter how different they are / but between those who have had to learn / to live at other latitudes / (even in inferior conditions) / and those who have never had to face / a culture other than their own" (27). Clearly, though, there is something fundamental about being in the place where you grew up, among people that know you and with whom you share a bond that requires no explanation. "I don't want to think. / Just see, hear and feel. / Note it all down before I lose my head, / drunk on this explosion of tropical / colors, smells and tastes. / I haven't been a part of a landscape like this / for so long" (58). The narrator's attempts to reconnect with this early childhood highlight the fact that it is not possible to erase the past, even if it does not dominate your present. The question is to determine what role it will play in one's contemporary reality. For Laferrière, it is the process of writing that allows him to grapple with these issues and to try to enunciate a space where both his past and present can coexist. As he states about his travels in Haiti in *The Return*: "As I move through this universe (the city, the people, the objects) that I've described so often, I don't feel like a writer, but more like a tree in its forest. I realize I didn't write those books to describe a landscape, but to continue being part of it" (121). Despite his success at creating a new life for himself in North America, Laferrière reveals that the past always remains dormant somewhere in the psyche, and it is up to each individual to determine how to reconcile it with the rest of one's life.

Despite the personal tone of the narrative, *The Return* is also a document that speaks more broadly, bearing witness to the social consequences of the Duvaliers' dictatorial regimes. Jean Hérald Legagneur, for example, asserts that Laferrière "combine l'imaginaire avec la nécessité de dire le social" (combines the imaginary with the necessity of speaking about social issues) (295). An important aspect of this social examination is Laferrière's revelation of the different strands of transgenerational exile that occur under the Duvaliers' bloody reigns. Speaking of the personal in the first instance, Laferrière commented in a 2000 interview that "François Duvalier a exilé mon père, et Jean-Claude Duvalier m'exilera vingt ans plus tard. Père et fils, présidents; père et fils, exilés" (François Duvalier exiled my father, and Jean-Claude Duvalier was to exile me twenty years later. Father and son, presidents; father and son, exiles) (*J'écris comme je vis*, 16). This intersection of the personal and political in his own life is complemented by reflections on wider aspects of transgenerational exile in the book. Indeed, the concept of generation is one to which Laferrière returns frequently in his work, arguing: "We're all cloistered in our decades" (75). Laferrière identifies different patterns of exile, such as the vertical traumas in the generations of Laferrière's paternal line who are affected by exile: "My nephew wants to be a famous writer. / . . . His father is a poet who gets death threats. / His uncle, a novelist living in exile. /He has to choose between death and exile. / For his grandfather it was death in exile" (78). There are horizontal traumas, as with the wife of a Manhattan restaurant owner where Laferrière's father ate every day for free because she recognized her own husband's story in that of her customer. Exile is experienced in a cross-generational way when Laferrière describes the physical attributes of his generation: "We all had the same emaciated look (wild eyes and dry lips). That's how you would recognize our generation" (69). And later we see Laferrière sitting across from his friend Rodney Saint-Éloi, Haitian writer and publisher, who is a more recent arrival in Montreal. "Here we are sitting, / Saint-Éloi and me. / Face to face. / Both of us from Haiti. / Him, scarcely five years ago. / Me, nearly thirty-five years back. / Thirty endless winters separate us. / That's the hard road he'll have to take" (51). However, despite these recurrent patterns of trauma, Laferrière rejects the inevitability of its continuation. He discovers on his father's death that Windsor had left a suitcase for him at the bank in New York. "The suitcase was waiting for me. / He had faith in his son's reflex. / What he didn't know / (shut up, you can't teach a dead man anything) / is that destiny is not passed from father to son. / The suitcase belongs to him alone. / The weight of his life" (50). The symbolism of this discovery is that Laferrière starts to enunciate a path that emphasizes transgenerational healing, rather than the perpetuation of transgenerational trauma. The different cycles he describes reject the idea that an exile is condemned like a mouse to run endlessly on a wheel, but instead has the possibility to change life patterns.

As we have already seen, part of Laferrière's strength of character comes from the powerful presence of women in his life. A direct consequence of the dictatorships, it was women who had to take on the role of sturdy providers in the absence of their male partners. Laferrière credits his grandmother Da as "la plus forte influence de ma vie" (the strongest influence in my life) (*J'écris comme je vis*, 17) and the one who allows him to thumb his nose at the dictators by having a happy childhood in spite of the terror that reigned in the country. Laferrière makes a number of observations about women and their place in history, firmly placing them in the role of quiet but influential history makers as opposed to powerful male directors of History. "My grandmother Da. My mother Marie. My sister Ketty. These women don't concern themselves with History but with daily life, which is an endless ribbon" (108). However, Laferrière clearly underlines that it is women who preserve and perpetuate Haitian histories and are therefore intrinsic to the continuing existence of the country. "My mother does not swim / in the great seas of History. / But all individual stories / are like rivers that run through her" (73). As we have seen in earlier chapters, it is women who are the unofficial but vitally important historians in many Caribbean societies. On a personal level, the narrator also credits his mother with authenticating his life, pointing out: "I keep coming back to her / in everything I write. / I spend my life interpreting / the slightest shadow on her brow. / Even from a distance" (87).

Laferrière has spent less time examining the consequences of male absence in his life, although *The Return* offers him the opportunity to reflect specifically on this situation with the death of his father. While Windsor Laferrière had to suppress his past life in order to survive post-exile—"I can still hear him yelling that he'd never had a child, or a wife or a country"

(45)—the narrator of *The Return* nonetheless acknowledges after hearing the news of his father's demise: "I got on the road early this morning. / No destination. / The way my life will be from now on" (3); and "My father's death has completed a cycle" (24). Indeed, as he later surveys his father in his casket, Laferrière comments that a dead father is "[a] star too blinding / to look at straight on" (44). Alongside these meditations on his relationship with his father, Laferrière introduces the presence of another male who has had a significant influence on his life, Martinican writer Aimé Césaire, author of the groundbreaking *Cahier d'un retour au pays natal* (*Notebook of a Return to The Native Land*). This book is one of two things Laferrière has kept with him since his exile to North America, the other being a "letter from my mother in which she explains, sparing no detail, how to live in a country she's never visited" (40). In one memorable scene, Laferrière plunges himself into a long bath with the book and falls into a reverie about his life. "I alternate mouthfuls of rum and pages of the *Notebook* until the book slides onto the floor. Everything is happening in slow motion. In my dream, Césaire takes my father's place" (21). Césaire therefore takes on a decisive symbolic role for the narrator, one who remains constant and present throughout his life, unlike his own father. As we have already seen in an earlier discussion, Césaire is also someone against whom Laferrière defines himself, which is another important role of the father in a son's life. Munro takes the relationship a step further, arguing that *The Return* "becomes a double eulogy to the father and to Césaire" (*Tropical Apocalypse*, 148). Returning to his notion of generation, the narrator elects to pass on his copy of the *Cahier* to his nephew Dany, who is representative of the next generation. "I slip the old water-warped copy / of *Notebook of a Return to the Native Land* / into my nephew's bag. / We need it before we leave. / Not when we return" (209). With this symbolic gesture, Laferrière sums up the importance of family and generation and the empowering qualities of literature.

It is the cyclical nature of life that draws together the different strands of Laferrière's journey of return. His spiritual and physical travels allow him to acknowledge the emptiness and loss that characterize exile, the death of his father, and their effects on memory. "He gave me birth. / I take care of his death. / Between birth and death, / we hardly crossed paths" (220). He reveals, moreover, that it is only through his mother that he is able to experience his father: "There is no picture / of us alone together. / Except in my mother's memory" (220). Significantly, though, *The Return* allows Laferrière to reflect on his personal philosophy, reinforcing yet again that it is not possible to view life in a linear and binary manner: "This is not winter.

/ This is not summer. / This is not the North. / This is not the South. / Life is spherical now" (226). The resolution he finds in the image of the sphere demonstrates his commitment to a life lived in relationship with others. It is a visual symbol that displaces the fixity of certain experiences and posits the possibility of viewing significant events in a different way. The closing lines of *The Return* take him back to the tranquility of his childhood, which he uses as a metaphor for the sense of closure he has found retracing his steps from Haiti to North America: "Someone has seen me smile / in my sleep too. / Like the child I was / in the happy times with my grandmother. / A time at long last recovered. / The journey is over" (227). For Laferrière, the memory of childhood provides him with a secure place from which to view the different phases of his life.

Tout bouge autour de moi

While *The Return* ends on a note of personal reconciliation, *Tout bouge autour de moi* (*The World Is Moving Around Me*) has a wider focus on Haiti and its people. No longer laced with humor and provocation, this book allows Haiti and its people to speak. It reveals Haiti's resilience, the optimism of its people and their capacity for survival, in the wake of the catastrophic earthquake of January 2010. While Laferrière's snapshot approach to his craft and his keen for eye for the immediacy of everyday detail are still evident, his eyewitness account of this natural disaster provokes in Laferrière a powerful evocation of Haiti's past, present, and future. It emerges that Laferrière was an unexpected witness to the event, having traveled to Haiti to take part in the Étonnants Voyageurs writers' festival. His close friend and fellow writer Rodney Saint-Éloi was an even more unexpected presence, as he had only arrived in the country a couple of hours before the earthquake, measuring 7.3 on the Richter scale, shook the nation. The sheer magnitude of its destruction put Haiti on the world map in an unprecedented manner, as the horror of the earthquake and its aftermath was watched around the world and generated a huge relief effort that drew in, among others, Hollywood stars. It suddenly became fashionable to be involved in Haiti's plight. In contrast to historical periods such as slavery, which left little written trace of its effects, this event was recorded in minute detail in both written and visual form. Laferrière's eyewitness account reveals how the 2010 earthquake was experienced by the Haitian people as well as detailing the processes of its memorialization in the early aftermath of the event. *The World Is Moving Around Me* provides a striking example of how History and histories are deeply connected and how the past is never separable from the present and future.

Laferrière in fact published two versions of the book, the first shortly after the disaster with Saint-Éloi's Montreal-based publishing house, Mémoire d'Encrier, and the second with Éditions Grasset of Paris in 2011. Munro details some of the changes between the two, which revolve principally around the idea that the earthquake constituted a definitive break in Haitian history in the first edition to one that is less optimistic about permanent change in the second (Munro, *Writing on the Fault Line*, 38–42). Other nonfictional works published over the next few years also express this more tempered approach to the long-lasting effects of the earthquake.[4] The analysis in this chapter will focus on the rewritten version of *The World Is Moving Around Me*, as it represents Laferrière's more recent understanding of the event and is also the basis for the English translation. Nonetheless, in the 2011 edition, Laferrière asserts that Haiti's earthquake constituted "[t]he fateful hour that cut Haitian time in two" (24), destined to be as significant as the Haitian revolution of independence in Haiti's history. Laferrière draws these two periods together, asserting that the revolution marked a time when the West turned its back on Haiti while the earthquake forced the world to finally take notice of Haiti. The arrival of Haiti into the international consciousness in 2010 provokes an analysis of the country's previous obscurement in the margins of history: "During the last weeks of January 2010, Haiti was seen more often than during the previous two centuries" (90). Laferrière observes that the West has traditionally relegated Haiti to a status defined by poverty and corruption, its troubles functioning as a warning to other nations who might be considering a revolution of independence. Yet Laferrière also questions whether this new "attraction" of Haiti in fact risks obscuring some of the highs and lows of its past. When a journalist suggests the Haitian earthquake has created a "Year Zero," Laferrière is skeptical: "I can't swallow this idea.... After all this time, people should know you can't erase the memory of a nation so easily.... The human landscape counts. Its memory will link the old and the new. Nothing is ever begun from scratch. It's impossible, in any case. All we do is continue" (81–82). Laferrière's reflections here pose important questions about a country's relationship to its past, about the level of attachment individuals should retain to events in history, and, more importantly, how one should treat a catastrophic contemporary event that is destined to become part of History with a capital "H."

The huge proliferation of documentation surrounding the earthquake—the endlessly unfolding images on television, the Haitian writers such as Laferrière and Edwidge Danticat who were quickly contacted for their "expert opinions" on the disaster, the journalists, the artists, and so forth—mark a completely different way of relating to history. As Thomas C. Spear, academic and another eyewitness to the earthquake, notes in Martin Munro's edited volume *Haiti Rising: Haitian History, Culture and the Earthquake of 2010*, "there are millions of perspectives of what was seen and felt, as with those of September 11, 2001" (Spear, "Point of View," 35). The likening of Haiti's earthquake to that of the collapse of New York's twin towers is significant, as the latter was perhaps the first "event" that truly changed the landscape of history making and witnessing by being broadcast in real time and continuously to millions of viewers around the world. Just as for Haiti, the world watched on horrified as continuous images of suffering and destruction played out across TV screens and in newspapers in the aftermath of 9/11. Indeed, the "ground zero" left by the razing of the twin towers was the precursor of the notion of "year zero" proposed in the wake of Haiti's crisis. As Laura Wagner observes in the same volume of *Haiti Rising*, it did not take long for the earthquake to turn into a narrative, "shifting from a lived event to a written-about one, leaving the realm of experience and entering the realm of reconstituted imagination" (15).

A brief glance over the table of contents of *Haiti Rising* gives a visual example of how the events of contemporary society may be memorialized for the future. The different parts of the book—titled "Survivor Testimonies," "Politics, Culture, and Society," "History," and "Haiti and Me"—underscore the impact of such an event on both the individual and collective level as eyewitnesses, academics, and Caribbean writers are called upon for their opinions. It also reveals the way in which history is not about singular events that remain unconnected to the past but forms part of a continuous narrative that shapes in part the way in which such an event is experienced and preserved. From his unique position as eyewitness to the earthquake, Laferrière reveals the interconnection of History and histories in a particularly poignant way. The fact that he is in Haiti at the time of the earthquake and has family members and friends he is anxious to make contact with after the event show how an external event affects an individual family. At the same time, though, Laferrière is conscious of his part in writing this event into history. He is interviewed as an expert, and *The World Is Moving Around Me*, among other writings, will form part of the "History" of the earthquake.

In "An Event without a Witness: Truth, Testimony and Survival," Dori Laub identifies three levels of witnessing in relation to his experience as a child survivor of the Holocaust: "the level of being a witness to oneself within the experience; the level of being a witness to the testimonies of others; and the level of being a witness to the process of witnessing itself" (75). Laferrière's recording of this important moment in history emphasizes its devastating impact and the different ways individuals struggle to digest it. Indeed, it is reminiscent of Cathy Caruth's characterization of trauma as the inability to experience an event directly. As Laferrière asserts, "I'm spending so much time on the moments that preceded the explosion because it's impossible to recreate the event itself. It lives within us in too intimate a fashion. No distance is possible with those kinds of emotions. The moment is eternally present" (42). Laferrière's dilemma relates particularly to Laub's third level of witnessing, which emphasizes the need to withdraw from the trauma in order to fully realize its impact. "Realizing its dimensions becomes a process that demands retreat" (Laub, 76). This dynamic process of moving forward and stepping back from trauma becomes the only way possible to "know" it. Otherwise, an event like the earthquake is destined to amplify in power to the point where a ten-second disaster can annihilate an entire civilization (Laferrière, *The World Is Moving*, 86). Laferrière records another strategy for coming to terms with the earthquake in the Haitian people's christening of it as Goudougoudou because of the sound it made at the moment of explosion. "Instead of fleeing, we have to confront 'the thing,' as they're calling it in the poorer districts. We have to name it if we intend to digest it" (46).

From the point of view of the contemporary historian, Laferrière attempts to place the earthquake within a wider context of history by returning to his notion of generations. He identifies a new generation of Haitians defined by a common vocabulary—"cracks, ruins, reconstruction, camps, tents, provisions"—replacing that of his own generation—"Aristide, *les chimères*, corruption, de facto government, eradication, and embargo"—and his father's before that—"Duvalier, dictatorship, prison, exile, *tonton-macoute*" (110). On a personal level, Laferrière recalls a conversation with his nephew Dany, who explicitly relates his generation to the earthquake while his uncle's is defined by the dictatorship (50). These statements identify patterns of transgenerational trauma in Haiti, but, significantly, there is the possibility of change, as the source of trauma is revealed as different for each generation. Like Laferrière's reflection about his father's suitcase in *The Return*, the possibility of liberation is underscored by the changing patterns of history. Indeed, Laferrière notes that in the wake of the earthquake one hears for the first time the word "reconstruction": "That's a new one. Even if most people don't really believe it" (111). While Laferrière may be skeptical about reconstruction, his statement nonetheless underlines that positive change is possible.

The potential for optimism in *The World Is Moving Around Me* is evident in Laferrière's reflection on his beloved grandmother, Da. While not neglecting the far-reaching destruction caused by the Haitian earthquake, a brief vignette describing the precious relationship between grandmothers and grandsons provides a personal insight into the resilience of Haiti and its people. As Laferrière observes: "My grandmother tore me from the claws of the dictator by teaching me something other than hatred and vengeance. This grandmother, on the other side of the net, is taking the horrible images in her grandson's head and replacing them with the songs and mythologies she can still find in her shaky memory" (68). Throughout the book, Laferrière transposes this observation of a single personal relationship into a more collective observation of the Haitian people, who are renowned for their resilient approach to hardship. He notes of his compatriots, for example: "Haiti's misfortune was not what moved the world: it was the way the Haitian people stood up to misfortune" (27); while Saint-Éloi remarks: "'What a country!' These people are so used to finding life in difficult conditions that they could bring hope down to hell" (32). There are numerous examples of Haiti's resilience in the book, embodied in the proverb that "in Haiti, if you're frightened one minute, you're dancing the next. This tried-and-true method keeps people from sinking into collective depression" (160). While it is important not to romanticize this idea of Haitian resilience, it nonetheless remains a trait that is much commented on by authors and critics alike. It becomes perhaps even more vital to focus on such an attitude when prospects for permanent change following the earthquake seem to recede with time.

Ultimately, then, *The World Is Moving Around Me* demonstrates that one of the effects of the earthquake is that it has knitted the Haitian community together more tightly, despite the depths of despair: "All these small acts bind us together and weave the great cloth of humanity" (43). Moreover, the literal trembling of the earthquake serves, like the first green shoots after a bush fire, as a place of regeneration for the poetry and artistry that are so synonymous with Haiti: "What art form will be the first to come forward after the earthquake?" (139). Martin Munro's 2014 publication *Writing on the Fault Line: Haitian Literature and the Earthquake of 2010* provides an exhaustive study of the differing literary reactions to the disaster. While he, too, expresses some reticence in viewing the earthquake as a history-altering event, he notes that the post-earthquake writings that are the subject of his book "are gestures of openness.... As such they deny the nationalist notion of Haitian exceptionalism and are expressions of a new, emergent post-earthquake cosmopolitanism" (226). *Writing on the Fault Line* thus ends on an optimistic note, as does *The World Is Moving Around Me*, with its emphasis on the unique qualities of this battered Caribbean land: "Haiti will continue to occupy the heart of the world for a long time to come" (173). The experience of the earthquake also provokes a rethinking of questions of national belonging and borders, with Laferrière coming to the realization that to be Haitian does not necessarily require you to live there. "Haiti is a place where you feel Haitian. It's not enough to be in Haiti to be useful to the country. That's what we discovered after the worldwide wave of generosity created by our situation. Things are not determined by place anymore" (146). In a sense, then, the 2010 earthquake provokes in Laferrière a new appreciation of his country of birth and strengthens his values about place and identity.

Dany Laferrière's body of work is as impressive as it is extensive. His varied books in *Une autobiographie américaine* provide valuable reflections on the themes of migration, history, and belonging and trace the trajectory of a writer successfully elucidating a new "American" approach to identity. He summarizes the lessons from this part of his life in the different gifts each place offers him. In America, he appreciates "[u]ne façon de vivre qui deviendra un style d'écriture. Une certaine liberté physique. Un sens du présent qui me pousse à toujours savoir où je suis" (a way of living that will become a way of writing. A certain physical freedom. A sense of the present that always pushes me to know where I am); Haiti brings "[l]e sens de l'Histoire" (the sense of History) and Europe "le sens de la mémoire" (the sense of memory) (*J'écris comme je vis*, 147). In the subsequent physical and emotional explorations he undertakes in works such as *The Return* and *The World Is Moving Around Me*, Laferrière refines this creative space. The work of this period is characterized by a deeper sensitivity than in his earlier books, revealing above all: "Il suffit de suivre la vie (sans protection) d'un individu ordinaire pour que se déroule une époque sous nos yeux" (It is enough to follow the life [without protection] of an ordinary individual in order to see an era unravel beneath your eyes) (*Un art de vivre*, 10). In this way, Laferrière contributes to a thought-provoking and compelling body of literature that engages with the past, is situated in the present, and looks to the future with openness. Above all, he demonstrates that for him, writing is life and life is writing.

CONCLUSION

Que des écrivains se rencontrent, que leurs poétiques se touchent, que leurs poétiques s'entraident est une chose précieuse. (That writers meet each other, that their poetics touch other, that their poetics help each other is a precious thing.)

—Édouard Glissant, *L'Imaginaire des langues*

In *Philosophie de la Relation*, Édouard Glissant states that Relation is defined by the imagination's capacity to connect, relay, and relate at one and the same time (72). It is particularly the ability to accommodate differences without being threatened by them that forms the foundation to his thought. The image of a rhizomatic network, which is inspired by these ideas, provides a visual framework for the present book. *Connecting Histories: Francophone Caribbean Writers Interrogating Their Past* reveals the way in which everything is connected in the intertwining of histories and History. The writers engage with different aspects of their personal and collective past through their autobiographical narratives, covering such areas as the individual and political, the linguistic, the literary, and the traumatic. While their style and emphasis vary, they all demonstrate that the writing space is a sheltering and challenging place with the power to transform their own lives as well as those of their readers.

Grande dame of francophone Caribbean literature Maryse Condé engages with her personal and national past through three autofictional narratives that explore distinct phases in her life—her childhood, the imagined past of her mother and grandmother, and the considerable period of time Condé spent in Africa as a young woman. In a way, her story also tells the history of her Caribbean homeland, as she must negotiate the consequences of slavery and colonialism for herself and her family, revealing a quest for selfhood that is marred by psychological ambiguity. At the same time, she unravels a rich cultural history of francophone writers and artists who were marginalized by French models of culture, a trait that is particularly apparent in her most recent autobiographical narrative. The story of Maryse Condé demonstrates the constant interrelationship between past and present, individual and collective; and the freedom she finds in embracing her individuality in all its complexity serves as a model of hopeful possibility. In the mature woman who pens the book *La Vie sans fards*, we see a steadfastly individual subject who is able to relate to the world widely as a result of filling in the gaps of her personal "herstory."

Gisèle Pineau forges a strikingly different path to her older compatriot and exposes an ongoing and often problematic relationship between the different strands of her upbringing. As a young person, she frequently appears torn between the competing influences of French and Creole cultures, and she struggles to find a meaningful place for herself. Her grandmother, Man Ya, plays an instrumental role in connecting her granddaughter to her Caribbean background, and this attachment to the island of Guadeloupe helps to liberate her from having to adopt either a French or Creole identity. Increasingly, Pineau's writings delineate a space where she is able to relate to the differing elements of her past without having to choose between them or to feel in conflict with them. Perhaps the most significant demonstration of the evolution of her thought is her stance in *Folie, aller simple*, where she brings to light the uniting strands that exist between all people, regardless of their differences. Pineau's writing is deeply passionate and highlights the urgent need to locate a sense of hope in a world that is often dominated by violence or misunderstanding.

Patrick Chamoiseau offers a more "traditional" example of autobiographical writing in this volume with his three-book study of his childhood, *Une enfance créole*. However, his emphasis is consistently on both the particular and the universal as seen through the model of the creolized imaginary. Each volume of his autobiography demonstrates both the uniquely Creole and the universal aspects of childhood, thereby allowing his readers to identify with many of the characters from his stories despite the fact that they may not have grown up in the Caribbean. The idea that the creolized imaginary is constructed in the intricate design of a mosaic where individual elements cannot always be isolated and where there is no one "root" from which it begins highlights the fact that we are all subject to a multitude of cultural, historical, and personal factors. His metanarrative style with constant commentaries on the unfolding text contributes to the notion that the written text is also subject to a variety of influences. Having frequently collaborated with Glissant on works of cultural history, Chamoiseau and his work are particularly fitting in a consideration of Relation.

Edwidge Danticat, Haitian born but living in the United States since the age of twelve, is an innovative writer who often takes on an advocate's role in relation to her country of birth. Although she has not lived permanently in the Caribbean for many years, Haiti and the diasporic Haitian community remain integral to her literary project. The passionate way in which she approaches her work is indicative of the ideological commitment that many immigrants retain to their birthplace, regardless of their "new" life in the immigrant land. Political and personal are therefore deeply linked in her work, and her approach sets about placing all elements in a uniting network, with Haiti often used as a specific example.

There is a distinct change of atmosphere with the arrival of Dany Laferrière in this book and his affinity to certain traditions in Haitian writing. While Haitian writers share many elements with their Martinican and Guadeloupean counterparts such as a traumatic past and the pressing need to carve out a meaningful identity for themselves in a postcolonial world, they also grapple with a range of different issues that deeply influence their work. The most prominent of these are the ongoing repercussions of the political dictatorships that have created generations of exiles and immigrants and the way in which significant contemporary events such as the 2010 earthquake are forcing a rethinking of history and memorialization in the present day. Laferrière's approach is characterized by his refusal to separate his life and his writing, enacting a lived philosophy that consistently underlines the inability to confine people or events to a particular category. His writing style, which moves between different genres even within the same work, creates a sense of connection within itself and also conditions the way in which he treats his subject matter. While his earlier works are underpinned by an apparently laid-back style and a love of provocation, his recent publications present him with the opportunity to explore more emotional and personal aspects of history in the making.

The voices of the writers themselves emerge clearly in this volume, as each has an important gift to bequeath to readers. While each author adopts a stance that is deeply individual and a reflection of his or her own unique experiences, they are united in their belief in the ultimate good of humanity. Their works have something to offer the increasing body of writing dedicated to postcolonialism and demonstrate that "the most promising avenue for the future exploration and amplification of Glissant's thinking is in the area of comparative, relational reading" (Gallagher, "Connection Failures," 32). However, most importantly, their offering is a human one, underlining Glissant's fundamental belief in "la nécessité vécue de ce fait: que toutes les cultures ont besoin de toutes les cultures" (the lived necessity of this fact: all cultures need all cultures) (*L'Imaginaire des langues*, 41). The contrasting strategies of these five Caribbean authors underscore the fact that reconciliation with a traumatic past is possible and that, ultimately, all histories are connected.

NOTES

Introduction

1. Recent titles that suggest a negative relationship with the past include Martin Munro, *Tropical Apocalypse: Haiti and the Caribbean End Times* (Charlottesville: University of Virginia Press, 2015); and Véronique Maisier, *Violence in Caribbean Literature: Stories of Stones and Blood* (Lanham, MD: Lexington Books, 2015).

2. The institute's website is at http://tout-monde.com. These terms come from Glissant's thought in *Poetics of Relation*, trans. Betsy Wing (Ann Arbor: University of Michigan Press, 1997), 169–79.

3. For information on the *comité*, see http://www.cnmhe.fr/.

Chapter 2

1. For an analysis of how Pineau exemplifies some of Glissant's ideas in her 2005 novel, *Fleur de Barbarie*, see Valérie Loichot, "'Devoured by Writing': An Interview with Gisèle Pineau," *Callaloo* 30, no. 1 (2007): 137–49.

2. For a consideration of the way this book reveals a "staged marginality" and an engagement with structures and ideas formed by metropolitan France, see Lorna Milne, "Working, Writing and the Antillean Postcolony: Patrick Chamoiseau and Gisèle Pineau," *Paragraph* 37, no. 2 (2014): 205–20.

Chapter 4

1. "Edwidge Danticat," Île en Île, at http://www.lehman.cuny.edu/ile.en.ile/paroles/danticat.html.

Chapter 5

1. Laferrière first published *Tout bouge autour de moi* with Rodney Saint-Éloi's Montreal-based publishing house Mémoire d'Encrier. Less than a year later, he practiced his art of rewriting and republished the work with Grasset, Paris, in 2011.

2. For an analysis of the significance of Laferrière's election to the Académie Française for the Haitian community, see Flore Zéphir, "Dany Laferrière and Michaëlle Jean: Two Haitian Diasporic Players on the World Stage," *Journal of Haitian Studies* 21, no. 1 (2015): 172–85.

3. For a useful definition of "Americanness" and "Americanization" in relation to Laferrière's works, see Stephanie Hopwood, "Port-au-Prince as Microcosm of the Americas: *Américanité* Meets Haitianisation in Dany Laferrière's *La Chair du maître*," *Australian Journal of French Studies* 52, no. 1 (2015): 66–67.

4. See, for example, Millery Polyné, ed., *The Idea of Haiti: Rethinking Crisis and Development* (Minneapolis: University of Minnesota Press, 2013); Paul Farmer, *Haiti after the Earthquake* (New York: Public Affairs, 2011); Amy Wilentz, *Farewell, Fred Voodoo: A Letter from Haiti* (New York: Simon & Schuster, 2013); Jonathan Katz, *The Big Truck That Went By: How the World Came to Save Haiti and Left Behind a Disaster* (New York: Palgrave Macmillan, 2013); and Emmanuelle Anne Vanborre, ed., *Haïti après le tremblement de terre: la forme, le rôle et le pouvoir de l'écriture* (New York: Peter Lang, 2014).

WORKS CITED

Primary Sources

Chamoiseau, Patrick.
———. *Childhood*. Translated by Carol Volk. Lincoln: University of Nebraska Press, 1999.
———. *School Days*. Translated by Linda Coverdale. Lincoln: University of Nebraska Press, 1997.
———. *Une enfance créole I: Antan d'enfance*. Paris: Gallimard, 1996.
———. *Une enfance créole II: Chemin d'école*. Paris: Gallimard, 1996.
———. *Une enfance créole III: À Bout d'enfance*. Paris: Gallimard, 2005.
Condé, Maryse.
———. *La Vie sans fards*. Paris: Lattès, 2012.
———. *Le Coeur à rire et à pleurer: contes vrais de mon enfance*. Paris: Laffont, 1999.
———. *Tales from the Heart: True Stories from My Childhood*. Translated by Richard Philcox. New York: Soho Press, 2001.
———. *Victoire, les saveurs et les mots*. Paris: Mercure de France, 2006.
———. *Victoire, My Mother's Mother*. Translated by Richard Philcox. New York: Atria Books, 2010.
Danticat, Edwidge.
———. *After the Dance: A Walk through Carnival in Haiti*. New York: Crown, 2002.
———. *Brother, I'm Dying*. New York: Alfred A. Knopf, 2007.
———. *Create Dangerously: The Immigrant Artist at Work*. New York: Vintage, 2011.
Laferrière, Dany.
———. *An Aroma of Coffee*. Translated by David Homel. Toronto: Coach House Press, 1993.
———. *Comment faire l'amour avec un Nègre sans se fatiguer*. Montreal: VLB, 1985.
———. *Dining with the Dictator (Le Goût des jeunes filles)*. Translated by David Homel. Toronto: Coach House Press, 1994.
———. *Down among the Dead Men (Pays sans chapeau)*. Translated by David Homel. Vancouver: Douglas and McIntyre, 1997.
———. *A Drifting Year (Chronique de la dérive douce)*. Translated by David Homel. Toronto: Douglas and McIntyre, 1997.

———. *Éroshima*. Montreal: VLB, 1987.
———. *Eroshima*. Translated by David Homel. Toronto: Coach House Press, 1991.
———. *How to Make Love to a Negro without Getting Tired*. Translated by David Homel. Toronto: Coach House Press, 1987.
———. *L'Énigme du retour*. Paris: Grasset, 2009.
———. *L'Odeur du café*. Paris: Le Serpent à Plumes, 2001.
———. *La Chair du maître*. Paris: Le Serpent à Plumes, 2000.
———. *Le Charme des après-midi sans fin*. Paris: Le Serpent à Plumes, 1998.
———. *Le Cri des oiseaux fous*. Paris: Le Serpent à Plumes, 2000.
———. *The Return*. Translated by David Homel. Vancouver: Douglas and McIntyre, 2010.
———. *Tout bouge autour de moi*. Paris: Grasset, 2011.
———. *Why Must a Black Writer Write about Sex? (Cette grenade dans la main du jeune Nègre est-elle une arme ou un fruit?)*. Translated by David Homel. Toronto: Coach House Press, 1994.
———. *The World Is Moving Around Me: A Memoir of the Haiti Earthquake*. Translated by David Homel. Vancouver: Arsenal Pulp Press, 2013.
Pineau, Gisèle.
———. *Exile According to Julia*. Translated by Betty Wilson. Charlottesville: University of Virginia Press, 2003.
———. *Folie, aller simple: journée ordinaire d'une infirmière*. Paris: Philippe Rey, 2010.
———. *L'Exil selon Julia*. Paris: Stock, 1996.
———. *Mes quatre femmes*. Paris: Philippe Rey, 2007.

Secondary Sources

Abraham, Nicolas, and Maria Torok. *The Shell and the Kernel: Renewals of Psychoanalysis*. Edited and translated by Nicholas T. Rand. Chicago: University of Chicago Press, 1994.
Alexander, Anne-Marie, et al. "A Conversation at Princeton with Maryse Condé." In *Feasting on Words: Maryse Condé, Cannibalism, and the Caribbean Text*, edited by Vera Broichhagen, Kathryn Lachman, and Nicole Simek, 1–28. Princeton, NJ: Program in Latin American Studies, Princeton University, 2006.
Alvarez, Julia. *Something to Declare*. New York: Plume, 1999.
Andrews, Mark. "Sarclages identitaires: l'imaginaire du jardin chez Gisèle Pineau." *Nouvelles Études Francophones* 27, no. 2 (2012): 45–58.
Anglade, Chantal, and Françoise Simasotchi-Brones. "Gisèle Pineau: 'Planter mes racines dans la terre créole . . . déracinée pour l'éternité.'" March 21, 2006. At http://www.remue.net/cont/Pineau_01entretien.html.
Anglesey, Zoe. "The Voice of the Storytellers: An Interview with Edwidge Danticat." *Multicultural Review* 7, no. 3 (1998): 36–39.
Antze, Paul, and Michael Lambek, eds. *Tense Past: Cultural Essays in Trauma and Memory*. New York: Routledge, 1996.
Artières, Philippe. "'Solitaire et solidaire,' entretien avec Édouard Glissant." In *Pour une littérature-monde*, edited by Michel Le Bris and Jean Rouaud, 77–86. Paris: Gallimard, 2007.
Bal, Mieke, Jonathan Crewe, and Leo Spitzer, eds. *Acts of Memory: Cultural Recall in the Present*. Hanover, NH: University Press of New England, 1999.
Benítez-Rojo, Antonio. *The Repeating Island: The Caribbean and the Postmodern Perspective*. Translated by James E. Maraniss. Durham, NC: Duke University Press, 1992.

Bernabé, Jean, Patrick Chamoiseau, and Raphaël Confiant. *Éloge de la Créolité*. Paris: Gallimard, 1989.
Berrouët-Oriol, Robert. "Négrophilie, schizophrénie, ou les Avatars de l'errance humaine." *Conjonction* 169 (April–June 1986): 60–67.
Bhabha, Homi. *The Location of Culture*. New York: Routledge, 2004.
Boisseron, Bénédicte. "Intimité: entretien avec Maryse Condé." *International Journal of Francophone Studies* 13, no. 1 (2010): 131–53.
———. "La Galerie de Dany Laferrière: une poétique de l'espace créole." *Nouvelles Études Francophones* 25, no. 1 (2010): 19–31.
Bongie, Chris. "Édouard Glissant: Dealing in Globality." *Postcolonial Thought in the French-Speaking World*, edited by Charles Forsdick and David Murphy, 90–101. Liverpool: Liverpool University Press, 2009.
Borer, Alain, Nicolas Bouvier, and Michel Chaillou, eds. *Pour une littérature voyageuse*. Paris: Éditions Complexe, 1992.
Braziel, Jana Evans. "'Caribbean Genesis': Language, Gardens, Worlds (Jamaica Kincaid, Derek Walcott, Édouard Glissant)." In *Caribbean Literature and the Environment: Between Nature and Culture*, edited by Elizabeth M. DeLoughrey, Renée K. Gosson, and George B. Handley, 110–26. Charlottesville: University of Virginia Press, 2005.
Brison, Susan J. "Trauma Narratives and the Remaking of the Self." In *Acts of Memory: Cultural Recall in the Present*, edited by Mieke Bal, Jonathan Crewe, and Leo Spitzer, 39–54. Hanover, NH: University Press of New England, 1999.
Britton, Celia M. "In Memory of Édouard Glissant." *Callaloo* 34, no. 3 (2011): 667–70.
———. *Language and Literary Form in French Caribbean Writing*. Liverpool: Liverpool University Press, 2014.
Burton, Richard D. "*Debrouya Pa Peche*, or *Il y a Toujours Moyen de Moyenner*: Patterns of Opposition in the Fiction of Patrick Chamoiseau." *Callaloo* 16, no. 2 (1993): 466–81.
———. *Le Roman marron: études sur la littérature martiniquaise contemporaine*. Paris: L'Harmattan, 1997.
Burton, Richard D., and Fred Reno, eds. *French and West Indian: Martinique, Guadeloupe, and French Guiana Today*. Charlottesville: University of Virginia Press, 1995.
Carruggi, Noëlle. "Écrire en Maryse Condé." In *Maryse Condé: rébellion et transgression*, edited by Noëlle Carruggi, 203–18. Paris: Karthala, 2010.
———, ed. *Maryse Condé: rébellion et transgression*. Paris: Karthala, 2010.
Caruth, Cathy. *Unclaimed Experience: Trauma, Narrative, and History*. Baltimore: Johns Hopkins University Press, 1996.
Casteel, Sarah Phillips. "New World Pastoral: The Caribbean Garden and Emplacement in Gisèle Pineau and Shani Mootoo." *Interventions* 5, no. 1 (2003): 12–28.
Certeau, Michel de. *The Writing of History*. Translated by Tom Conley. New York: Columbia University Press, 1988.
Chamoiseau, Patrick. *Césaire, Perse, Glissant: les liaisons magnétiques*. Paris: Philippe Rey, 2013.
———. *Écrire en pays dominé*. Paris: Gallimard, 1997.
———. Preface to *L'Écologie ou la passion du vivant: quarante ans d'écrits écologiques*, by Garcin Malsa, 9–11. Paris: L'Harmattan, 2008.
———. *Texaco*. Paris: Gallimard, 1992.
———. *Un dimanche au cachot*. Paris: Gallimard, 2007.
Chamoiseau, Patrick, and Raphaël Confiant. *Lettres créoles: tracées antillaises et continentales de la littérature; Haïti, Guadeloupe, Martinique, Guyane 1635–1975*. Paris: Gallimard, 1999.

Chamoiseau, Patrick, and Rodolphe Hammadi. *Guyane: traces-mémoires du bagne*. Paris: Caisse Nationale des Monuments Historiques et des Sites, 1994.

Clark, Vèvè. "Je me suis réconciliée avec mon île: une interview de Maryse Condé." *Callaloo* 12, no. 1 (1989): 85–133.

Collins, Jo. "Bricolage and History: Edwidge Danticat's Diasporic Life Writing in *After the Dance*." *Life Writing* 10, no. 1 (2013): 7–24.

Condé, Maryse. "Chercher nos vérités." In *Penser la créolité*, edited by Maryse Condé and Madeleine Cottenet-Hage, 305–10. Paris: Karthala, 1995.

———. *Crossing the Mangrove*. Translated by Richard Philcox. New York: Anchor-Doubleday, 1995.

———. "Finally Edwidge Arrived." In *Edwidge Danticat: A Reader's Guide*, edited by Martin Munro, 163–67. Charlottesville: University of Virginia Press, 2010.

———. *Hérémakhonon*. Paris: 10/18, 1976.

———. "How to Become a So-Called Caribbean Writer: A User's Manual." Translated by Dawn Fulton. *Massachusetts Review* 51, no. 4 (2010): 673–77.

———. "Itinéraire d'une écrivaine des Caraïbes." Lectured delivered at the Alliance Française of Perth, Australia, July 8, 2005.

———. *The Journey of a Caribbean Writer*. Translated by Richard Philcox. London: Seagull Books, 2014.

———. *La Civilisation du bossale: réflexions sur la littérature orale de la Guadeloupe et de la Martinique*. Paris: L'Harmattan, 1977.

———. *La Parole des femmes: essai sur des romancières des Antilles de langue française*. Paris: L'Harmattan, 1979.

———. "Liaison dangereuse." In *Pour une littérature-monde*, edited by Michel Le Bris and Jean Rouaud, 205–16. Paris: Gallimard, 2007.

———. *Mets et merveilles*. Paris: Lattès, 2015.

———. *Ségou: la terre en miettes*. Paris: Laffont, 1985.

———. *Ségou: les murailles de terre*. Paris: Laffont, 1984.

———. *Traversée de la mangrove*. Paris: Mercure de France, 1989.

Condé, Maryse, and Madeleine Cottenet-Hage, eds. *Penser la créolité*. Paris: Karthala, 1995.

Crosta, Suzanne. "Marronner le récit d'enfance: *Antan d'enfance* de Patrick Chamoiseau et *Ravines du devant-jour* de Raphaël Confiant." 1999. At http://www.lehman.cuny.edu/ile.en.ile/docs/crosta/chamoiseau_confiant.html.

Dainese, Francesca. "Entretien avec Dany Laferrière." *Voix Plurielles* 12, no. 1 (2015): 393–97.

Danticat, Edwidge. *Breath, Eyes, Memory*. New York: Soho Press, 1994.

———. Introduction to *Haiti noir*, edited by Edwidge Danticat, 10–15. New York: Akashic Books, 2011.

———. "Living and Loving through Tragedy." *Sojourners* (March 2010): 10–11.

Dash, J. Michael. *Culture and Customs of Haiti*. Westport, CT: Greenwood Press, 2001.

———. "Martinique Is (Not) a Polynesian Island: Detours of a French West Indian Identity." *International Journal of Francophone Studies* 11, nos. 1–2 (2008): 123–36.

———. "Remembering Édouard Glissant." *Callaloo* 34, no. 3 (2011): 671–75.

Delas, Daniel. "Dany Laferrière, un écrivain en liberté." *Notre Librairie* 146 (2001): 88–90.

Deleuze, Gilles, and Félix Guattari. *Mille Plateaux*. Paris: Éditions de Minuit, 1980.

Douglass, Ana, and Thomas A. Vogler, eds. *Witness and Memory: The Discourse of Trauma*. New York: Routledge, 2003.

Doubrovsky, Serge. *Autobiographiques: de Corneille à Sartre*. Paris: Presses Universitaires de France, 1988.
Essar, Dennis F. "Time and Space in Dany Laferrière's Autobiographical Haitian Novels." *Callaloo* 22, no. 4 (1999): 930–46.
Eyerman, Ron. *Cultural Trauma: Slavery and the Formation of African American Identity.* Cambridge: Cambridge University Press, 2001.
Fanon, Frantz. *Peau noire, masques blancs*. Paris: Seuil, 1952.
Farmer, Paul. *Haiti after the Earthquake*. New York: Public Affairs, 2011.
Felman, Shoshana, and Dori Laub. *Testimony: Crises of Witnessing in Literature, Psychoanalysis, and History*. New York: Routledge, 1992.
Forsdick, Charles. "Traveling, Writing." In *Edwidge Danticat: A Reader's Guide*, edited by Martin Munro, 99–116. Charlottesville: University of Virginia Press, 2010.
Foucault, Michel. "Film and Popular Memory: An Interview with Michel Foucault." *Radical Philosophy* 11, no. 11 (1975): 24–29.
Fulton, Dawn. *Signs of Dissent: Maryse Condé and Postcolonial Criticism*. Charlottesville: University of Virginia Press, 2008.
Gallagher, Mary. "Connection Failures: Discourse on Contemporary European and Caribbean Writing in French." *Small Axe* 14, no. 3 (2010): 21–32.
———. *Soundings in French Caribbean Writing since 1950: The Shock of Time and Space.* Oxford: Oxford University Press, 2002.
Gasparini, Philippe. "Autofiction vs autobiographie." *Tangence* 97 (2011): 11–24.
Gauvin, Lise. "Un rapport problématique." In *L'Écrivain francophone à la croisée des langues: entretiens*, 35–47. Paris: Karthala, 1997.
Ghinelli, Paola. *Archipels littéraires: entretiens avec Chamoiseau, Condé, Confiant, Brival, Maximin, Laferrière, Pineau, Dalembert, Agnant*. Montreal: Mémoire d'Encrier, 2005.
Githire, Njeri. "Horizons Adrift: Women in Exile, at Home, and Abroad in Gisèle Pineau's Works." *Research in African Literatures* 36, no. 1 (2005): 74–90.
Glissant, Édouard. *Caribbean Discourse: Selected Essays*. Translated by J. Michael Dash. Charlottesville: University of Virginia Press, 1989.
———. *Faulkner, Mississippi*. Paris: Stock, 1996.
———. *The Fourth Century*. Translated by Betsy Wing. Lincoln: University of Nebraska Press, 2001.
———. *L'Imaginaire des langues: entretiens avec Lise Gauvin (1991–2009)*. Paris: Gallimard, 2010.
———. *La Case du commandeur*. Paris: Gallimard, 1981.
———. *La Cohée du Lamentin (Poétique V)*. Paris: Gallimard, 2005.
———. *Le Discours antillais*. Paris: Gallimard, 1981.
———. *Le Quatrième siècle*. Paris: Gallimard, 1964.
———. *Mémoires des esclavages: la fondation d'un centre national pour la mémoire des esclavages et de leurs abolitions*. Paris: Gallimard, 2007.
———. *The Overseer's Cabin*. Translated by Betsy Wing. Lincoln: University of Nebraska Press, 2011.
———. *Pays rêvé, pays réel*. Paris: Seuil, 1985.
———. *Philosophie de la Relation: poésie en étendue*. Paris: Gallimard, 2009.
———. *Poetics of Relation*. Translated by Betsy Wing. Ann Arbor: University of Michigan Press, 1997.
———. *Poétique de la Relation (Poétique III)*. Paris: Gallimard, 1990.
———. *Soleil de la conscience (Poétique I)*. Rev. ed. Paris: Gallimard, 1997.

———. *Tout-monde*. Paris: Gallimard, 1993.
———. *Une nouvelle région du monde (Esthétique I)*. Paris: Gallimard, 2006.
Glissant, Édouard, and Patrick Chamoiseau. *Quand les murs tombent: l'identité nationale hors-la-loi?* Paris: Galaade, 2007.
Green, Mary Jean. "Maryse Condé's *Victoire*: Thinking Back through Her Mothers." *Nottingham French Studies* 53, no. 3 (2014): 297–313.
Griffiths, Jennifer Lee. *Traumatic Possessions: The Body and Memory in African American Women's Writing and Performance*. Charlottesville: University of Virginia Press, 2009.
Halbwachs, Maurice. *On Collective Memory*. Translated by Lewis A. Coser. Chicago: University of Chicago Press, 1992.
Hamilton, Paula. "The Knife Edge: Debates about Memory and History." In *Memory and History in Twentieth-Century Australia*, edited by Kate Darian-Smith and Paula Hamilton, 9–32. Oxford: Oxford University Press, 1994.
Hardwick, Louise. *Childhood, Autobiography and the Francophone Caribbean*. Liverpool: Liverpool University Press, 2013.
———. "'J'ai toujours été une personne un peu à part': questions à Maryse Condé." *International Journal of Francophone Studies* 9, no. 1 (2006): 111–24.
Hellerstein, Nina. "Violence, mythe et destin dans l'univers antillais de Gisèle Pineau." *LittéRéalité* 10, no. 1 (Spring–Summer 1998): 47–58.
Hirsch, Marianne. "The Generation of Postmemory." *Poetics Today* 29, no. 1 (2008): 103–28.
Hopwood, Stephanie. "Port-au-Prince as Microcosm of the Americas: *Américanité* Meets Haitianisation in Dany Laferrière's *La Chair du maître*." *Australian Journal of French Studies* 52, no. 1 (2015): 65–72.
Hutton, Patrick H. *History as an Art of Memory*. Hanover, NH: University Press of New England, 1993.
Île en Île. "Gisèle Pineau." September 2, 2012. At http://www.lehman.cuny.edu/ile.en.ile/paroles/pineau.html.
Jurney, Florence Raymond. "Entretien avec Gisèle Pineau: réflexions sur une oeuvre ancrée dans une société mondialisée." *Nouvelles Études Francophones* 27, no. 2 (2012): 107–20.
Katz, Jonathan. *The Big Truck That Went By: How the World Came to Save Haiti and Left Behind a Disaster*. New York: Palgrave Macmillan, 2013.
King, Nicola. *Memory, Narrative, Identity: Remembering the Self*. Edinburgh: Edinburgh University Press, 2000.
Knepper, Wendy. "In/justice and Necro-Natality in Edwidge Danticat's *Brother, I'm Dying*." *Journal of Commonwealth Literature* 47, no. 2 (2012): 191–205.
———. *Patrick Chamoiseau: A Critical Introduction*. Jackson: University Press of Mississippi, 2012.
LaCapra, Dominick. *Writing History, Writing Trauma*. Baltimore: Johns Hopkins University Press, 2001.
Laferrière, Dany. "Discours de réception de Dany Laferrière." Académie Française, May 28, 2015. At http://www.academie-francaise.fr/discours-de-reception-de-dany-laferriere.
———. "A Heart of Serenity in the Storm." In *Edwidge Danticat: A Reader's Guide*, edited by Martin Munro, vii–viii. Charlottesville: University of Virginia Press, 2010.
———. *I Am a Japanese Writer*. Translated by David Homel. Vancouver: Douglas and McIntyre, 2010.
———. *J'écris comme je vis: entretien avec Bernard Magnier*. Lyon: La Passe du Vent, 2000.

———. *Je suis fatigué.* Port-au-Prince: Les Éditions Mémoire, 2001.
———. *Je suis un écrivain japonais.* Paris: Grasset, 2008.
———. "Je voyage en français." In *Pour une littérature-monde*, edited by Michel Le Bris and Jean Rouaud, 87–101. Paris: Gallimard, 2007.
———. *L'Art presque perdu de ne rien faire.* Montreal: Boréal, 2011.
———. *Les Années 80 dans ma vieille Ford (Chroniques parues dans Haïti-Observateur de 1984 à 1986).* Montreal: Mémoire d'Encrier, 2005.
———. *Un art de vivre par temps de catastrophe.* Edmonton: University of Alberta Press, 2010.
Lambek, Michael, and Paul Antze. Introduction to *Tense Past: Cultural Essays in Trauma and Memory*, edited by Paul Antze and Michael Lambek. New York: Routledge, 1996.
Larrier, Renée. *Autofiction and Advocacy in the Francophone Caribbean.* Gainesville: University Press of Florida, 2006.
Laub, Dori. "An Event without a Witness: Truth, Testimony and Survival." In *Testimony: Crises of Witnessing in Literature, Psychoanalysis, and History*, by Shoshana Felman and Dori Laub, 75–92. New York: Routledge, 1992.
Le Bris, Michel, and Jean Rouaud, eds. *Pour une littérature-monde.* Paris: Gallimard, 2007.
Le Goff, Jacques. *History and Memory.* Translated by Steven Rendall and Elizabeth Claman. New York: Columbia University Press, 1992.
———. *The Medieval Imagination.* Translated by Arthur Goldhammer. Chicago: University of Chicago Press, 1988.
Legagneur, Jean Hérald. "*L'Énigme du retour* de Dany Laferrière ou quand imaginaire et urgence du social se transforment en *Cahier du retour au pays natal*." *Voix plurielles* 10, no. 2 (2013): 295–311.
Lejeune, Philippe. *Le Pacte autobiographique.* Paris: Seuil, 1975.
Leservot, Typhaine. "Maryse Condé: Post-Postcolonial?" In *Postcolonial Thought in the French-Speaking World*, edited by Charles Forsdick and David Murphy, 42–52. Liverpool: Liverpool University Press, 2009.
Lewis, Barbara. "Tales from the Heart: A Conversation with Maryse Condé." *Black Renaissance* 5, no. 2 (2003): 94–104.
Leys, Ruth. *Trauma: A Genealogy.* Chicago: University of Chicago Press, 2000.
Licops, Dominique. "Métaphores naturelles et identité culturelle dans l'oeuvre de Gisèle Pineau." *Nouvelles Études Francophones* 27, no. 2 (2012): 90–106.
———. "Reading and Danger: The Emerging Writer in Maryse Condé's and Gisèle Pineau's Autofiction." *Women in French Studies*, special issue (2012): 248–64.
Lionnet, Françoise. *Autobiographical Voices: Race, Gender, Self-Portraiture.* Ithaca, NY: Cornell University Press, 1989.
Loichot, Valérie. "'Devoured by Writing': An Interview with Gisèle Pineau." *Callaloo* 30, no. 1 (2007): 328–37.
Lyons, Bonnie. "An Interview with Edwidge Danticat." *Contemporary Literature* 44, no. 2 (2003): 183–98.
Maisier, Véronique. *Violence in Caribbean Literature: Stories of Stones and Blood.* Lanham, MD: Lexington Books, 2015.
Makward, Christiane. "Entretien avec Gisèle Pineau." *French Review* 76, no. 6 (2003): 1202–15.
Mardorossian, Carine M. *Reclaiming Difference: Caribbean Women Rewrite Postcolonialism.* Charlottesville: University of Virginia Press, 2005.

Mathis-Moser, Ursula. *Dany Laferrière, la dérive américaine*. Montreal: VLB, 2003.
McCusker, Maeve. "De la problématique du territoire à la problématique du lieu: un entretien avec Patrick Chamoiseau." *French Review* 73, no. 4 (2000): 724–33.
———. "On Slavery, Césaire, and Relating to the World: An Interview with Patrick Chamoiseau." *Small Axe* 30 (2009): 74–83.
———. *Patrick Chamoiseau: Recovering Memory*. Liverpool: Liverpool University Press, 2007.
———. "'Troubler l'ordre de l'oubli': Memory and Forgetting in French Caribbean Autobiography of the 1990s." *Forum of Modern Language Studies* 40, no. 4 (2004): 438–50.
Milne, Lorna. *Patrick Chamoiseau: espaces d'une écriture antillaise*. Amsterdam: Rodopi, 2006.
———. "Working, Writing and the Antillean Postcolony: Patrick Chamoiseau and Gisèle Pineau." *Paragraph* 37, no. 2 (2014): 205–20.
Miraglia, Anne Marie. "Dany Laferrière, l'identité culturelle et l'intertexte afro-américain." *Présence Francophone* 54 (1999): 121–39.
Morgan, Janice. "Re-Imagining Diversity and Connection in the Chaos World: An Interview with Patrick Chamoiseau." *Callaloo* 31, no. 2 (2008): 443–53.
Morrison, Toni. *The Bluest Eye*. New York: Holt, Rinehart & Winston, 1970.
Moudileno, Lydie. "Positioning the 'French' 'Caribbean' 'Woman' Writer." In *Feasting on Words: Maryse Condé, Cannibalism, and the Caribbean Text*, edited by Vera Broichhagen, Kathryn Lachman, and Nicole Simek, 123–46. Princeton, NJ: Program in Latin American Studies, Princeton University, 2006.
Munro, Martin, ed. *Edwidge Danticat: A Reader's Guide*. Charlottesville: University of Virginia Press, 2010.
———. *Exile and Post-1946 Haitian Literature: Alexis, Depestre, Ollivier, Laferrière, Danticat*. Liverpool: Liverpool University Press, 2007.
———, ed. *Haiti Rising: Haitian History, Culture and the Earthquake of 2010*. Kingston: University of the West Indies Press, 2010.
———. "Inside Out: A Brief Biography of Edwidge Danticat." In *Edwidge Danticat: A Reader's Guide*, edited by Martin Munro, 13–25. Charlottesville: University of Virginia Press, 2010.
———. "Master of the New: Tradition and Intertextuality in Dany Laferrière's *Pays sans chapeau*." *Small Axe* 9, no. 2 (September 2005): 176–88.
———. *Tropical Apocalypse: Haiti and the Caribbean End Times*. Charlottesville: University of Virginia Press, 2015.
———. *Writing on the Fault Line: Haitian Literature and the Earthquake of 2010*. Liverpool: Liverpool University Press, 2014.
Murdoch, H. Adlai. "Autobiography and Departmentalization in Chamoiseau's *Chemin d'école*: Representational Strategies and the Martinican Memoir." *Research in African Literatures* 40, no. 2 (2009): 16–39.
Naudillon, Françoise. "Le Continent noir des corps: représentation du corps féminin chez Marie-Célie Agnant et Gisèle Pineau." *Études Françaises* 41, no. 2 (2005): 73–85.
Nesbitt, Nick F. *Caribbean Critique: Antillean Critical Theory from Toussaint to Glissant*. Liverpool: Liverpool University Press, 2013.
———. "Le Sujet de l'histoire: mémoires troublées dans *Traversée de la mangrove* et *Le coeur à rire et à pleurer*." In *Maryse Condé: une nomade inconvenante*, edited by Madeleine Cottenet-Hage and Lydie Moudileno, 113–20. Jarry, Guadeloupe: Ibis Rouge, 2002.
———. "Stepping Outside the Magic Circle: The Critical Thought of Maryse Condé." *Romanic Review* 94, nos. 3–4 (2003): 391–404.

———. *Voicing Memory: History and Subjectivity in French Caribbean Literature.* Charlottesville: University of Virginia Press, 2003.
Nora, Pierre. "Between Memory and History: Les Lieux de Mémoire." In *History and Memory in African-American Culture*, edited by Geneviève Fabre and Robert O'Meally, 284–300. Oxford: Oxford University Press, 1994.
Onyeoziri, Gloria Nne. "Gisèle Pineau et l'oralité mondialisée." *Nouvelles Études Francophones* 27, no. 2 (2012): 17–29.
Pfaff, Françoise. *Entretiens avec Maryse Condé.* Paris: Karthala, 1993.
Picanço, Luciano. "Rêver des voix égarées: l'utilisation de l'autobiographie onirique dans *Écrire en pays dominé* de Patrick Chamoiseau." *Nottingham French Studies* 51, no. 2 (2012): 192–203.
Pineau, Gisèle. "Écrire en tant que Noire." In *Penser la créolité*, edited by Maryse Condé and Madeleine Cottenet-Hage, 289–95. Paris: Karthala, 1995.
———. "L'Identité, la créolité et la francité." In *La Culture française vue d'ici et d'ailleurs*, edited by Thomas Spear, 217–24. Paris: Karthala, 2002.
———. *La Grande Drive des esprits.* Paris: Le Serpent à Plumes, 1993.
Pineau, Gisèle, and Marie Abraham. *Femmes des Antilles: traces et voix cent cinquante ans après l'abolition de l'esclavage.* Paris: Stock, 1998.
Polyné, Millery, ed. *The Idea of Haiti: Rethinking Crisis and Development.* Minneapolis: University of Minnesota Press, 2013.
Prophète, Jean L., and Carrol F. Coates. "Dany Laferrière and the Autobiography of Disorderly Past Times." *Callaloo* 22, no. 4 (1999): 947–49.
Pulitano, Elvira. "An Immigrant Artist at Work: A Conversation with Edwidge Danticat." *Small Axe* 15, no. 3 (2011): 39–61.
———. "Landscape, Memory and Survival in the Fiction of Edwidge Danticat." *Anthurium: A Caribbean Studies Journal* 6, no. 2 (2008): 1–16. At http://anthurium.miami.edu/volume_6/issue_2/pulitano-landscape.
Radstone, Susannah. "Reconceiving Binaries: The Limits of Memory." *History Workshop Journal* 59 (2005): 134–50.
Rand, Nicholas T. "Introduction: Renewals of Psychoanalysis." In *The Shell and the Kernel: Renewals of Psychoanalysis*, by Nicolas Abraham and Maria Torok, 1–22. Edited and translated by Nicholas T. Rand. Chicago: University of Chicago Press, 1994.
Ricoeur, Paul. *Memory, History, Forgetting.* Translated by Kathleen Blamey and David Pellauer Chicago: University of Chicago Press, 2004.
Rosello, Mireille. *The Reparative in Narratives: Works of Mourning in Progress.* Liverpool: Liverpool University Press, 2010.
Roumain, Jacques. *Gouverneurs de la rosée.* Port-au-Prince: Imprimerie de l'État, 1944.
Sankara, Edgard. *Postcolonial Francophone Autobiographies: From Africa to the Antilles.* Charlottesville: University of Virginia Press, 2011.
Sansavior, Eva. *Maryse Condé and the Space of Literature.* London: Legenda, 2012.
Scharfman, Ronnie. "Criss-Crossing the Mangrove: The Literary Nomadics of Maryse Condé." In *Feasting on Words: Maryse Condé, Cannibalism, and the Caribbean Text*, edited by Vera Broichhagen, Kathryn Lachman, and Nicole Simek, 199–214. Princeton, NJ: Program in Latin American Studies, Princeton University, 2006.
———. "A Fugue of Legacies: A Meditation for Maryse Condé." *Romanic Review* 94, nos. 3–4 (2003): 457–64.
Schnepel, Ellen M. "The Other Tongue, the Other Voice: Language and Gender in the French Caribbean." *Ethnic Groups* 10 (1993): 243–68.

Schwarz-Bart, Simone. *The Bridge of Beyond*. Translated by Barbara Bray. London: Heinemann, 1982.

———. *Pluie et vent sur Télumée Miracle*. Paris: Seuil, 1972.

Shea, Renee H. "The Dangerous Job of Edwidge Danticat: An Interview." *Callaloo* 19, no. 2 (1996): 382–89.

———. "A Family Story: Danticat Talks about Her Newest—and Most Personal—Work." In *Edwidge Danticat: A Reader's Guide*, edited by Martin Munro, 187–93. Charlottesville: University of Virginia Press, 2010.

———. "Travelling Words with Edwidge Danticat." *Poets and Writers Magazine* (January–February 1997): 42–51.

Sourieau, Marie-Agnès. Afterword to *Exile According to Julia*, by Gisèle Pineau, 171–87. Charlottesville: University of Virginia Press, 2003.

Spear, Thomas C., ed. *La Culture française vue d'ici et d'ailleurs*. Paris: Karthala, 2002.

———. "Point of View." In *Haiti Rising: Haitian History, Culture and the Earthquake of 2010*, edited by Martin Munro, 35–42. Kingston: University of the West Indies Press, 2010.

Sroka, Ghila. *Conversations avec Dany Laferrière: interviews de Ghila Sroka*. Montreal: La Parole Métèque, 2010.

Sturken, Marita. "The Wall, the Screen, and the Image: The Vietnam Veterans Memorial." *Representations* 35 (1991): 118–42.

Suárez, Lucía M. "Gisèle Pineau: Writing the Dimensions of Migration." *World Literature Today* (Summer–Autumn 2001): 9–21.

Tervonen, Taina. "Biographie des territoires, entretien avec Dany Laferrière." *Africultures* 23 (1999): 101–3.

Thomas, Bonnie. *Breadfruit or Chestnut? Gender Construction in the French Caribbean Novel*. Lanham, MD: Lexington Books, 2006.

Thompson, Robert Farris. *Flash of the Spirit: African and Afro-American Art and Philosophy*. New York: Vintage, 1984.

Trouillot, Evelyne. "The Right Side of History." In *Edwidge Danticat: A Reader's Guide*, edited by Martin Munro, 168–74. Charlottesville: University of Virginia Press, 2010.

Vanborre, Emmanuelle Anne, ed. *Haïti après le tremblement de terre: la forme, le rôle et le pouvoir de l'écriture*. New York: Peter Lang, 2014.

Veldwachter, Nadège. "Interview with Gisèle Pineau." *Research in African Literatures* 35, no. 1 (2004): 180–87.

Vergès, Françoise. *La Mémoire enchaînée: questions sur l'esclavage*. Paris: Albin Michel, 2006.

Vitiello, Joëlle. "Poétiques haïtiennes-québécoises: Dany Laferrière, Emile Ollivier et Gérard Etienne." In *Poétiques et imaginaires: francopolyphonie littéraire des Amériques*, edited by Pierre Laurette and Hans-George Ruprecht, 349–59. Paris: L'Harmattan, 1996.

Wagner, Laura. "Salvaging." In *Haiti Rising: Haitian History, Culture and the Earthquake of 2010*, edited by Martin Munro, 15–23. Kingston: University of the West Indies Press, 2010.

Walcott-Hackshaw, Elizabeth. "Home Is Where the Heart Is: Danticat's Landscapes of Return." *Small Axe* 27 (2008): 71–82.

Wilentz, Amy. *Farewell, Fred Voodoo: A Letter from Haiti*. New York: Simon & Schuster, 2013.

Zéphir, Flore. "Dany Laferrière and Michaëlle Jean: Two Haitian Diasporic Players on the World Stage." *Journal of Haitian Studies* 21, no. 1 (2015): 172–85.

INDEX

Abraham, Nicholas, 17, 35, 38
Africa, 25, 27, 43–44, 47–48, 68, 79, 119
Antillanité, 76, 79
archipelago, 6, 8, 10, 11
autobiography/autofiction, 20, 22, 32, 80, 83, 84

Benítez-Rojo, Antonio, 6, 102
Britton, Celia, 7, 22
brokenness, 4, 6, 14, 17, 20, 38, 51, 71–72, 73, 109

Caruth, Cathy, 16, 18, 36, 142
Certeau, Michel de, 14, 15, 29, 38, 71–72
Césaire, Aimé, 8, 11, 13, 25, 27, 46–47, 76, 123, 126, 128, 138
Chamoiseau, Patrick, 4, 17, 21, 53, 55, 59, 76–99, 138, 147; *À Bout d'enfance*, 95–98; *Antan d'enfance/Childhood*, 82–88; *Césaire, Perse, Glissant: les liaisons magnétiques*, 77, 78, 95, 99; *Chemin d'école/School Days*, 88–95, 103, 105; *Chronique des sept misères/Chronicle of the Seven Sorrows*, 80; *Écrire en pays dominé*, 80–81; *Éloge de la créolité/In Praise of Creoleness*, 76, 79–80; *Guyane: traces-mémoires du bagne*, 82; *Lettres créoles*, 80; *Quand les murs tombent: l'identité nationale hors-la-loi?*, 7–9, 27, 30, 51–52; *Solibo magnifique/ Solibo Magnificent*, 80; *Texaco*, 76, 86; *Un dimanche au cachot*, 93
colonization/colonialism, 4, 17, 29, 35, 68, 126
Columbus, Christopher, 4, 13
Comité pour la mémoire de l'esclavage, 13
Condé, Maryse, 4, 13, 17, 21, 24–49, 100–102, 105, 120–21, 125, 146–47; *Desirada*, 27; *Hérémakhonon*, 29, 43–44; *The Journey of a Caribbean Writer*, 27; *La Civilisation du bossale*, 27; *La Vie sans fards*, 24–25, 27, 36, 42–48; *Le Coeur à rire et à pleurer/Tales from the Heart*, 32–37; "Liaison dangereuse," 25, 29; *Mets et merveilles*, 27; *Ségou*, 27; *Traversée de la mangrove/Crossing the Mangrove*, 27–28; *Victoire, les saveurs et les mots/ Victoire, My Mother's Mother*, 21, 32, 36–42
Confiant, Raphaël, 53, 55, 76–77, 79, 93
connection/connectivity, 3, 5–8, 10, 14–15, 17, 22, 29, 31, 35–36, 39, 41, 48, 51, 58, 63–64, 67, 70, 73, 102–4, 106–7, 111–15, 119
Cottias, Myriam, 13
créoliste writers, 29–30, 34, 51, 53, 55, 77, 88, 102
Créolité, 76, 78–79
creolization, 7–9, 11, 62, 76–77, 79, 81, 84
cultural cannibalism, 29–30, 34

Danticat, Edwidge, 4, 16–17, 21, 100–119, 141, 148; *After the Dance*, 107–11; *Breath Eyes Memory*, 100–101, 103; *Brother, I'm Dying*, 111–16; *Create Dangerously*, 104, 106, 116–19; *Haiti noir*, 104, 111; *Krik Krak*, 103
Dash, J. Michael, 8, 120
diaspora/*dyaspora*, 104, 107, 114, 118–19
diversalité, 77, 79, 81, 96, 98–99, 103
Doubrovsky, Serge, 20
Douglass, Ana: and Thomas Vogler, 7, 12–13, 16, 18

earthquake in Haiti (2010), 116, 139–44
exile, 31, 112, 115–16, 120–21, 125, 127–28, 130–31, 133–39, 142

Fanon, Frantz, 27, 33, 46, 89
forgiveness, 14–15
fugue, 6

Gallagher, Mary, 4, 20, 148
Gauvin, Lise, 11, 105
Glissant, Édouard, 6–14, 20, 22, 38, 50–51, 65, 67, 76, 78, 81–82, 97–98, 109–10, 122, 146, 148–49; *La Case du commandeur/The Overseer's Cabin*, 7, 110; *La Terre magnétique*, 95; *Le Discours antillais/Caribbean Discourse*, 7, 10, 14, 66, 82; *Le Quatrième Siècle/The Fourth Century*, 7, 110; *Mémoires des esclavages*, 7, 10, 51; *Pays rêvé, pays réel*, 130; *Philosophie de la Relation*, 7, 124, 146; *Poétique de la Relation/Poetics of Relation*, 6–7; *Quand les murs tombent: l'identité nationale hors-la-loi?*, 7–9, 27, 30, 51–52; *Soleil de la conscience/Sun of Consciousness*, 7; *Une Nouvelle Région du monde*, 7, 10
Goff, Jacques le, 13–14
grandmothers, 38–39, 56–63, 65–66, 86, 113, 121, 128, 137, 139, 143

Hardwick, Louise, 20–21, 32, 95
Hirsch, Marianne, 17–18, 63
history and memory, 6–8, 10, 12–14, 27, 39, 65, 84, 103, 118

history/histories, 5, 13, 21, 30–31, 35, 41, 51, 56–57, 62, 66, 69–70, 80, 86, 102, 107–8, 111–14, 116–19, 137, 140–41, 144–46
Holocaust, 12, 14, 142

identity, 4, 8, 9, 19, 26–32, 36, 46, 53–55, 57–58, 60–62, 79, 90–92, 94, 102, 104, 119, 122, 124–25, 127–31, 133, 144–45
imaginaire, 9, 11, 76–77, 79, 85, 97–99, 105
independence of Haiti, 4, 109, 140

Knepper, Wendy, 78–79, 82, 84–85, 88, 96, 111–12

LaCapra, Dominick, 19
Laferrière, Dany, 4, 16–17, 21, 100, 102, 116–18, 120–45; *Autobiographie américaine/American Autobiography*, 127–33; *Cette grenade dans la main du jeune Nègre est-elle une arme ou un fruit?/Why Must a Black Writer Write about Sex?*, 127, 129, 148; *Chronique de la dérive douce/A Drifting Year*, 127–29; *Comment faire l'amour avec un Nègre sans se fatiguer/How to Make Love to a Negro without Getting Tired*, 122, 127, 129; *Éroshima/Eroshima*, 127; *J'écris comme je vis*, 121, 127, 136–37, 144; *Je suis fatigué*, 122; *Je suis un écrivain japonais/I am a Japanese Writer*, 124–25, 128; "Je voyage en français," 125–26; *L'Énigme du retour/The Return*, 120, 125–26, 128, 131, 133–39, 144–45; *L'Odeur du café/An Aroma of Coffee*, 127; *La Chair du maître*, 127; *Le Charme des après-midi sans fin*, 127; *Le Cri des oiseaux fous*, 121, 128; *Le Goût des jeunes filles/Dining with the Dictator*, 127; *Les Années 80 dans ma vieille Ford*, 121–22; *Pays sans chapeau/Down Among the Dead Men*, 127, 130–33, 135; *Tout bouge autour de moi/ The World Is Moving Around Me*, 120, 131, 139–45, 117; *Un art de vivre par temps de catastrophe*, 128, 145
landscape, 8, 10, 51, 59–62, 65–67, 71, 74, 86, 91–92, 109–10, 125–26, 131–32

language, 25, 28–29, 33–34, 45, 55, 58, 60–61, 81, 86–91, 94, 96, 102, 105–6
Lejeune, Philippe, 20
Lionnet, Françoise, 6
littérature-monde, 28–29, 52, 125–26, 132

maternal, 35–37, 40–42, 44–45, 131, 137–38
McCusker, Maeve, 20, 81–87, 97
memory, 10–12, 17–19, 21, 60, 63, 70, 73, 82–84, 88, 97, 107, 113, 118–19, 134, 139–41, 144
Munro, Martin, 100, 104–6, 116–17, 119–20, 130, 138, 140–41, 143–44

nature, 8, 10, 51, 59–62, 65–67, 71, 74, 86, 91–92, 109–10
Négritude, 46, 79
Nesbitt, Nick, 5, 21–22, 29–30, 39

personal narratives, 3
Pineau, Gisèle, 4, 17, 50–75, 147; "Écrire en tant que Noire," 52–53, 56, 75; *Femmes des Antilles*, 3, 21; *Folie, aller simple*, 54, 70–74; *L'Exil selon Julia/Exile According to Julia*, 53–54, 56–62; *Mes quatre femmes*, 62–70
poetry, 11
postmemory, 63
post-traumatic stress disorder (PTSD), 16, 59, 66

relation, 6–12, 30, 46, 48, 68, 71, 76–77, 81, 84, 88, 95, 97–99, 146–47
rhizome, 6, 9–10, 22, 52, 63, 79, 84, 103, 108, 146
Ricoeur, Paul, 14, 19
Rosello, Mireille, 15
rupture, 4, 6, 14, 17, 20, 38, 51, 71–72, 73, 109

slavery, 4–5, 7–8, 11, 13, 15, 17, 38, 56, 58–60, 68–70, 89–91, 101–2, 110, 139

Taubira, Christiane, 13
Torok, Maria, 17
Tout-monde, 7, 9, 22, 81
trauma, 5, 11, 14, 16, 18–19, 56–57, 63–65; transgenerational, 12, 16–17, 62–70, 134, 137, 142

Vergès, Françoise, 13, 15
Vogler, Thomas: and Ana Douglass, 7, 12–13, 16, 18

"working through," 15, 19, 34–35, 54–55, 57, 63
writing, 5–6, 16, 35, 40, 47–48, 52, 54–57, 60, 63, 72–73, 78–81, 95, 116–17, 123–27, 133, 135–36, 144–46

www.ingramcontent.com/pod-product-compliance
Lightning Source LLC
Chambersburg PA
CBHW030625230426
43661CB00053B/2146